Watching Women's Liberation, 1970

Friedan
(Rudolph
and TV Actors)

Watching Women's Liberation, 1970

Feminism's Pivotal Year on the Network News

1. Search
Miss Amaka 1968
Pageant as
defing event
(Dow + 2)

BONNIE J. DOW

UNIVERSITY OF ILLINOIS PRESS
Urbana, Chicago, and Springfield

Library of Congress Cataloging-in-Publication Data
Dow, Bonnie J.
Watching women's liberation, 1970 : feminism's pivotal year on
the network news / Bonnie J. Dow.
pages   cm
Includes bibliographical references and index.
ISBN 978-0-252-03856-3 (cloth : alk. paper)
ISBN 978-0-252-08016-6 (pbk. : alk. paper)
ISBN 978-0-252-09648-8 (ebook)
1. Women on television. 2. Feminism on television. 3.
Feminism—Press coverage—United States—History—20th
century. 4. Women's rights—Press coverage—United States—
History—20th century. 5. Television broadcasting of news—
United States—History—20th century. 6. Feminism—United
States—History—20th century.
I. Title.
PN1992.8.W65D693   2014
305.420973'09047—dc23   2014002446

In memory of my mother

Contents

Acknowledgments   ix

Introduction: 1970   1

1. The Movement Meets the Press:
   The 1968 Miss America Pageant Protest   29

2. The Movement Makes the News: Network News
   Feature Stories on Women's Liberation in 1970   52

3. Magazines and the Marketing of the Movement:
   The March 1970 *Ladies' Home Journal* Protest   95

4. Fixing the Meaning of the Movement: ABC's May 1970
   "Women's Liberation" Documentary   120

5. Making a Spectacle of the Movement:
   The August 26, 1970, Women's Strike for Equality   144

6. After 1970: Second-Wave Feminism,
   Mediated Popular Memory, and Gloria Steinem   168

Notes   201

References   215

Index   231

Acknowledgments

This book has taken much longer to complete than I imagined when I first began to write it. As a result, the list of people who have facilitated it, in various large and small ways, is long. Its true genesis can be traced to one of my first courses in graduate school at the University of Kansas, almost thirty years ago, when Karlyn Kohrs Campbell introduced me to what she then termed "the rhetoric of contemporary feminism." It was an apt label at a time when the second wave of U.S. feminism was not the somewhat distant memory it is today. Karlyn enabled my introduction to feminism as a living and breathing set of ideas rather than as a historical relic and started me on the path to my life's work as an academic. I am indebted to her in more ways than I can express.

I am also very grateful to Bill Regier, director of the University of Illinois Press, for maintaining his interest in this project despite the fact that it took five more years to complete than I said it would; to Danny Nasset, my editor at Illinois who shepherded it efficiently and supportively through the review and revision process; and to Dawn Durante, Jennifer Clark, and Karen Hallman at the press, who were helpful in multiple ways during the journey to production. Most importantly, this would be a very different book without the generosity of the three anonymous reviewers whose suggestions dramatically improved it.

This project first took shape during the decade I spent at the University of Georgia. My initial collection of much of the news coverage that I treat in it was facilitated by a research grant from the UGA Women's Studies Program that funded my first trip to Vanderbilt's Television News Archives. I am grateful for the efficiency and professionalism of the staff at the archives—then and now—and I also thank the librarians at UGA's Peabody Awards Archives, who brought my attention to ABC's 1970 "Women's Liberation" documentary that is the topic of chapter 4. During my time at UGA, a variety of graduate students in the Department of Speech Communication provided able and enthusiastic research assistance at various stages in this project's development, particularly Paul Achter, Cindy Dietz Skalicky, Becky Kuehl, Jon Hoffman, and Gordon Stables. I extend a special note of warmth and appreciation to the five students in the Seminar on Second-Wave Feminist Rhetorics that I taught at UGA in 2002: Kristan Poirot, Ashli Quesinberry Stokes, Wendy Atkins-Sayre, Kristy Maddux, and Tasha Dubriwny. They not only generated research and insights that have informed my thinking in multiple ways since then, but they provided one of the most satisfying teaching experiences of my career. Several of the papers produced in that seminar were subsequently published, and I have taken great pleasure in drawing on those essays in the writing of this book.

I have presented various portions of this project as invited lectures over the past decade or so, and each audience of colleagues and students has prodded my thinking in important ways. For inviting me to share my ideas and for receiving them generously, I thank the communication departments and/or the women's studies programs at the University of Wisconsin, the University of Illinois, the University of Maryland, Boston College, Northwestern University, Texas A & M University, Ohio University, St. Mary's College of Notre Dame, Villanova University, Wabash College, University of Wisconsin-Milwaukee, DePauw University, Albion College, and the University of Richmond.

By the time I arrived at Vanderbilt University in 2006, this book had stalled, pushed aside by other projects, administrative work, and life's vicissitudes. The College of Arts and Science, in particular Dean Carolyn Dever, enabled its rejuvenation and then its completion with two research leaves, for which I am profoundly grateful. In the Department of Communication Studies, I have had the great fortune to work in one of most congenial environments imaginable, and for that I thank my colleagues: Kass Kovalcheck, Vanessa Beasley, Claire King, Paul Stob, Carole Kenner, John English, M. L. Sandoz, Neil Butt, Diane Banks, and Stephanie Covington. I also thank former Vanderbilt Communication Studies major Taylor Imboden Brown for her keen research skills. Various members of the Women's and Gender Studies community at Vanderbilt have given me informal feedback on parts of this project over the past several years, and I am grateful for that as well.

In 2010 and 2011, I was privileged to participate in a yearlong seminar on Representation and Social Change at the Robert Penn Warren Center for the Humanities at Vanderbilt, an experience that enriched this project by exposing me to the smart thinking of my colleagues—about their work and my own—from other disciplines. I thank Executive Director Mona Frederick and the staff of the Warren Center for their support of that seminar, and I am especially appreciative of the intellectual companionship and thoughtful feedback on my work offered by the members of the seminar, in particular Laura Carpenter, Terry McDonnell, Eddie Wright-Rios, and Anne Morey.

Julia T. Wood of the University of North Carolina at Chapel Hill, my sometime coauthor and always-dear comrade in the feminist scholarly community in Communication Studies, has been overwhelmingly supportive of this book, even when it took time away from other projects that we were working on together. She improved its introduction immeasurably, in her always gracious yet incisive style, and I thank her for that as well as for the priceless perspective she brings to my thinking about my work and my life.

John M. Murphy, my colleague at three different institutions over the years, read parts of the manuscript of *Watching Women's Liberation* at different moments in its evolution, and he ably acted as a naïve reader when I needed smart feedback from someone who was not immersed in the second wave. He is not, however, naïve about how to make an argument clearer and about how to gently correct problematic prose. I owe him a great deal for his kindnesses in these areas and many others.

Lisa Maria Hogeland, my colleague in Women's Studies at my first academic home, the University of Cincinnati, as well as my intellectual companion and beloved friend for twenty-plus years, remains my touchstone and ideal reader on all matters related to the study of the second wave of U.S. feminism. She turned her talents toward improving this book every time I asked for her help, reading almost every word of it over the years. She is my personal hero for doing so, and she made the final product much smarter than it otherwise would have been.

The search for images to illustrate *Watching Women's Liberation* presented a number of challenges, and I thank John Lucaites for some initial advice on handling them. I also am deeply appreciative of the help I received from a number of people who made personal efforts that allowed me to reprint important photographs. Among them are Lauren Wendle and Patricia Fried, whose late father Lawrence Fried took the well-known photo of Gloria Steinem that appeared on the cover of *Newsweek* in 1971; Mary Brooks, the daughter of Jaquie

Davison, who allowed me to reprint Davison's photo in chapter 5; and Robin Morgan and Alix Kates Shulman, who graciously gave me permission to reprint photos of the 1968 Miss America Pageant protest that came from their personal collections. I also thank my Vanderbilt colleague Paul Stob, whose technological wizardry was indispensable for the screen captures that appear in chapter 2. The College of Arts and Science and the Office of the Vice Provost for Research at Vanderbilt also have my gratitude for the generous subsidy they provided to cover the cost of permissions associated with the reprinting of previously published photographs.

I also acknowledge the assistance of Taylor & Francis Publishers in allowing me to reprint portions of chapters 4 and 5 that first appeared, respectively, as "'Fixing' Feminism: Women's Liberation and the Rhetoric of Television Documentary," *Quarterly Journal of Speech* 90 (2004): 55–80; and "Spectacle, Spectatorship, and Gender Anxiety in the Television Coverage of the 1970 Women's Strike for Equality," *Communication Studies* 50 (1999): 143–157.

Last, but by no means least, I thank my family and friends in Nashville. John and Christopher Sloop respected this project and its importance to me and gave me the gifts of time, space, and solitude that I needed to finish it. The many women, too numerous to name, who form the community that enriches my life every day were a crucial support in ways they will never know. Their smarts, strength, and sisterhood are a continuing reminder that the impact of the second wave of U.S. feminism is profound and long lasting.

Everyone I have named here has made this project better; responsibility for all weaknesses that remain is my own.

Watching Women's Liberation, 1970

Introduction
1970

If the 1960s belonged to the blacks, the next ten years are ours.

—Lucy Komisar (1970) on "The New Feminism"
in the *Saturday Review* (p. 55)

On September 7, 1968, roughly one hundred women from several states convened on Atlantic City's famed boardwalk to protest the Miss America Pageant. They passed out a ten-point press release titled "No More Miss America!" (1970) that was created by a group calling itself New York Radical Women (NYRW). The document outlined their objections to the annual event and all it represented, beginning with its perpetuation of "The Degrading Mindless-Boob-Girlie Symbol" (p. 584). The protestors marched, they carried signs, they sang, they performed guerilla theater (crowning a live sheep Miss America and parading a life-size Miss America puppet in chains representing beauty standards). They also threw bras, high heels, and other trappings of femininity into a Freedom Trash Can, which, despite later reports that alleged bra burning at the event, they did not light on fire. That night during the pageant itself, several protestors entered the auditorium and draped a Women's Liberation banner over the balcony. Chanting "no more Miss America" and "freedom for women," they released stink bombs, supposedly containing Toni Home Permanent Solution (Toni was a pageant sponsor), before they were ejected by police and a few were arrested. During the mayhem, the network television cameras broadcasting the pageant never wavered from the stage (Hanisch, 1998).

Despite ample camera presence at the pageant, none of the three television networks carried a story about the protest on their nightly news.[1] It received widespread coverage from newspapers and the wire services, however, and the events on the boardwalk that day quickly came to represent "the moment when the women's movement made its debut on the national stage" (Collins, 2009, p. 194). The 1968 Miss America Pageant protest also precipitated a period of rapid development for what is now termed the "second wave" of feminism in the United States, yet that movement would not be the subject of a nightly network news broadcast until early 1970, almost a year and a half later.[2] The networks quickly made up for lost time, however, and devoted more airtime to reporting on the women's movement that year than they ever would again.

The year 1970 was *the* pivotal year in the launching of what was then called "women's liberation" into mediated public consciousness in the United States. A deluge of national print and broadcast stories pushed the movement to public prominence, offering viewers and readers various narratives about its origins, its members, and its meaning. The Big Three network news divisions would produce more than twenty discrete reports on the movement and/or activities in 1970, including a three-part series on CBS, a six-part series on NBC, and a half-hour documentary on ABC. By mid-year, all of the networks had weighed in with their portraits of the movement; by the end of August, each would send reporters to multiple U.S. cities to cover the movement's largest event thus far: the Women's Strike for Equality planned by the four-year-old National Organization for Women (NOW). Designed to dramatize the movement's issues, the strike also was a purposeful intervention into what NOW's leaders saw as feminism's developing image problem.

Although 1968's Miss America Pageant protest proved to be the first real success among feminists' early attempts to attract media attention, 1970 was the year that their media activism would finally bear fruit on national television. In addition to the voluminous attention to the Women's Strike for Equality, network news would cover feminists' disruption of Senate hearings on the birth control pill in January and the sit-in by a hundred women at the offices of the *Ladies' Home Journal* in March. Scenes from the Miss America Pageant protest finally appeared on national television screens that year as well, in feature stories on the movement that cemented the importance of the 1968 events—and the mythology of bra burning—to the mediated narrative of the women's movement. Bra burning was the first and most tenacious media-created misconception about feminism's second wave, but it would not be the last. Over the course of 1970, as leaders and members of the multifaceted women's liberation movement struggled with the movement's growing numbers, ideological conflicts, and evolving political goals, they also would grapple with its dramatically increasing visibility.

Watching Women's Liberation focuses on the national television news narratives about the second wave that proliferated in 1970, a year in which the networks' eagerness to make sense of the movement for their viewers was accompanied by feminists' efforts to use national media for their own purposes. The interaction of these efforts produced coverage that was distinguished by its contradictions—it ranged from sympathetic to patronizing, from thoughtful to sensationalistic, and from evenhanded to overtly dismissive. The effects of the movement's heightened public profile proved to be equally unpredictable. Even negative coverage had positive outcomes for movement growth; at the same time, some feminist media activism that proved surprisingly successful had an adverse effect on movement cohesion.

The multiplicity of news coverage and its consequences reflected feminism's own variety and attendant instability in 1970, when it lacked the clearly defined goals, such as "stop the war" or "end Jim Crow," attached to other contemporaneous countercultural efforts. The relationship between the two major wings of women's liberation, the liberal feminism primarily represented by NOW and the radical faction made up of various small groups, was politically antagonistic in many ways, and each wing faced internal discord as well. In 1970, NOW had existed for four years but was not yet the singular public voice of feminism that it would become during the Equal Rights Amendment (ERA) campaign, and the ERA's materialization as a key feminist goal in the public mind was in its early stages, although media reports would facilitate that process as the year wore on. At the same time, the radical feminist groups that had begun to form in various cities three years earlier were in organizational and ideological flux as they negotiated their political identities and priorities, including their relationship to other countercultural movements from which most of their members had emerged. Some early groups, such as NYRW, had already splintered, and its offshoots that would become important to second-wave theorizing, such as New York–based Redstockings, were barely a year old. In short, radical feminism was a movement in transition that "did not yet have a clearly defined politics" (Hole and Levine, 1971, p. 136).

The year 1970 proved a turning point for the movement and its image politics, as "two way, interactive, reflexive and historically specific struggles over meaning" between movement actors and news workers played out on television screens (Barker-Plummer, 2010, p. 146). Furthermore, 1970 was the year that network news programs gave their most sustained attention to the second wave *as a movement*—as a public phenomenon with broad social implications and as a collective of diverse political actors working for social change. The volume and variety of network coverage of the movement itself fell off sharply after 1970 and shifted in perceptible ways as news reports became increasingly issue-centered around topics such as abortion, the ERA, rape law reform, and various antidiscrimination actions spearheaded by institutionalized feminist interest groups.[3]

In a series of case studies examining every network news report produced about women's liberation in 1970, *Watching Women's Liberation* complicates conventional wisdom about the second wave's interaction with mass media. The established narrative holds that national media functioned primarily as feminism's enemy and not its ally in this early period, consistently framing "feminists and feminism as illegitimate, deviant, unlike 'real' women and extremist" and effecting an overall "marginalization" of the movement's ideas, actors, and activism (Barker-Plummer, 2010, pp. 175–176). These claims are all true to some degree, but they are not true of all coverage, including early network news reports. Such generalizations do not account for the significance of particular moments in the trajectory of mass media engagement with the second wave, the historical circumstances that gave rise to them, and their meaning-making potential in their specific contexts. That potential was the product of the interaction, and in some cases the collision, of multiple factors: the movement's complex history and structure, including its varying ideological and political commitments that affected feminists' media practices; journalists' reliance on news values, routines, and formats that shaped their coverage of the movement; and feminism's intersection with and challenges to existing cultural narratives and ideologies about gender, race, class, and sexuality that circulated in its historical milieu.

The stories that network news told about women's liberation in 1970 were a product of the tumultuous times in which they were produced, demonstrating the ways in which the movement was "a complex and moving target" (Barker-Plummer, 2010, p. 174). That context affected everyone involved: the news workers (including sympathetic women reporters familiar with gender discrimination) who would rely on sex-race and feminism–civil rights analogies to frame the movement's meaning; the feminists, who struggled to negotiate their political identities and commitments in the face of the distorting mirror of media attention; and the American television news viewer watching women's liberation unfold on a television screen that had been broadcasting images of political unrest for a decade or more. Typically presumed to be a middle-aged, middle-class, white male by news producers, such a viewer was likely to see the movement as yet another bewildering assault on his privileged status.

Women themselves, although rarely a target audience for national network news, were watching as well, and thousands flocked to join the feminist groups that mushroomed in the wake of 1970's media onslaught (Freeman, 1975). After the August 1970 Strike for Equality, a CBS News poll found that 1 in 5 Americans over age eighteen reported that they had "read or heard about women's liberation" (quoted in Hole and Levine, 1971, p. 269). Equally as striking, interviews with movement members between 1969 and 1971 revealed that women who joined feminist groups before the end of 1969 did so because of personal contacts, but about a quarter of those who joined *after* 1969 "decided to look into the movement entirely on the basis of what they had learned from the mass media" (Carden, 1974, pp. 32–33).

That public understanding of a social movement is largely dependent on mass media depictions of it is a truism of the scholarship on media and social movements. A movement's media image "tends to become 'the movement' for wider publics and institutions who have few alternative sources of information, or none at all, about it," and feminism is no exception (Gitlin, 1980, p. 3). Although the 1960s resides in cultural memory as the one in which social change movements of various kinds exploded onto newspaper pages and television screens, second-wave feminism was a latecomer to this wave of public protest. By the time women's liberation made the news, feminists had some sense of what they were up against with a mainstream media that had been covering public turmoil over the Vietnam War, civil rights, and youth discontent for several years. They met the general tendencies revealed by that coverage with media strategies that reflected the diversity of the movement itself.

Movements, Media Strategies, and Women's Liberation

In the broadest terms, the relationship between social movements and mass media is characterized by interdependency: movements need media to make news, and media need movements so that they can make news out of them. More specifically, movements need mass media to get out their message in order to mobilize members, to validate their importance as a "player," and to create public awareness and sympathy that can be used to put pressure on those in power to attend to the movement's demands. From this perspective, "no news is bad news" (Gamson and Wolfsfeld, 1993, p. 116). In return, movements provide mass media with good copy, especially when they stage dramatic demonstrations and/or use disruptive, confrontational tactics. Yet this relationship is hardly balanced—"social movements need the media more than the media need them"—and the burden of adaptation falls heavily on movement actors (Huddy, 1997, p. 184). Because reporters work in very structured ways (although often unconsciously so), movements that "use" mass media successfully tend to be those that organize their events and their messages in ways that work with news organizations' preexisting logics and routines.

An enormous number of potential news stories present themselves in any given day; those events and/or issues that get reported are those that fit well with news values: "the profession-specific values on which journalists call in constructing stories" (Bradley, 2003, p. 77). In addition to their commitment to general journalistic values such as balance, objectivity, and accuracy, news workers operate within institutional traditions that news scholars variously refer to as routine practices, strategic rituals, or professional news norms, all of which are rooted in the qualities that influence what stories are worth covering and how they will be framed (Bennett, 1988; Bradley, 2003; Fishman, 1980; Gans, 1979; Gitlin, 1980; Jamieson and Campbell, 2006; Tuchman, 1978b).

Common news norms include a focus on conflict/drama, deviance, and human interest (exemplifying the value of individualism), as well as an emphasis on events rather than issues, and on the potential connection of those events to topics of recent and recognized public concern. The rise of broadcast news added additional criteria, including a story's capacity to yield "good pictures" and the need to tell it quickly and thus simply. Finally, some factors just make particular stories easier to report. News workers are attracted to stories that happen during business hours, preferably on weekdays, and that allow them to meet press and broadcast deadlines. They also tend to find routinely scheduled events (e.g., public meetings, trials, press conferences) convenient to cover, and they appreciate accessible spokespersons (such as media representatives and organizational leaders) who can comment on the meaning of events (Tuchman, 1978b).

These criteria clarify the problems and possibilities faced by social movements in their quest for media attention. Although dramatic demonstrations catch media attention, focus on the drama can take the place of reporting on the message; that is, the spectacle of the *event* supplants analysis of the *issue*. Challengers who use "an act of disorder to force their way" into the media spotlight "enter defined as upstarts, and the framing of the group may obscure any message it carries" (Gamson and Wolfsfeld, 1993, p. 122). Moreover, of the factors most likely to produce helpful media coverage for movement groups (coverage that helps the movement to gain standing in the public sphere, to disseminate the movement's preferred frame for its message, and "to gain sympathy from relevant publics"), the existence of a professional organizational structure and the appointing of representatives specifically designated for interacting with media are among the most important (Gamson and Wolfsfeld, 1993, p. 121). Without these elements, movements look disorganized, and reporters assume that disorganized entities are unlikely to be taken seriously by those in power and therefore merit less serious treatment. Organizational coherence generally coincides with message coherence, and news workers tend to find movements with easily understandable messages and goals—oriented toward legal, legislative, and institutional change—easy to understand and to write about.

Feminists' awareness of these tendencies, an awareness that, for many, arose not just from witnessing previous media-movement interactions but also from participating in them, did not result in a unified response. The battle over the media image of women's liberation that erupted in 1970 was fought on a variety of fronts inside and outside the movement, and it reflected the disparate organizational and ideological origins of the two major factions in the movement that developed separately but roughly simultaneously in the mid- to late 1960s.

The initial rumblings of what would become the liberal wing of women's liberation surfaced in 1963, when Betty Friedan published *The Feminine Mystique,* a critique of middle-class, white women's oppression as housewives that became a key text for liberal feminism. That same year, the Presidential Commission on the Status of Women, created by John F. Kennedy and initially chaired by Eleanor Roosevelt, released its report, *American Women,* that detailed the limited opportunities and discrimination women faced in education, employment, the law, and politics. The 1966 creation of NOW, with Friedan as its first president, was the eventual product of these intersecting events (Eisenmann, 2010).[4]

On a different front, white women in civil rights and New Left groups began to circulate documents critiquing movement sexism by 1964. The resistance to their efforts and the subsequent fallout within the Left would lead to the influential radical feminist groups that began to form in in New York, Chicago, Boston, and Gainesville, Florida, by 1967; two national conferences for those initially calling themselves "radical women" would occur in 1968 (Giardina, 2010; Freeman, 1975). By that point, the two primary branches of what mass media would generally refer to as "the women's liberation movement" were taking shape.[5] The liberal branch, largely identified with NOW, was composed of older women with experience in media, government, and politics and was concerned primarily with issues of public discrimination (e.g., education, employment, and pay equity). The radical branch was composed of younger women, many of whom had been active in other countercultural movements and who brought the skills they learned there to their theorizing and activism.

Liberals and radicals would cohere around support for the repeal of laws criminalizing abortion, but their ideological emphases and their political practices—like their origin stories—were quite distinct in most ways. Reformist liberal feminists focused their efforts on cultivating positive media coverage and on influencing the courts, legislative bodies, government agencies, and electoral politics. They also worked with existing interest groups with similar goals, such as the American Civil Liberties Union and the National Association for the Advancement of Colored People (NAACP). Women in the radical branch, in contrast, rejected liberalism and saw themselves as working toward a grassroots cultural and political revolution that would entail the elimination of what were then termed "sex roles." Most radical groups practiced consciousness-raising (CR), the analysis of power relations between men and women in a variety of contexts, both private and public, a focus that can be broadly labeled "sexual politics." CR, a small-group process in which women shared their thoughts and experiences about living in a male-defined and male-dominated culture, enabled the recognition that what women had viewed as personal problems were, rather, political problems produced by the disparities in power between men and women under patriarchy. Hence, the well-known phrase, "the personal is political" (Hanisch, 1978b; Sarachild, 1978).

The media strategies developed by these two broad groups of women, like their politics, differed. Feminists in the liberal branch of the movement, because of previous experience dealing with the press (and because many worked in media organizations), practiced "media pragmatism," an approach designed to maximize favorable coverage by establishing functional relations with news media (Barker-Plummer, 1995, p. 312). For example, NOW's leaders tailored events to attract media coverage, made sure that they had a coherent, specific message on such occasions, and provided representatives who knew how to talk to the press. Because NOW was primarily concerned with issues of public discrimination—for instance, the organization staged several early protests against gender discrimination in public facilities—their equality-based discourse was familiar to news workers steeped in the traditions of U.S. liberalism. NOW's self-framing of itself as a civil rights group—an NAACP for women—made its discourse and goals easy to understand and to communicate for news workers who saw the analogy to civil rights rhetoric from the previous two decades (Barker-Plummer, 2002).

Radical feminist goals and activities were far more difficult to fit into traditional news categories that emphasized public events and policy issues.[6] Radical feminists were concerned with issues outside the bounds of liberalism's concern with equal treatment under the law—issues such as sex-role stereotyping, male-female relationships, oppressive images of women, rape, pornography, and sexuality—and their analysis of those topics initially took place in CR groups and in somewhat ephemeral movement media rather than in public places. Compounding this problem was the fact that radical women's liberation groups were usually leaderless because they saw hierarchy as patriarchal; thus, they had no officers to speak *for* them to the press. Without official sources, news workers would talk to anyone they could find, appointing some members of the movement as leaders without their consent.

Familiar with negative news treatment of countercultural movements in the 1960s, radicals were suspicious of reporters and viewed mainstream media as

"little more than the handmaiden and voice of the establishment power structure" (Hole and Levine, 1971, p. 267). They often refused access to reporters who
were not women, motivated by their belief that men would not understand their
concerns and would misrepresent them as well as by their hope that news organizations could be pressured into hiring more women in the same way that the
civil rights movement had stimulated the hiring of black journalists (Freeman,
1975). Terming this strategy "media subversion," Bernadette Barker-Plummer
(1995) notes that radical feminists' "refusal to embed any media logic into their
communications sometimes extended into outright hostility where women
sabotaged attempts to cover movement events because they were suspicious
of how that coverage would turn out" (pp. 317–318). Motivated by their general
distrust of mainstream media, radical feminists prioritized the creation of their
own alternative publications, and a feminist print culture developed rapidly
after 1968.[7]

Ultimately, the different approaches that liberal and radical feminists took
to dealing with news media were related to their differing rhetorical purposes
and presumed audiences when they took their issues public. NOW structured
its issues carefully to fit criteria for newsworthiness; through media exposure,
they sought not just to attract members but also to win the approval of opinion
leaders (presumed to be male) and to produce legislative and judicial change.
When radical feminists sought media attention, their purpose was to take CR to
a public stage and to recruit women to the movement, thus precipitating a shift
in consciousness that would lead to the revolution they envisioned. As Ellen
Willis, a founding member of NYRW, remarked in 1998, "the primary task of the
early radical feminists was public consciousness-raising—getting these new
and controversial ideas out to women everywhere" (quoted in Bradley, 2003,
p. 49). The 1968 Miss America Pageant protest, which Willis helped to plan,
was an early example of this strategy.

Second-wave feminists' varying media strategies produced varying results,
but previous studies of mainstream news' treatment of the women's movement
and its issues emphasize some broad themes in the coverage, such as the tendency to depict the movement and its adherents as angry, deviant, and unnatural,
qualities that worked to make movement activities newsworthy at the same time
that they cast them as irrelevant to most Americans (Ashley and Olson, 1998;
Barker-Plummer, 2010; Bradley, 2003; Douglas, 1994; Mendes, 2011). Many stories "separated feminists and feminist concerns from those that were perceived to
be the characteristics of women in general," and the negative reactions of "ordinary women" became a recurring feature of reports on the movement, while the
opposition of men was usually invisible (Bradley, 2003, p. 89; see also Douglas,
1994; Dow, 1999; Rhode, 1995). Because feminists did not represent the views of

all women, such stories implied, their claims reflected their personal failings as "ugly, humorless, disorderly man-haters" who would be happy, "normal" women if only they were pretty and sexually satisfied (Douglas, 1994, p. 189).

Such characterizations were more common for feminists categorized as radical or militant, appellations sometimes claimed by activists themselves but also freely dispensed by journalists. In some cases, radical was a label applied to grievances that foregrounded topics conventionally defined as personal or private, and thus outside the limits of legitimate public protest. Such issues were the focus of early radical feminist activism such as the 1968 Miss America Pageant protest or the 1969 disruption of the New York City Bridal Fair. In other cases, the radical or militant tag was applied on the basis of behavior and was used to describe feminists who, regardless of their ideology, engaged in actions deemed unruly or confrontational. The bar for what counted as transgressive behavior was, however, particularly low for women; at a basic level, public feminist activity breached the boundaries of the gendered division between public and private that made any social protest a violation of women's proper sphere (Douglas, 1994; Dow 1999).

Conclusions about news media treatment of women's liberation take note of particularities arising from feminists' violation of gender expectations, but they also reflect general tendencies in mainstream mass media coverage of countercultural movements. For example, like those of student activists in the 1960s, the protests of the younger branch of the second wave often were depicted as "simultaneously dangerous and ineffectual, deeply subversive yet of little consequence" (Douglas, 1994, p. 155). As in early coverage of the New Left, a search for feminist leaders to speak for the cause elevated some voices that did not—and could not—speak for the diverse interests of the movement but that served journalistic purposes nonetheless (Gitlin, 1980). And, as was the case in some coverage of civil rights, confrontation itself—rather than the reasons behind it—became the focus of reporting, and opportunities for those who engaged in it to "speak in their own voices and to assume active subject positions" were rare (Bodroghkozy, 2012, p. 59). In later stages of both the antiwar movement and the civil rights movement, moderate leaders became increasingly newsworthy and moderate demands increasingly acceptable. The same was true for feminism by the early 1970s, when Gloria Steinem achieved her status as the widely recognized face of feminism and support for moderate demands that could be met within the system (e.g., passage of the ERA) received positive media treatment, a process that facilitated and gained strength from the marginalization of radical voices calling for a social and cultural revolution (Bradley, 2003; Douglas, 1994; Dow, 2004; van Zoonen, 1992).

In other important ways, however, the early second wave is not a neat analog to the protest movements that preceded it. With the exception of abortion, which had emerged as a public policy issue in some states by 1970, many of the issues on which feminists, particularly radical feminists, focused did not have acknowledged status as topics of public concern. Thus, part of the rhetorical challenge feminists faced was simply making their grievances salient in a context in which those grievances could be (and were) depicted as frivolous, particularly in comparison to those raised by other movements. Being taken seriously as political actors was a central obstacle feminists faced, and the moral authority that came to be attached to both civil rights and the antiwar movement eluded women's liberation. Sexism could not be vividly illustrated by photos or television footage of children being napalmed, or of protestors being hosed down by firemen, attacked by police dogs, and gassed by state troopers; in short, "the most basic and pernicious forms of female oppression did not lend themselves to visual documentation" (Douglas, 1994, p. 187).

Even so, when network television reporters began to cover women's liberation, they made use of the medium's visual capacity in ways that sometimes supported and other times undermined feminist claims. Sustained analysis of the images that accompanied verbal news discourses about the movement is mostly absent from the body of work just discussed, but television news is distinguished by its visuality. As I argue next, the potential meanings and influence of television news narratives about second-wave feminism are most fully comprehended through close readings of the verbal *and* visual features of news texts in relation to the specific historical, rhetorical, institutional, and political contexts that operated within and on the movement and mass media. Attention to the interacting forces that enabled and constrained the diverse portraits of the movement offered by network news in 1970 generates a rich and textured narrative that both confirms and confounds existing generalizations about news media and women's liberation.

Rhetorics of News

Watching Women's Liberation constructs a historicized narrative of national broadcast representation of the second wave as it evolved over the course of a single, pivotal year. This focused approach allows me to acknowledge important distinctions among different types of coverage—print versus television, hard news or event-centered reporting versus soft feature or trend stories and documentary—as well as to recognize the diverse strategies reporters used within these formats to construct strikingly different narratives for explaining women's liberation to their audiences. Such variances become most apparent through close analysis of the verbal and visual content of news reports.

I approach news about the movement at the level of individual news stories, thus yielding insights into their meaning-making potential that a more fragmented and decontextualized mode of reading cannot. Close critical analysis of texts at this level is "more flexible" in that it "aspires to a level of complexity" that "remains true to the actual complexity and contradictoriness of media artifacts" (Gitlin, 1980, p. 303). The greater depth possible with this method enables identification of not only the strategies that come to typify treatment of a topic but also of those that are idiosyncratic; importantly, it also allows for appreciating the significance of both. My use of the term "strategies" derives from my background in rhetorical studies and my stance as a rhetorical critic. I view television news, then and now, as a rhetoric, an attempt to advocate for a chosen perspective. Regardless of conscious intention on the part of news workers, news discourse functions persuasively through choices of words and images; it makes some positions and points of view more palatable than others; and it constructs a partial (in all senses of the term) and particular reality for what a topic such as women's liberation does and should mean to the assumed media spectator.

A rhetorical perspective emphasizes the ways in which discourse is always produced with an audience in mind, and I bring this sensibility to understanding not only what feminists believed themselves to be up to when they took their issues to a public stage, but also to understanding how news workers were always already addressing an imagined viewer when they represented those issues and activities. If news addresses its viewers as citizens, to whom it presumably provides "knowledge about the real historical world, knowledge that will lead to action *in* the world," then the subject position of "citizen" is generally assumed to be occupied by white males, an assumption that reverberates in specific ways when the topic is feminism, as I will elaborate shortly (Thornham, 2007, p. 85, emphasis in original; see also Schudson, 1995).

Sensitivity to context is important to understanding rhetorical impact as well. I situate the case studies of news discourse in this book in relationship to each other, to print reporting of the period, and to the historical events and people that they purport to represent, as well as to various other discourses to which they explicitly and implicitly allude. These discourses include, at different moments, the history and rhetoric of the second wave, the rhetorical tactics and representation of previous and contemporaneous movements for social change, and the norms of news as a discursive genre as well as changes taking place in the news industry around 1970. The intentions of movement actors, when they sought and participated in media coverage, and the intentions of journalists, when they framed their reports about feminist activities, also form a key context for the representations that resulted, and I offer insight into those motivations as well. I am, however, primarily interested in what appeared *on the screen* and, given the context(s) in which it appeared, how it might have been understood by members of the national viewing audience, most of whom would have had no direct experience with movement politics.

Importantly, I am less interested in separating fact from fiction or truth from (mis)representation than I am in making arguments for understanding these texts and their contexts in particular ways (although I am often interested in the rhetorical impact of errors of fact and omission). Generally, my critical practice is "an argumentative activity in which the goal is to persuade the audience that their knowledge of a text will be enriched if they choose to see a text as the critic does, while never assuming that that particular 'way of seeing' is the only or the best way to see that text (or that all audiences do, in fact, see it that way)" (Dow, 1996, p. 4; see also Dow, 2001). The extended narrative of network reporting in 1970 that results from this approach is my interpretation of the trajectory of the movement's mediated meaning and momentum over the course of that singularly influential year, and my ultimate objective is to provide unique depth and perspective on the rhetorical power of the visions of women's liberation offered by national broadcast media.

I use the term "visions" quite deliberately, because I attend closely to the visual, as well as the verbal, strategies of network television news texts. With rare exceptions (e.g., Douglas, 1994), the research on representations of second-wave feminism focuses on print texts, and even analyses that account for television news neglect sustained scrutiny of the often complex and contradictory function of images in the context of broadcast news narratives. Yet visuality is fundamental to the impact of television news; equally important, Western culture's relationship to women also is largely governed by the visual, and femininity "is bound up very closely with the way in which the female body is perceived and represented" (Betterton, 1987, p. 7). Thus, one of the challenges faced by feminists who were captured by television cameras was simply being subjected to the norms generally used for visually representing women, whether in pornography, fine art, advertising, or film.

Because news workers assumed that the consumers of news—particularly hard news dealing with topics of public concern—were men, their reporting on feminism often deployed conventions of visual representation that were presumed to appeal to male spectators. One of those conventions was the display of female bodies as objects for what film theorist Laura Mulvey (1975/1999) has called "the determining male-gaze" (p. 62). The camera work in many television news stories about feminist protest operated from a seemingly common-sense assumption that women's bodies functioned as objects of visual display for men and that they were, as a result, always ripe for evaluation (Douglas, 1994). A corollary to the problem of objectification is the tendency to reduce groups of women acting in public to nothing more than sheer spectacle. Art critic John Berger's (1972) famous formulation that "men act and women appear" is useful for elucidating the tendency of broadcast journalists to frame masses of women engaged in protest as an entertaining and amusing phenomenon that did not require explanation of its import by the participants (p. 46).

Unlike liberal feminist calls for equal opportunity, radical feminist ideology was complicated and unfamiliar, and it proved difficult to communicate within the brevity required by television news. Many reports simply represented the radical movement through images of transgressive behavior rather than through explication of issues. Certain images of radical protest functioned as stock footage for network stories; for example, scenes of a brief disruption by members of Washington D.C. Women's Liberation at the Senate hearings on the birth control pill in January of 1970 appeared in no fewer than five different network stories that year. The national broadcast stories of 1970 also had recurring, although less incendiary, stock footage for liberal feminism. Demands for employment opportunity were routinely illustrated with images of dronelike secretaries at rows of desks, and the activities of liberal feminists themselves were depicted through footage of meetings at which mostly middle-aged, middle-class, professionally garbed women sat quietly listening to speakers or holding composed discussions of issues; in fact, one NBC reporter described the look of a 1970 NOW meeting as "interchangeable with the PTA."

Network reports thus accomplished the delineation of liberal or moderate versus radical or militant feminist demands and behavior visually as well as verbally. Some reporting stressed radicals' violation of decorum, social consensus, and gender expectations by representing them with images characterized by excess and exaggeration, yet underscored liberals' moderation by depicting them with unremarkable, almost mundane, visuals and framing them in respectful and conventional medium shots when they spoke to the camera. Radicals were more likely to be the subject of extreme close-ups, which violate expectations for interpersonal distance, signify hostility or distrust toward the subject, and contribute to an impression of deviance (Fiske, 1987). For women specifically, extreme close-ups imply that "their images, like their emotions, are disproportionate, over-the-top, and uncontrollable; they cannot contain themselves, nor can they be contained (not even by the parameters of the medium itself)," a description that aptly captures the attitude of some reporting on radical feminism (King, 2007, p. 134). When national television news reports focused on radical feminist groups rather than individuals, they featured images of casually dressed, long-haired, and intense-looking young women sitting on the floor in private spaces, creating a stark contrast with the organized and "ladylike" demeanor of liberal feminist groups held in public meeting rooms. Although not named as such, these were usually images of CR groups.

CR presented a unique representational challenge for news workers, one that usefully illustrates the ill fit between news practices and radical politics. In important ways, CR was the heart of radical feminism; it recruited women to the movement, served as an organizing tool for radical feminist protest, and produced feminist theory; many early feminist analyses published in the various movement publications that multiplied after 1968 were written as a result of CR. By the early 1970s, thousands of such groups existed across the country (Shreve, 1989). But their political importance to women's liberation was not amenable to media representation, to say the least. As Tuchman (1978b) has observed, "much of the [radical] movement's political emphasis was upon thinking about issues, women's place in the world, and 'changing people's heads'" (p. 139). It was a *process* rather than an *event*, and its significance was hard to capture in a sound bite or an image.

CR flew in the face of the norms of news culture: men were barred from meetings; the gatherings were purposely leaderless; they were held at night and on weekends; and they were laborious and emotional (Tuchman, 1978a). CR was a highly inductive group process that challenged news workers' preference for representing individuals with clearly stated claims; as Patricia Bradley (2003) usefully puts it, "mass media do not have a place for 'cooperative behavior' on their encoding templates" (p. xv). One reporter compared representing CR to "trying to nail Jell-O to the wall," and only one network report in 1970 explicitly mentioned the process (Mills, 1997, p. 43). Radical protest actions, on the other hand, were camera-friendly and had clear news value, and images of confrontational and disruptive women became a signifier for radical feminism in the public mind.

However, not all visual strategies employed by network news workers worked *against* feminism, and several of the reports I discuss in the case studies refused the temptation to depict women's liberation as sensationalized spectacle. The negative aspects of reporting on the second wave have received far more attention than the positive ones, a phenomenon that works against recognition of some news workers' inventive use of the camera's rhetorical capabilities to legitimate feminist grievances, as several stories from 1970 illustrate. Equally as noteworthy, the visual inclusion of women of color in some of those reports implicitly incorporated them within the movement's constituency, something that, as I discuss shortly, news reports almost always refused to do verbally.

Finally, the news reports from 1970 functioned as implicit (and sometimes explicit) discourses about gender. This dynamic manifested at every level, from assumptions about the audiences for those reports, to their verbal and visual framing, to their deep concern with what women's liberation might mean for men, even more so than for women. At a basic level, network news itself was a "masculine narrative," in terms of those who produced it and those who were assumed to consume it, particularly so in 1970 (Rakow and Kranich, 1991, p. 8). Harvey Molotoch noted in 1978 that "news is a man's world," and the news business was about "men talking to men" (p. 180). Women in positions of power were even rarer in network news than they were at national newspapers; middle-aged white men ran newsrooms, and "their interests, their biases, [and] their backgrounds" dominated news reporting (Mills, 1997, p. 43). This same type of man was assumed to be the audience for news, regardless of who did the reporting. Thoughtful treatment of feminist issues was not easy to come by because men were assumed to lack interest in it, and many of the qualities of early network coverage of women's liberation are made easier to understand once one realizes that reporters often were operating under the premise that they were explaining the sometimes shocking behavior of angry women to an audience of middle-aged white men much like themselves.

Much early print coverage, in contrast, appeared on the women's pages of newspapers and in women's magazines, venues in which the assumption of a female audience shifted the valence of the reporting and allowed it to be somewhat sympathetic, or, at the least, less dismissive (Tuchman, 1978a). Many feminists saw such soft news venues as a ghetto that undercut the movement's political status, but the women's pages, particularly in the *New York Times*, gave important exposure to the early movement at a time when it otherwise would not have been covered at all (Bradley, 2003).[8] For example, the *Times*'s reports on the 1968 Miss America Pageant protest were written by staff from the paper's Style section (formerly the women's page). Network news had no corresponding section targeted to "women's interests," and when women's liberation became the focus of national television reporting in 1970, it bore the full brunt of its conflicts with masculine news values. Yet there were exceptions, and a few of the sympathetic network feature stories from that year imply a targeted audience of women viewers.

Cultural ideologies about gender also played a consistent role in the content of verbal and visual television reporting on the movement, as some visual strategies already discussed exemplify. Ironically, as feminists took their issues to the public stage, they found themselves being framed through the very same cultural logics of gender that they were critiquing. These logics included, for example, an obsession with the femininity and physical attractiveness of feminists as well as adherence to a rigid gender binary under which any departures from or questioning of conventional white, middle-class standards for femininity became part of the context used to interpret feminist activism. Women's assumed *difference* from men, as well as feminists' assumed *difference* from ordinary women, were implicit or explicit framing devices in much movement coverage, demonstrating the always interactive nature of gender definitions.

By taking their grievances public, feminists challenged the privileging of the public sphere as a male-dominated space, threatening masculinity by asserting a prerogative reserved for men. Moreover, radical feminists explicitly called the immutability of gender definitions into question through their analyses of the workings of patriarchy as a socially constructed system, rather than as the "natural" order of things. News reports often implied that feminists' violation of gender norms stemmed from their deviant personal psychologies rather than from their politics, making their femininity—their credibility as women—the issue. This pathologizing of feminist complaints had a corollary effect of obscuring many feminists' longtime identity as activists, erasing the considerable experience they possessed as political thinkers and actors. Just as leftist men refused to recognize sexism as a political issue rather than a personal problem, so did many news workers.

Thus, understandings of feminists' deviance were grounded in the perils that their behavior and discourse posed to cultural notions of femininity *and* masculinity. Much coverage of the second wave was suffused with a palpable sense of *gender anxiety;* an implicit (and sometimes explicitly articulated) unease with the threat that feminists posed to the stability of traditional gender norms. Although it was perhaps most obvious in the images of women practicing karate that appeared in both print and broadcast stories about the movement and that "overflowed with anxieties about female anger, male castration, and the possible dissolution of amicable heterosexual relations" (Douglas, 1994, p. 188), gender anxiety took a variety of forms in national reporting on feminism.

Such anxiety was evident quite early on in the mythical association of feminism and bra burning that resulted from print coverage of the 1968 Miss America Pageant protest. Media obsession with "the supposed burning of bras" communicated "the fear that women might, by abandoning cosmetics and delicate costuming, lose their femininity, i.e., their sexual and companionship utility for men" (Molotoch, 1978, p. 182). Some reporting on the movement implied that feminists both hated men and wanted to *be* men, endangering not just their own femininity but men's masculinity as well. This last variation is clearly visible in the network coverage of the 1970 Women's Strike for Equality, in which ABC commentator Howard K. Smith warned of the dangers of "defeminization" (and its corollary implications for masculinity) lurking behind calls for women's liberation.

On the other hand, illustrating one of the many contradictions in early television reporting on feminism, attention to gender differences also resulted in sympathetic stories that invoked women's roles as mothers and caregivers as a rationale for feminist reforms. To put it more broadly, some feminist demands received approving media treatment when linked to a certain kind of deserving victim whose suffering merited attention, a variation on what Torres (2003) and Bodroghkozy (2012; see also Gray, 1997) have theorized as the preferred "civil rights subject" in news representations of civil rights struggles. Network reports in the 1960s foregrounded certain "worthy Negroes," depicting them as hardworking and responsible and thus as "eminently worthy beneficiaries of the rights and equality" they demanded (Bodroghkozy, 2012, p. 48, 90). Similarly, network stories on feminism gave credence to some movement claims when they constructed a preferred feminist subject through their poignant portraits of struggling white single mothers, deserted by their husbands, who deserved to benefit from liberal feminist demands for child care, equal pay, and employment opportunity. Thus, while it did not always manifest in exactly the same way, the (always raced and classed) difference that women embodied was a consistent presence in reporting on the movement.

The general backdrop of gender anxiety in early network news coverage of the second wave was a crucial context for the warm welcome that mass media provided for the always composed, conventionally attractive, and heterosexually active Gloria Steinem after she became active in movement politics in 1970 (predictably, media accounts rarely failed to note her difference from most feminists). Coverage of Steinem functioned as a counterweight to negative frames for women's liberation that were established by the time she rose to prominence as a feminist icon, and the existing momentum of the movement and of its mediated identity were what made that rise possible. Such relationships between earlier and later reporting provide an additional warrant for close attention to 1970. Television's sustained attention to the movement that year performed decisive and long-lasting rhetorical and definitional work that would profoundly affect the movement's image politics.

Rhetorics of Race and Sexuality

A key aspect of that definitional work concerned the role of race in the movement. Though women's liberation intersected with the claims and activities of the civil rights movement in multiple ways, the mediated misconception that the second wave of U.S. feminism was an entirely white phenomenon is as old as the bra-burning myth. Studies of the movement's representation concur that news reports defined the movement as dominated by and centrally concerned with white women, and the belief that this was the reality of the movement, rather than a construction of it, has had a great deal of traction in critiques of second-wave politics (Barker-Plummer, 2010; Bradley, 2003). Wini Breines (2007) has summarized it this way:

> The accepted historical narrative of youthful second wave feminism has been that it was a white movement due to its racism. Black women were not welcome or were repelled by white women's racism. Feminist racist attitudes and racial bias had led to such a narrow conception of women's discrimination and liberation, of gender, that African-American women could not see themselves in the movement. (p. 8)

Yet, as Breines (2007) goes on to argue, this narrative is "too simple" (p. 8). Such claims fly in the face of white second wavers' (including veterans of civil rights activism) earnest attempts to engage with race in their critiques of patriarchy; moreover, they erase the participation of many women of color in both radical and liberal groups and activities.

For example, African American lawyer and activist Flo Kennedy was a key player in the 1968 Miss America Pageant protest (which targeted the pageant's racism as well as its sexism), and African American Cellestine Ware was one of the founders of New York Radical Feminists in 1969. In 1970, Ware published *Woman Power,* an analysis of the growth of women's liberation that included a chapter discussing black women's relationship to the movement. Toni Cade Bambara's important edited collection of race, class, and gender theorizing, *The Black Woman,* appeared in 1970 as well, the year that Jamaican American Aileen Hernández, a cofounder of NOW, took office as the organization's second president. Moreover, members of the Third World Women's Alliance, a group of feminists of color, marched in the 1970 Women's Strike for Equality, where black women were among the featured speakers (Roth, 2003, Hunter, 1970).

Certainly, the largest and most publicly visible feminist groups in the 1970s were dominated by white women, but the claims that that these groups were unconcerned with the role of race in their issues and that they were uniformly hostile to women of color are not borne out by the historical record. Equally as important, such a perspective erases leftist black women's parallel organizing around gender issues during the second wave. For example, by 1968, black women in the Student Non-Violent Coordinating Committee had formed the Black Women's Liberation Committee that later became the Third World Women's Alliance. In addition, prominent black feminists and civil rights advocates such as Pauli Murray (a cofounder of NOW) and Eleanor Holmes Norton chose to work against race and gender discrimination through existing male-dominated liberal organizations such as the American Civil Liberties Union (Hartmann, 1998), and, at the other extreme, the Black Panther Party's newspaper indicated the group's links to women's liberation activism in New York as early as 1969 (Lumsden, 2009). Several of the women involved in the founding of the National Black Feminist Organization in 1973 had been active in NOW, the National Women's Political Caucus, and *Ms.* magazine.

A limited view of what counted as feminism in the 1970s, one perpetuated by the narrowness of some histories as well as by cultural memories constructed through mass media, is responsible for the simplistic explanation that the second wave was a consistently white and racist movement. Such a perspective "negates the agency of feminists of color," as it disregards the political contexts they negotiated in their own communities when women's liberation ideas and organizing began to emerge in the mid-1960s (Roth, 2003, p. 6). Leftist women of color experienced a deep race-based loyalty to their male counterparts, a factor that limited their affiliation with white feminists (against whom they measured their relative deprivation) as well as their motivation to reject their movements of origin, despite the sexism they experienced there (Springer, 2005). Because leftist white women did not experience racial oppression, their ability to feel and to act upon their oppression as women (their relative deprivation in comparison to their white male colleagues) was less constrained.

In countercultural movements, white leftist women's primary emphasis on gender was a targeted rhetorical response to their particular relationship with white leftist men, who saw race and class as the privileged categories of oppression and viewed gender as a distraction. White feminists countered by creating a "universalist gender ideology, one that privileged gender oppression above others," a move that was intended to make the case for feminism stronger but that alienated women of color by "blur[ring] racial and ethnic differences among women" (Roth, 2003, p. 188). The epigraph for this chapter is one example: Komisar's claiming of the 1970s for women, rather than blacks, glossed over those who occupied both categories.

News workers exacerbated these tensions when they "mostly failed to 'see' feminists of color within the majority white liberation movement" or to notice their independent organizing, "effectively whitewashing the movement by underreporting the women of color who were there" (Barker-Plummer, 2010, p. 191).[9] A corollary to the whiteness of news media depictions of the movement was news workers' failure to recognize links between the interests of white women and women of color; the latter were usually used to represent race rather than gender and never their intersections. For the most part—and I will note some key exceptions—news media did not represent women of color as a movement constituency, thus reinforcing the impression of women of color that feminism was a "family quarrel between white women and white men" (Morrison, 1971, p. 15).

Yet a focus on the presence or absence of women of color and their concerns in news coverage of feminism is only one—although certainly the prevailing—way to tell the story of the politics of race in the movement and its representation. I come at this issue from a new direction in my analysis, focusing on the ways that the topic of race was raised repeatedly in early second-wave coverage, both explicitly and implicitly, through reporters' uses of sex-race, sexism-racism, and feminism–civil rights analogies to make sense of feminist politics. Such analogies were rooted in the history of the movement itself, in which they had served various purposes for white feminists, and news workers familiar with civil rights discourse adapted them to their own ends as they sought to frame feminism in meaningful ways for a presumed white public.

In multiple ways, "the sex/race analogy was a foundational rhetorical strategy for the emergent Women's Liberation Movement" (Hogeland, 1998, p. 129). NOW analogized itself to the NAACP, and sexism-racism analogies were used in the earliest stages of radical feminism's development as well (Evans, 1979). In two different documents issued in 1964 and 1965, white Student Non-Violent Coordinating Committee members Mary Hayden and Casey King critiqued the sexism in the organization that relegated women to subordinate clerical and housekeeping roles, concluding that "assumptions of male superiority are as widespread and deep rooted and every much as crippling to the woman as the assumptions of white supremacy are to the Negro" ("SNCC Position Paper [Women in the Movement]," 1964/1979, p. 234; see also Hayden and King, 1965/1979). Because "white male politicos saw the race issue as morally legitimate, while dismissing feminism as 'a bunch of chicks with personal problems,'" white feminists relied on the sexism-racism comparison as a rhetorical device for leftist men specifically (Willis, 1992, p. 112). Hayden's and King's critiques resonated with many countercultural white women, and they are accorded key importance in histories of the radical second wave's development (e.g., Echols, 1989; Evans, 1979; Giardina, 2010; Rosen, 2000). At the same time, the chilly reception black movement women gave to these early feminist documents exhibited their indignation over the ways that white women's discourse about race and its relationship to sexism ignored their unique experiences (Anderson-Bricker, 1999).

News workers' use of race-sex analogies in the coverage I discuss is thus another demonstration of the interaction of movement strategies and media framing, as well as of the contradictory results. In some cases, when sexism was implicitly compared to racism to diminish the importance of the former and to establish the greater significance of the latter, they were treated as competing rather than intersecting claims. In others, a feminism–civil rights analogy was used as a legitimation device to bring the imprimatur of reasonableness to feminist demands for equality; for example, news reports echoed NOW's recurring deployment of an analogy between its equality goals and those of the moderate civil rights movement.[10] In all cases, the analogies worked to separate the concerns of white women and women of color and suggested a limited understanding of the intersections of feminist and race politics, but their presence challenges the claim that the topic of race was routinely absent from media constructions of women's liberation.

I am, however, well aware that by focusing on national news media coverage of the ideas and activities produced primarily by white feminists, I am participating in the centralizing of a partial account of what counts as the second wave that feminist scholars have rightly criticized. But this was the version of feminism to which most Americans were exposed, and my analyses elucidate the complexities of the rhetorical contexts and constraints that enabled its production and that put in place longstanding and limited notions about the meaning of feminism.[11]

Ultimately, my conclusions are constrained by the limits of the coverage itself, which, in addition to its underrepresentation of the role of women of color in feminist activism, gave minimal attention to sexuality issues and their importance to the movement, offering a picture of the second wave that was both white *and* heterosexual at a time when many liberal and radical feminists identified as lesbian. The often-decried media conflation of "feminist" and "lesbian" was not a characteristic of early television coverage, which completely neglected the movement's crucial conflicts over sexuality in 1970. That year, the "lesbian issue" exploded in New York movement circles, provoking the gay-straight split that would rend and realign radical feminist groups, produce important movement theorizing, and culminate in a media maelstrom late that year over the public outing and print media censure of radical feminist Kate Millett (Poirot, 2004, p. 222; see also Poirot, 2009).

Previously dubbed "the high priestess" of women's liberation by the *New York Times,* Millett was the author of the much-heralded *Sexual Politics,* an analysis of sexism in literature that was published in August 1970 and that landed her on the cover of *Time* (Prial, 1970, p. 30). Just a few months later, *Time* would out Millett as bisexual in a December article that claimed the disclosure "discredited her as a spokeswoman" for the movement ("Women's Lib: A Second Look," 1970, p. 50). The article precipitated a show of support from a variety of feminists and put sexuality and its relationship to second-wave politics briefly in the spotlight—in the press although not on national television—in a fashion that was internally productive for the movement if not for its public image (Klemesrud, 1970).

In all senses, network news coverage of women's liberation displayed far more interest in the movement's implications for women's relationships to men than in its implications for women's relationships to each other, a tendency linked to assumptions about the primary audience for national news. Although conflicts over lesbian sexuality and its political implications were a vital issue for the East Coast–based second-wave circles on which national media tended to focus, no viewer would know this from the national broadcast stories in 1970. Yet, this outcome, like news reports' narratives about the movement's relationship to race, was the product of interaction between feminists' choices and news practices and cannot easily be attributed solely to media homophobia/heterosexism.

For different reasons, liberal and radical feminists were loath to expose the conflicts over sexuality to media scrutiny. As president of NOW, Betty Friedan had famously termed lesbians a "lavender menace" in 1969, fearing the negative impact on the movement's public image if it was associated with "man-haters" and a "bunch of dykes" (Jay, 1999, p. 137). Within a year, Friedan would oversee what has come to be known as the "lesbian purge" of NOW, which resulted in the departure of a number of lesbians from the organization (Poirot, 2009, p. 270, see also Gilmore and Kaminski, 2007). By 1971, after Friedan had left NOW's leadership, the organization would acknowledge lesbian oppression as a "legitimate concern of feminism" and would pass a series of resolutions affirming that "a woman's right to her own person includes the right to define and express her own sexuality" (Carabillo, Meuli, and Csida, 1993, p. 223).

Some radical groups were wary of the lesbian issue as well, but not for public relations reasons; for example, some radical feminists viewed lesbianism as a sexual rather than political issue and were concerned with the ways that butch-femme lesbian relationships mimicked patriarchal heterosexuality (Echols, 1989). Lesbian feminists in the movement forced a confrontation over the issue in May 1970 at the Second Congress to Unite Women, a gathering of primarily New York–based feminist groups. Outraged over the lack of programming on lesbian issues at the congress, they staged an intervention in which they took to the stage in t-shirts reading Lavender Menace, distributed a manifesto titled "The Woman-Identified Woman" (destined to become a principal document in lesbian feminist theorizing), and launched a discussion of the oppression of lesbians in a heterosexist culture. One of the instigators, Karla Jay (1999), described the event as "the single most important action organized by lesbians who wanted the women's movement to acknowledge our presence and needs" (p. 137).

Even so, those involved understood the events as an intramovement argument that needed to be sorted out in private, a stance that was about "protect[ing] the privacy and freedom of the women" involved (Barker-Plummer, 2010, p. 164). According to Jay (1999), when ABC's Marlene Sanders—who had been given some access to the congress to gather material for her documentary on the movement—was discovered to be filming the proceedings, one of the Menaces stole her film. Jay's recounted rationale was that that media coverage would have prevented the exchange from being "free and unfettered"; certainly, some women could not afford to be featured on national television discussing their lesbian identity (1999, p. 144).

Similar to television news' erasure of black women, the virtual absence of lesbianism from early network coverage serves as an unusually clear example of the gap between the political life of the feminist movement in 1970 and its representation in mass media. Because lesbian sexuality had limited presence in national television news representations of the second wave in 1970, its presence in this project is limited as well, and, as is the case with black women's feminist activism, lesbian feminist activism has a parallel history to which I give limited attention (see, e.g., Abbott and Love, 1972; Faderman, 1991; Jay, 1999). Even so, those rare moments in the coverage when sexuality issues are explicitly featured or implicitly alluded to (or made more present by their surprising absence) enable my analysis of the intersections of movement politics and media strategies that facilitated the production of narrow and heterosexist mediated visions of the second wave.

Overview

Watching Women's Liberation proceeds chronologically through case studies of network television's early narratives of second-wave feminism that developed over the course of 1970. I underscore the interaction that produced those narratives with a structure that alternates chapters examining coverage of feminist media activism with those that treat network news' feature stories designed to introduce the movement to viewers. In a broad sense, these case studies illustrate the evolution of a consensus among the networks over the course of the year, one that coalesced around the reasonableness of women's demands for public equality, particularly in the workplace, and that eventually seized on the ERA as a sensible solution.

Yet this narrative was far from seamless and it was contested in different news stories and within the movement itself. Many of the examples of reporting I discuss feature moments of excess, a term referring to potential meanings and implications that "stand beyond the reach" of the "web of significance" in which they are embedded (Nichols, 1991, p. 142). That is, some strategies of representation in these network stories are an uneasy fit with the overall narrative about women's liberation constructed by network news in 1970, and, at another level, with the narrative constructed by scholars about the nature of news coverage of feminism generally. Each of the case studies described at tends to the significance of one or both of these two levels of excess, drawing attention to those verbal and visual textual features—and their meaning-making potential—that "contest, qualify, resist, and refuse" dominant mediated interpretations of second-wave feminism (Nichols, 1991, p. 142).

Chapter 1 begins at the beginning, with an analysis of national press coverage of the feminist protest at the 1968 Miss America Pageant, the event that put women's liberation on the national media map and that would have a continuing presence in print and broadcast interpretations of the movement. News reports about the events in Atlantic City feature the earliest appearance of many strategies for making sense of the movement, strategies that would reappear in national broadcast stories in 1970 along with film footage of the pageant protest that established its importance to feminism's public narrative. My discussion of the protest and its reverberations inside and outside the movement highlights an often overlooked aspect of the events of September 7, 1968: that the first Miss Black America Pageant, sponsored by the NAACP, was held the same night just down the boardwalk. The *New York Times* covered the two pageants in tandem, and my reading of that coverage focuses on reporters' early efforts to construct a narrative about the relationship between feminist and civil rights activism, an emphasis that would reappear in 1970's wave of national television reporting.

Chapter 2 begins the story of 1970's "grand press blitz," when a barrage of print stories on the movement set the stage for network news' first reports on women's liberation (Freeman, 1975, p. 148). I couple a discussion of all three networks' first, brief, hard news reports on feminist protest in January—the disruption of the Senate birth control pill hearings by a women's liberation group—with an extensive analysis of the two series of lengthy soft feature stories (nine total) on women's liberation broadcast by CBS and NBC in March and April.[12] On one level, both network series created a sort of moderate middle ground of acceptable feminism anchored by their legitimation of liberal feminist issues related to workplace discrimination, but they diverged sharply in other ways that indicated key differences in their purposes and their imagined audiences.

The CBS and NBC series provide a sort of baseline for national television representations of the movement in 1970; between them, they display the wide range of rhetorical strategies—visual and verbal, skeptical and supportive—contained in early network reports. The CBS stories offered a generally dismissive and visually sensationalized *narrative about the movement,* particularly its radical contingent, displaying the gender anxiety assumed to afflict its male target audience. CBS's three reports serve as the paradigmatic case of a type of negative coverage of women's liberation that too often is taken to represent the entirety of that coverage; in particular, its implicit and explicit comparisons of liberal and radical groups' behavior and goals functioned to demarcate what were presented as the movement's reasonable versus its extremist elements. In a stark contrast, the NBC series presented a generally sympathetic *narrative about the movement's issues* that unified radical and liberal concerns rather than using the latter to marginalize the former. NBC's reports gave less attention to characterizing the movement itself than to establishing sexism as a social problem—a process to which its use of images was essential—and several of the network's stories suggested a target audience of women.

Chapter 3 focuses on the March 18, 1970, sit-in at *Ladies' Home Journal* (*LHJ*), a crucial episode in feminist media activism that had dramatic internal and external consequences for women's liberation. Conceived as a radical action by a small group of women incensed at the demeaning portrayal of women in a publication that touted itself as "the magazine women believe in," the *LHJ* protest was an unpredictable success, precipitating significant changes in editorial and employment practices at women's magazines. That outcome was the product of several factors, including the emphases of the print and broadcast coverage of the *LHJ* events as well as the action's timing among a wave of protests and discrimination complaints launched in 1970 by women employees of major media institutions. Equally important was the recognition of the magazine's editors—and those of their sister publications—that incorporating and com-modifying women's liberation was more profitable than resisting it, processes that would soon escalate across all forms of mass media.

At the same time, the results of the *LHJ* protest caused considerable contro-versy within the radical movement itself, exacerbating tensions over feminism's increasing media presence, as well as over what many radicals saw as liberal co-optation of the movement's revolutionary goals. ABC's exclusive story on the *LHJ* sit-in that ran on the night of the protest is a revealing exemplar of the latter process. Reporter Marlene Sanders, a feminist sympathizer who was invited to the protest by its planners, represented the action through an equality-centered narrative that emphasized the protestors' critique of employment discrimina-tion at the magazine while downplaying their more controversial analysis of the sexual politics and sexism that were integral to the publication's editorial and advertising content. In effect, she deradicalized the action by foregrounding its liberal demands, illustrating a tendency that would be even more pronounced in the documentary on the movement that she produced in late May.

That ABC documentary, my focus in chapter 4, was the third lengthy network news portrait of the movement to appear in as many months. Succinctly titled "Women's Liberation," it is 1970's key example of a supportive reporter's self-conscious effort to represent the movement fairly; relatedly, it also serves as the most developed example of network news' reliance on race-sex and feminism—

civil rights analogies. In her memoir of her reporting career (Sanders and Rock, 1988), Sanders makes clear that she saw the documentary as an intervention into poor media treatment of the movement, echoing the contention of many feminists that the movement's image problems resulted from reporting by men. Refuting negative stereotypes about women's liberation (including, importantly, man-hating) was among the program's central strategies, as was an analogy to (a nostalgic memory of) the moderate civil rights movement. Sanders's effort to package feminism in comprehensible and commonsensical terms that would make sense to her imagined white male viewer resulted in an evolutionary liberal narrative that narrowed the meaning of the movement in crucial ways, diminishing rather than demonizing its radicalism and presenting the ERA as the answer to what ailed women. Ultimately, the ABC documentary prompts recognition that sympathetic reporting that failed to encompass the movement's ideological and political complexity cannot be neatly categorized as positive or negative. Rather, the story Sanders told was both *limited and limiting* in its containment of feminism within the "masculinist and rationalist epistemologies" that undergird mainstream news as a genre (Barker-Plummer, 2010, p. 147).

By the time of the August 26, 1970, Women's Strike for Equality, the topic of chapter 5, women's liberation seemed poised for its triumphal moment in the media spotlight. The House of Representatives had passed the ERA a few weeks earlier, and all three networks had produced stories that linked this outcome to the movement's momentum. The strike seemed to confirm that momentum: involving tens of thousands of women in the United States and abroad, it was the subject of more national print and broadcast attention than any other feminist event that year. Despite the strike's inclusion of an array of liberal and radical feminist groups, it was an instance of media activism conceived and controlled by NOW, and it put the organization's media pragmatism on full display. Confounding NOW's careful planning, and in a reversal of the *LHJ* protest dynamics, the reports on the strike took an essentially liberal action and presented it as a radical one. Featuring almost no discussion of the three carefully chosen issues—abortion, equal pay, and child care—that the event was designed to dramatize, the network reports instead presented a narrative of feminist deviance, visually depicting the masses of women protestors as an entertaining spectacle. In a departure from the diversity of earlier national television reports, the three networks converged in their emphasis on what they presented as the disturbing, underlying objective of the movement as a whole: its radical assault on traditional gender roles, an implication they depicted as alternately absurd and alarming. Apprehended as a whole, their coverage of the August 26 events offers the clearest example of the gender anxiety that manifested in reporting on the movement in 1970.

The Strike for Equality was the final major movement story of 1970 as far as the networks were concerned, and it represented the culmination of feminism's growing visibility that year. Despite the tone of the networks' strike coverage, the event's impact on the movement's growth and public profile produced the results its planners wished for, and it signaled the beginning of the ascendance of liberal feminism—and its issues—as the only feminism in the public mind. Yet, as the television coverage of the strike also portended, when radical feminism disappeared from national television screens and was no longer available to serve as liberal feminism's extremist other, movement opponents were able to recast reformist issues such as the ERA as public signifiers of feminist radicalism. In chapter 6, I discuss this consequence as well as other ways in which the television news narratives produced in 1970 influenced developments in the movement and its network television representation in the decade that followed, concluding that the failure of ERA ratification in 1982 seemed to mark the end of the second wave in the eyes of national media, ushering in a postfeminist media perspective. I also take up another key element in the post-1970 context in this final chapter: the rise of Gloria Steinem as feminism's enduring media icon.

Steinem barely appeared in the network coverage of feminism from 1970, save a brief and unidentified shot of her at a Strike for Equality rally. She was not yet a key movement figure for news media that year, and I approach her role in the movement's media history through a reading of HBO's 2011 documentary *Gloria: In Her Own Words*. Framed as biography, *Gloria* also constructs a version of popular memory about the second wave, and it serves as a useful coda to the story I tell about 1970. My reading of Steinem's history—and the story told about it in the documentary—illuminates the ways that early mediated narratives about women's liberation and their interaction with the movement's own media strategies facilitated Steinem's emergence as the antidote to feminism's image problems. *Gloria* is a study in contradictions, simultaneously visually displaying and verbally disavowing the role of mass media in Steinem's rise as a feminist celebrity. Yet, told primarily through television footage, much of it from 1970, the documentary is inescapably a story about media and the movement. As such, it demonstrates the enduring power of many of the problematic strategies of early movement coverage: it positions white, middle-class, heterosexual women as feminism's primary constituents and beneficiaries; it molds the movement's meaning toward a moderate middle ground; and its search for a saleable story marginalizes the radical voices that did so much to shape the second wave's remarkable intervention into American culture.

Challenges by
reflection
of Media

CHAPTER 1

The Movement Meets the Press

The 1968 Miss America Pageant Protest

> "Bra-burner" became the put-down term for feminists of my
> generation. . . . Had the media called us "girdle-burners," nearly
> every woman in the country would have rushed to join us.
>
> —Carol Hanisch (1998), member of New York Radical Women and
> participant in the 1968 Miss America Pageant protest (p. 199)

The Miss America Pageant was the first or second most popular television event for eight of ten years in the 1960s (Watson and Martin, 2004). In many families, mine included, watching it was an annual ritual, and presidential candidate Richard Nixon commented in 1968 that it was the only program that his daughters Tricia and Julie had been allowed to stay up late to watch (Cohen, 1988). The pageant's visibility as a recurring referendum on American womanhood made it an ideal target for feminist intervention, as the members of NYRW no doubt realized when they searched for an outlet for their political energies. As Carol Hanisch (1970) recounted shortly afterward, the group conceived of the 1968 protest as a "zap action" that would "[use] our presence as a group and/or media to make women's oppression into a conscious social issue" (p. 133).[1]

The protest and the media attention to it accomplished that goal, and the events in Atlantic City on September 7, 1968, quickly became an origin story—inside and outside the movement—for the public emergence of women's liberation ideas and activities. The protest's occurrence and the images it produced became an enduring element of cultural memories of the second wave. Early print feature stories on the movement from 1969 would include photos of the Miss America Pageant protestors (e.g., Babcox, 1969), and images from that

Saturday's events would surface in multiple network news stories about the movement in 1970, when the event had gained a retrospective importance that warranted its inclusion in television news narratives about women's liberation.

NYRW was the first radical feminist group in New York City, and it was formed in 1967 by several women who hoped to extend the critiques forwarded by other radical movements to include an analysis of women's oppression. In fact, NYRW held its meetings at the offices of the Southern Conference Education Fund, a civil rights group with which Carol Hanisch was affiliated (Dicker, 2008). Many of the members of NYRW also were or had been active in the Student Non-Violent Coordinating Committee, the Congress of Racial Equality, Students for a Democratic Society, and the Youth International Party (Yippies), organizations from which they were becoming increasingly alienated for reasons that included those groups' dismissal of women's issues and women's leadership. Like radical feminism generally, NYRW did not have much of a public profile in 1968, but their attack on a cherished American institution would be the event that "marked the end of the movement's obscurity" (Echols, 1989, p. 93).

Robin Morgan (1992), a member of NYRW (as well as Students for a Democratic Society, the Congress of Racial Equality, and the Yippies) and a key organizer of the Miss America Pageant protest, called it "the first major action in the current wave of feminism in the United States" (p. 21). In the chapter of her memoir titled "The Origins of the Second Wave of Feminism," Sheila Tobias (1997) perhaps put it most succinctly when she noted that the protest "both helped publicize and would later haunt the women's movement" (p. 86).[2] As most accounts acknowledge, what "haunted" the women's movement was the specter of bra burning. No bras were burned at the 1968 protest, and feminist historians, as well as participants and observers of the protest, have long attempted to dispel this misconception.[3] Regardless, bra-burning became what Ruth Rosen (2000) calls "the most tenacious media myth about the women's movement," a "sexy trope" that "became a symbolic way of sexualizing—and thereby trivializing—women's struggle for emancipation" (pp. 160–161). Contending that, post-1968, bra-burning became an "international icon of women's liberation," Hilary Hinds and Jackie Stacey (2001) concur that it was cast as "tame, domestic, and petty" and depicted as "a kind of self-indulgence similar to a ridiculous concern with sexual pleasure" (pp. 157–158).

Bras were only one of many items that were tossed into the Freedom Trash Can on the Boardwalk in Atlantic City on September 7, 1968—also included were girdles, high heels, cosmetics, eyelash curlers, wigs, and issues of *Cosmopolitan*, *Playboy*, and *Ladies' Home Journal*. The rumor that the trash can would be ignited—and the later assumption that it had been—was begun by Robin Mor-

Figure 1. Robin Morgan throws a bra into the Freedom trash can. From *Saturday's Child: A Memoir*, courtesy of Robin Morgan.

gan's interview with *New York Post* reporter Lindsy Van Gelder a few days earlier. In that conversation, Morgan identified herself as a member of the Yippies and drew connections between the Miss America Pageant action and other New Left protests. Seizing on these links, Van Gelder wrote a lead to her story that read as follows: "Lighting a match to a draft card or a flag has been a standard gambit of protest groups in recent years, but something new is due to go up in flames on Saturday. Would you believe a bra-burning?" Further heightening the effect, the *Post* gave the story a headline that read, "Bra Burners and Miss America" (quoted in Van Gelder, 1992, p. 81). The Miss America Pageant protest occurred less than two weeks after the tumultuous 1968 Democratic National Convention in Chicago, and, given that many members of NYRW had leftist movement experience, Van Gelder's analogy to the burnings of draft cards and flags was not out of place.

On the other hand, the comparison did not bode well for a nascent movement that had little credibility with either the Left or with mass media, both of which viewed feminist claims with derision in contrast to the matrix of national and international political issues and events gripping the nation in late 1968. By that point, two beloved national political figures had been assassinated, a presidency had been brought down by controversy over the Vietnam War, black and white students had occupied several buildings at Columbia University, and riots had erupted in the streets of Chicago during the Democratic National Convention. Years later, Van Gelder (1992) recalled that she had been assigned to write a "humor piece" on the protest after her editors had a "thigh-slapping reaction" to the NYRW press release; in fact, she also noted that the Yippies's Steering Committee had a similar reaction when Robin Morgan informed them of NYRW's plans (p. 81).

Van Gelder, who would go on to become an active feminist and a regular writer for *Ms.,* was sympathetic to the aims of the protest, and the bra-burning reference was part of her effort to make connections to other movements in which such public burnings had "moral weight" (p. 81). As she later put it, she was trying to "speak in a language that the guys on the city desk could understand" as well as "to speak in code to the radicals of our generation" (p. 81). The ultimate backfire of her good intentions portended the difficulty radical feminists would have in gaining traction for their critique of sexual politics, even when aided by supportive journalists. Bra burning quickly became a decontextualized (and fictional) trope that would function as shorthand for the frivolousness of feminist goals.

Van Gelder's effort to link the protest to existing countercultural discourses cohered with the intentions of the protestors themselves, who brought the analytical skills they had learned in previous activism and had honed through CR to their critique of the pageant. In a CR session about the pageant, NYRW members concluded that the protest would be an ideal way "to unite women by taking on those issues that spoke to the oppression we all experienced in our daily lives" (Hanisch, 1998, p. 198). Robin Morgan's (1992) description of the protest, originally written in 1968 and published in various New Left outlets, defended the pageant as an appropriate target because of its "perfect combination of American values—racism, militarism, capitalism—all packaged in one ideal symbol: a woman" (p. 25). In addition to the pageant's propagation of the "Mindless Sex-Object Image," a black woman had never been a finalist, the winner would entertain the troops in Vietnam, and "the whole million dollar pageant corporation is one commercial shill game to sell the sponsor's products" (Morgan, 1992, p. 26). Participant Judith Duffett's (1968) account of the protest was even more direct about the systemic nature of the feminist critique, maintaining that "our purpose was *not* to put down Miss America but to attack the male chauvinism, commercialization of beauty, racism and oppression of women symbolized by the pageant" (p. 4, emphasis in original).

The "No More Miss America" flyer distributed at the protest outlined the critique of racism, militarism, and capitalism; in addition, it argued that the contest promoted the "win-or-you're-worthless competitive disease," the ideal of women as "young, juicy, and malleable," and the "Madonna-Whore combination" within which women must be both "sexy and wholesome."[4] It charged that the pageant encouraged women to be "inoffensive, bland and apolitical" because conformity was "the key to the crown," and it claimed that "real power to control our own lives is restricted to men, while women get patronizing pseudo-power, an ermine cloak and a bunch of flowers." Finally, the feminists contended that the pageant "exercises thought control . . . to enslave us all the more in high-heeled, low-status roles; to inculcate false values in young girls;

to use women as beasts of buying; to seduce us to prostitute ourselves before our own oppression."

But the coverage of the Miss America Pageant protest would feature almost none of the feminists' analysis that connected the action to leftist concerns, and the *New York Times*'s multiple stories on the pageant, on the protest, and on the Miss Black America Pageant held the same day provide early examples of the problems of event-centered reporting that would plague feminists as they attempted to use mass media to bring attention to their issues. The tendencies for representing women's liberation that emerged in the *Times,* the nation's "newspaper of record" that was especially influential among the media elite, laid important groundwork for the narratives about the movement that took shape in later print and broadcast reporting.[5] Although bra burning may be the most potent media-constructed cultural memory of this early feminist action, it has overshadowed other legacies important to understanding mass media framing of second-wave feminism for public consumption.

In the broadest sense, the Miss America Pageant protest coverage indicated how fundamentally mainstream news media and the radical movement were working at cross-purposes, even when sympathetic women reporters (from the *Times*'s Style section, no less) were involved. The protestors' analysis of the political ills that the pageant symbolized received much less attention than did the spectacle of the protest itself, the demeanor and appearance of the protestors, and the conflict generated by the reactions of spectators and counterprotestors. While not overtly dismissive, the *Times*'s coverage did little to give the protest and its participants political credibility, framing the event as a motley collection of women who had creative tactics but an incoherent message. This interpretation was bolstered by reporters' comparisons of feminist and civil rights protests that were precipitated by the juxtaposition of the Miss America and Miss Black America Pageants on September 7.

Providing early examples of the sex-race analogies that would become a recurring theme in reporting on women's liberation, the *Times*'s stories demonstrated the vastly different levels of cultural authority attached to claims of sexism and racism in 1968, when racial discrimination was a recognized social problem in elite national media and sexism was a term often encapsulated by quotation marks. Although the politics of sexism received short shrift in the reporting on the events of September 7, the challenge to cultural gender politics that the protestors' presence and behavior represented did not, and accounts of the protest and its aftermath showcase early manifestations of the persistent role that gender ideologies would play in reporters' and spectators' attempts to make sense of women's liberation.

Published, but surrounded by Pageant.

The Protestors and the Press

Freedom Trash Can

On September 8, the day after the pageant, the *Times*'s Sunday edition carried a lengthy account of the protest, headlined "Miss America Pageant Picketed by 100 Women" (Curtis, 1968a), along with a boxed sidebar on the results of the pageant. Titled "Illinois Girl Named Miss America" (1968), the pageant story indicated in its second paragraph that Judith Anne Ford was the first blond to win the title in ten years. When the new Miss America was asked for her reaction to the protest in the last paragraph of the brief story, she replied, "It was just too bad. I'm sorry it happened" (p. 81).

The first three paragraphs of the *Times*'s story on the protest itself managed to describe the scene at the action as well as to include brief snippets of the protesters' critique of beauty politics, their labeling of the pageant as racist, and their intent to boycott pageant sponsors. Charlotte Curtis, the *Times*'s Style section editor, covered both the pageant and the protest. Curtis's lead featured a description of the Freedom Trash Can and its contents (with no mention of burning bras) as well as noted that the women were "armed with a giant bathing beauty puppet."[6] She also described the chains encircling the puppet and included the feminists' claim that they represented "the chains that tie us to these beauty standards against our will." The story provided a vivid picture of the protest, describing the live sheep that the demonstrators crowned Miss America and noting that the women were peaceful and stayed behind police barricades.

Curtis's story lacked overt editorializing; for instance, she did not label the demonstrators as "militant," a tag that news workers would come to use repeatedly in reference to feminist protestors. Generally, her account is a good example of a standard "five W's" formula (who, what, when, where, why) of event reporting. Describing the group as "mostly middle-aged careerists and housewives, with a sprinkling of 20 year olds and grandmothers," she also detailed their geographic diversity and implicitly noted the reach of the movement when she wrote that some came from as far away as Bancroft, Iowa, and Gainesville, Florida. Curtis gave particular attention to the older women at the protest, including the grandmother of NYRW member Kathie Amatniek, who was chided by Amatniek for talking with a male spectator and who "promised to do better."[7] At another point, Curtis mentioned a sixty-eight-year-old member of the Jeannette Rankin Brigade, a women's antiwar group, who threw a high-heeled shoe into the Freedom Trash Can. Such vignettes upped the human-interest quotient, and the implication of absurdity attached to the description of grandmothers at the protest brought the news value of deviance into play, but they gave little insight into the "why" of the events. The multiple mentions of television cameras and photographers in Curtis's story implicitly offered simple attention seeking as a motivation for the action, and she explicitly observed at one point that the protestors "escalated their activities when the cameramen arrived."

The absence of a leader to succinctly lay out the purposes of the protest resulted in a story that tacitly put Robin Morgan in that role, even as she was quoted as describing the protest as "a simultaneous cooperative effort conceived and executed by a number of people." Of the NYRW members present, Morgan had the most presence in the *Times* report, in which Curtis described her as a "poet, former child actress, and a housewife" rather than as the experienced political activist that she was. Curtis noted that the protestors "belonged to what they called the Women's Liberation Movement," yet she gave no other details about their purpose or structure, and Morgan's quoted comment that "we don't want another Chicago" (in reference to the protestors' promise to the Atlantic City mayor that they would be "orderly and quiet") came closest to linking the demonstration with her (and other protestors') leftist politics. In fact, Morgan was never quoted on the politics of the protest, only its logistics, and most of her discourse in the story focused on the concerns of the mayor, who was worried about the highly flammable boardwalk (which had caught fire just the week before), followed by her assurance that "just a symbolic bra-burning" was planned. Because she was quoted so extensively, and because Curtis gave more biographical information on her than on anyone else mentioned in the story, Morgan became the dominant voice of the demonstrators.

Reporters seek out the most recognizable figures present to give focus to a story, and Morgan fit that bill. She had acquired fame as a child because of her role on the popular television series *I Remember Mama* from 1950 to 1956; she was adept at speaking with the press; and she and Curtis were already acquainted (Morgan, 2001). In fact, Morgan was credited by other protestors for milking her media contacts from her famous past, thus ensuring ample coverage of the action. At the same time, her centrality to the resulting coverage did not go unnoticed within the movement; "some women felt Morgan took control of the action and resented her for that" (Echols, 1989, p. 95), and Carol Hanisch (1998) would later call Morgan "a bit of a press hound" (p. 199). Morgan's role in the *Times*'s story appears to give credence to these charges, but attributing her visibility solely to her own choices is overly simplistic.

Consistent with their commitment to CR, a resolutely egalitarian process in which all participants were treated as experts, NYRW's position was that any woman at the protest was as qualified as any other to talk about what it meant. Yet the varying responses this stance produced in Curtis's story—which quoted different women decrying high heels, girdles, and dishwashing along with the "enslavement" of beauty standards—worked against message coherence for the action. Presumably, the protestors were united by their wish for an end to the Miss America Pageant (recall that the press release title was "No More Miss America!"), but their professed goal was simply to raise the consciousness of the public, particularly potential movement members, about the problematic politics of the pageant. Such a purpose fit poorly with the event-centered values of reporting that favored a focus on the colorful and conflict-ridden spectacle of the protest. In fact, NOW leaders at the time, who understood such issues well, were reportedly displeased with the protest for just this reason: they believed that demonstrations "were best utilized for specific ends, not mass consciousness-raising" (Bradley, 2003, p. 61).

The *New York Times*'s coverage of the protest illustrates especially well the ways that norms of event-centered reporting worked against the construction of political credibility for the protestors as well as the related ways that they undermined the possibilities for communicating the feminists' complex political analysis of what the pageant symbolized. For example, in a typical journalistic search for "balance" combined with a standard "conflict" frame, Curtis included a depiction of the public reaction to the protest in the latter half of her story. The contrast between the report's count of the "nearly 100 demonstrators" and their "650 generally unsympathetic spectators" created an impression of the feminists as vastly outnumbered, although the spectators were no doubt pageant fans who had planned to be there regardless and did not turn up simply to oppose the protest.

However, Curtis's featuring of the reaction of male spectators is noteworthy, given how rarely coverage of the movement would feature men's opposition to feminism rather than women's. In much coverage, men remained "above the fray as seemingly objective onlookers, never opponents, in the feminist struggle" (Rhode, 1995, p. 701). Yet Curtis quoted one man who called the protesters "vulgar," and another man was quoted as telling the feminists to "throw yourselves" into the Freedom Trash Can because "it would be a lot more useful." Yet another told them to "go home and wash your bras." Curtis also noted the presence of three counterpicketers led by a 1967 Miss America runner-up who wore a sign that said, "There's Only One Thing Wrong with Miss America. She's Beautiful."

Such reactions not only provided the conflict important to the newsworthiness of such a story, they also indicated the violation of gendered expectations at the root of that conflict; for example, protesting in public made the feminists vulgar, and their proper place was at home. The implication of the counterpicketer's sign was that the protestors hated Miss America because she conformed to traditional beauty norms and they did not, a harbinger of what would become a recurring characterization of feminists as "unfeminine, unappealing women" who "sought to get through political flamboyance what they were unable to get through physical attractiveness" (Douglas, 1994, p. 156). Such interpretations cohered with news workers' penchant for focusing on individuals; in other words, Miss America herself was under attack, not the pageant, and the women attacking her were motivated by their personal, not political, grievances. That the new Miss America—rather than, for instance, a representative of the pageant organization—was asked for her opinion of the protest further bolstered this personalization strategy.

The spectacle and "facticity" of the Miss America Pageant action took precedence over the "analytic explanations of the everyday world as a socially experienced structure"; in other words, the protestors' critique of the various "isms" represented by the pageant was supplanted by the conflict between the feminists and their opposition on the boardwalk (Tuchman, 1978b, p. 134). The Miss America Pageant protest planners were clearly attempting to link their action to issues that already had significant cultural visibility; that is, they extended to the Miss America Pageant the analyses of racism, capitalism, etc., that they had learned in their previous movement experience and they laid them out in their press release (such analysis also was targeted at gaining credibility for the action with male leftists). Yet, as Hanisch (1970) later lamented, the document was "too long, too wordy, too complex, too hippy-yippee-campy" (p. 132), and the easy to observe and report *event* of the protest became the focus.

Although very little of the language of the press release made it into the coverage of the action, links between feminism and other contemporaneous social movements—notably civil rights—would surface in other explicit and implicit ways in the reports. In particular, the contrast between the reporting on the Miss America Pageant protest and the Miss Black America Pageant illustrates the uphill struggle early feminists faced as they were forced to compete for legitimacy with issues that already had standing on the media agenda.

Feminism, Racism, and Miss Black America

The second of the ten points in the "No More Miss America" press release was titled "Racism with Roses" and read as follows: "Since its inception in 1921, the pageant has not had one Black finalist, and this has not been for a lack of test-case contestants. There has never been a Puerto Rican, Alaskan, Hawaiian, or

Mexican-American winner. Nor has there ever been a true Miss America—an American Indian."[8] However, reflecting journalistic norms, this feminist grievance was not as important in warranting the attention to race in the subsequent reporting as was the event of the first Miss Black America Pageant, which was, hardly coincidentally, held the very same evening, right down the boardwalk.[9]

Early in the story on the protest, Charlotte Curtis noted that the protestors "denounced the beauty contest's 'racism,'" although her use of quotation marks can be taken to indicate skepticism of the claim. Yet, after describing the feminist action, she spent the last ten paragraphs of a thirty-four–paragraph story detailing aspects of the first Miss Black America Pageant. Curtis segued by writing that the Miss America Pageant protest "was not the only protest going on here today," and she included a quotation from Miss Black America Pageant sponsors calling their pageant "a positive protest." A pageant organizer claimed, "there's a need for the beauty of the black woman to be paraded and applauded as a symbol of universal pride," adding that they were "not protesting against beauty" but "because the beauty of the Black woman has been ignored. It hasn't been respected." A specific accusation of racism was absent (ignored by whom? not respected by whom?), although present between the lines. At this point, Curtis noted that "at least a few" of the Miss America Pageant protestors were "Negroes," and she described them as "not sure what they should do about" the Miss Black America Pageant.

Curtis set sexism and racism against each other in these paragraphs with a subtle "gotcha!" strategy, creating the implication that the mostly white Miss America Pageant protestors could hardly claim racism as one of their grievances if black people supported beauty pageants (and that perhaps sexism was a small price to pay for black advancement). The somewhat equivocal reactions that Curtis included from the two Miss America Pageant protestors that she quoted on the issue supported this implication. The first, Bonnie Allen, described as a "Negro Bronx housewife" (while the race of the white protestors went unmarked) said, "I'm for beauty contests. But then again, maybe I'm against them. I think black people have a right to protest." Maxine Leeds Craig (2002) has usefully interpreted this confusing statement as a reflection of Allen's "intersectional disempowerment," arguing that, as a black woman, she was caught between gender solidarity with the Miss America Pageant protest and race solidarity with the Miss Black America Pageant, "neither of which adequately addressed her situation" (p. 5).

Robin Morgan, who supplied the second quotation, was clearer but also cautious when she said, "We deplore Miss Black America as much as Miss White America, but we understand the black issue involved." Allen's and Morgan's statements indicated an unwillingness to challenge the moral weight of a position taken against racism, even if that position was imbricated with sexism, a sign of the drastically different levels of political salience attached to women's liberation and civil rights in 1968. Feminists, particularly white feminists like Morgan who had worked for civil rights, had a difficult time negotiating those occasions when the interests of the movements appeared to collide.

The impression that the second wave was a white women's movement that was almost entirely insensitive to racial issues is ahistorical, but finding support for that impression is easy in mainstream media coverage of the movement, where "an unrecognized institutional reluctance appeared to exist that mitigated against the promotion of black membership in the women's movement" (Bradley, 2003, p. 72). For example, not only were there at least two black women, Bonnie Allen and Flo Kennedy, among the Miss America Pageant protestors, but Kennedy, a well-known lawyer and activist by this point (she had represented Valerie Solanas after Solanas famously shot Andy Warhol in June 1968), led the march of the protestors up the boardwalk. According to eyewitness accounts, she also talked with reporters about the pageant's racism (Giardina, 2010; Morgan, 2001). Kennedy should have been as recognizable to Curtis as Morgan was, but she went unmentioned in the story on the protest. Allen, the only black protestor so identified in Curtis's story, was labeled as a "housewife," and her only role in the story was to comment on the race issue, reflecting a common tendency of reporters to view white women as experts only on gender and black women as experts only on race.

The moves that Curtis made in her story on the Miss America Pageant protest are an example of how difficult reporters found arguments for what has come to be called intersectionality; that is, she used claims of racism to discredit claims of sexism rather than understanding their interrelationships.[10] Her positioning of the two protests as competitive and contradictory would be solidified by the additional stories on the two pageants that the *Times* ran the following day. On Monday, September 9, Curtis's (1968b) lengthy story on the Miss America Pageant winner was coupled with Judy Klemesrud's (1968) article on the results of the Miss Black America Pageant. The two stories, positioned side by side on the same page, shared a headline that reached across eight columns: "Along with Miss America, There's Now Miss Black America."[11] Curtis's story on the new Miss America did not mention the protest, but it did include an account of the winner's reactions to being asked about other issues of the day. The new Miss America was asked about her opinion on the Chicago Democratic convention ("I hate to talk about this. It's so controversial"), hippies ("I wouldn't want to be one"), whether "a Negro" should become Miss America ("as long as she's the prettiest"), and whether a woman should be president of the United States (depends on whether she's "qualified").

These queries about current issues reflected not just the tenor of the times but also journalists' bias toward easily accessible representative voices with institutional status. If many Americans considered Miss America "the standard for an ideal woman," as a CBS story on women's liberation would assert in 1970, then those who wore the crown were suitable for offering a "woman's perspective" on current topics, particularly those involving young women. Asking Miss America contestants and winners about their perspectives on feminism, in particular, would become a common tactic for reporters in the years that followed (Dow, 2003).

Miss America's response that a black woman should win the crown if she's "prettiest" was unintentionally ironic in the context of the *Times*'s paired stories on the two pageants and their treatment of the winners' appearances. The differing tones of the stories were initially signaled by their leads. Klemesrud's story on the new Miss Black America, Saundra Williams, noted in its first line that the winner "wears her hair natural, does African dances, and helped lead a student strike at her college last spring. She's what the new black woman is all about." The lead to Charlotte Curtis's story on the new Miss America mentioned hair as well, but stopped there: "What matters about 18-year-old Judith Anne Ford, besides her becoming Miss America of 1969 early today, is the color of her hair. The Illinois gymnast is the first blonde to win the title in 11 years."

Figure 2. Miss Black America 1969, Saundra Williams © 2013 Associated Press.

Whereas Curtis's story went on to depict Miss America shying away from mentions of politics and calling herself and other pageant contestants "just regular girls—not at all different from anybody else," Klemesrud's account of Miss Black America's politics was considerably less circumspect. Klemesrud quoted the Miss Black America Pageant sponsors' comment that they were protesting the "white stereotype" of Miss America, thus making the antiracist motives of the pageant more explicit than had Curtis's earlier story. Moreover, the "student strike" referred to in the lead was further explained as an action led by Williams to desegregate a restaurant in the Maryland town where she attended college, and the article also mentioned her membership in the NAACP.

Williams appeared to agree with the feminists' critique of the racism of the Miss America Pageant when she commented, "Miss America does not represent us because there has never been a black girl in the pageant. With my title, I can show black women that they too are beautiful even though they do have large noses and thick lips." However, the article also recounted that she looked "bored when asked about the 100 women demonstrators, mostly white, who had picketed the Miss America Pageant," and her only comment was, "They're expressing freedom, I guess. . . . To each his own." The contradictions here are somewhat striking; that is, Williams appeared dismissive of the feminists' critique of beauty politics while she was, by her own admission, engaged in a similar enterprise.

On one level, Klemesrud's inclusion of Williams's comment about the Miss America Pageant protestors cohered with the general tendency of the stories on the two protests to put sexism and racism in competition. Yet, on another level, Williams's remark may reflect the difficult relationship between black and white women activists that often turned on black feminists' disdain for what they saw as whites' misguided priorities. For example, Lumsden (2009) gives several examples of disapproving mentions of "bra burners" in her analysis of the treatment of women's liberation in black periodicals between 1968 and 1973, although she also argues that those periodicals' coverage of some aspects of feminism was often supportive.

Side by side, Curtis's and Klemesrud's reports on the two beauty contest winners created a rather sharp contrast. The Miss America organization took pains not to create controversy, and Curtis's story on Judith Anne Ford, in which she noted that Ford was asked by pageant officials not to comment on the "competing Miss Black America pageant," reflected this, giving credence to the eighth point in the press release distributed by the Miss America Pageant protestors:

> The Irrelevant Crown on the Throne of Mediocrity. Miss America represents what women are supposed to be: inoffensive, bland, apolitical. If you are tall,

short, over or under what weight The Man prescribes you should be, forget it. Personality, articulateness, intelligence, and commitment—unwise. Conformity is the key to the crown—and, by extension, to success in our Society.

Yet Klemesrud's story on Miss Black America presented Saundra Williams as someone who precisely possessed the "personality, articulateness, intelligence, and commitment" that Judith Anne Ford lacked in Charlotte Curtis's report.

Klemesrud's positive description of Saundra Williams's political activism exemplified one strand of the differing approaches national media took to non-violent civil rights actions and to Black Power tactics. The former were linked to "decent but aggrieved blacks who simply wanted to become a part of the American Dream," while the latter were constituted as "threats to the very notion of citizenship and nation" (Gray, 1997, p. 350). Moderate civil rights activism, particularly the kind represented by the NAACP and by what was described in the *Times* story as the "silent protest march" that Williams led against the segregated Maryland restaurant, was unlikely to be threatening or extreme to regular readers of the *Times* by 1968. The assassination and martyrdom of Martin Luther King Jr., coupled with the rise in visibility of the Black Panther Party and its reputation for violence, created a context in which Williams's politics were hardly remarkable. Her activism was of the safe and admirable sort, given that the discrimination she faced at the Maryland restaurant had supposedly been made illegal by the 1964 Civil Rights Act. Journalism reflects "common sense" perceptions of the world, and the existence of public racial discrimination, as well as the necessity of resisting it, had become common sense in elite media by 1968. Klemesrud's appraisal of Williams as "what the new black woman is all about" reflected a dominant perspective of her time, particularly within the *New York Times,* which had been a pioneer in positive national coverage of the nonviolent civil rights movement in the South (Roberts and Klibanoff, 2007).

Feminists faced a very different situation; they were fighting for precisely the kind of recognition of their grievances that civil rights activists had already achieved. The protestors were attempting to politicize the pageant and to make its sexism, among other sins, visible to the public. They succeeded in making themselves quite visible, but the accusations did not stick, so to speak, to the pageant itself. That Curtis's lengthy Monday story on the pageant outcome did not even mention the protest indicates that the latter was not taken seriously enough in 1968 to fully rupture the conventional Miss America narrative. Williams's activism was folded into her identity as a "new black woman," but Miss America's disinterested approach to current events was presented as unremarkable in a report that read as though the feminist protest did not even occur. In these stories, "white beauty queens" still "wore their crowns for themselves," but "black beauty queens stood for the race" (Craig, 2002, p. 70).

The reports on the two pageants and the protest are early indicators of news workers' elision of intersectionality, a tendency that worked against the recognition of feminism's political status as well as contributed to the whitewashing of women's liberation. Sexism, as a cultural malady, simply did not possess the same resonance as racism, and the *Times*'s treatment of the two protests reflected and reproduced this impression. Both actions critiqued beauty standards, but the Miss Black America Pageant had the imprimatur of the NAACP, and the pageant's figurehead, Saundra Williams, was given activist credentials while the political histories of the Miss America Pageant protestors went unmentioned. And, crucially, all of the *Times*'s stories indicated a tendency to depict black and white women's interests as antagonistic, despite feminists' efforts to link those interests.

Feminism, Femininity, and Miss America

The coverage of the Miss America Pageant action demonstrated that second-wave feminism, particularly its radical factions, faced the problems of many movements: making a complex analysis of a social phenomenon accessible and concrete, maintaining ideological commitments in the face of pressure to moderate them for public consumption, and creating enough drama to get attention without being reduced to sheer spectacle. Yet feminists faced some additional and unique challenges that arose from cultural ideologies about gender, and multiple accounts of the Miss America Pageant protest illustrate the central role that gender expectations attached to white, middle-class womanhood played in reactions to the action. These reactions, characterized by a preoccupation with the femininity (or lack thereof) of the protestors and a related insistence on interpreting the feminists' critique of the pageant as the outcome of personal frustration rather than political analysis, make clear that such activism was viewed as deeply transgressive.

Feminists saw the Miss America Pageant as symptomatic of the ways that femininity was constituted and evaluated with male consumers in mind, as the first point in the press release made clear:

> The pageant contestants epitomize the roles we are all forced to play as women. The parade down the runway blares the metaphor of the 4-H Club county fair, where the nervous animals are judged for teeth, fleece, etc., and where the best "Specimen" gets the blue ribbon. So are women in our society forced daily to

Figure 3. Miss America Pageant protestors with signs in Atlantic City, 1968. © 2013 Associated Press.

compete for male approval, enslaved by ludicrous "beauty" standards we ourselves are conditioned to take seriously.

Widely disseminated photographs of the protest show an effort by feminists to make this point visually as well—next to a sign stating "Welcome to the Miss America Cattle Auction," they carried a large poster depicting a kneeling, naked woman whose body parts were partitioned and labeled with terms derived from meat processing, for example, rib, rump, loin. Yet the same cultural norms that made it reasonable for women to compete for scholarship money by parading their bodies in swimsuits and evening gowns influenced news reports of feminist protest as well. Movement coverage reflected the assumption that women's physical appearance and appeal were always relevant; for example, Charlotte Curtis noted the age and apparel of protest participants in her story, mentioning that Robin Morgan was attired in "a black and white pajama suit."

Eyewitness accounts detail the presence of this mode of thinking among observers of the Miss America Pageant protest. Judith Duffett (1968) reported that hecklers shouted, among other things, "You're just jealous—you couldn't be Miss America if you were the last man on earth" and "Get back on your broom," as well as suggested that the protesters must be lesbians (p. 54). Similarly, Robin

Morgan (2001) recounted that a spectator also yelled "Dykes! Commies! Lezzies! You don't deserve to be Americans!" and she noted that, while the experienced leftists among the protestors were used to being called communists, they were taken aback at the lesbian accusation (p. 261). Yet the performance of masculinity that public protest represented, coupled with the critique of Miss America as a heterosexual, feminine ideal, was apparently enough to warrant such reactions. For "normal" women to do such things was unnatural; the protestors must, therefore, be lesbians.

The theme of women's obligation to function as sexually appealing objects was accompanied by its corollary: women's competition with other women for the approval of men. That many feminists refused to participate in beauty politics was a clear message of the protest; at issue was their motivation. A few days after the protest, in a *New York Post* column, Harriet Van Horne (1968) called the protesters "sturdy lasses" in "sensible shoes" (not difficult to decipher as code for "lesbian," or, at the least, unfeminine) and wrote that she discarded her invitation to attend the protest because "this lady of the press usually has something nicer to do on Saturday night than burn her undergarments on the boardwalk in Atlantic City. And I suspect the deep-down aching trouble with these lassies is that they haven't" (p. 38). She thus neatly forwarded the bra-burning myth as well as the notion that the protesters, whom she labeled "unstroked, uncaressed, and emotionally undernourished" were driven less by ideology than by their failure as objects of heterosexual appeal (Van Horne, 1968, p. 38). If it was the case, as a feminist remarked in an appearance on the David Susskind show shortly after the protest, that "every day in a woman's life is a walking Miss America contest" (quoted in Hanisch, 1998, p. 198), then one of the unfortunate perceptions created by the events in Atlantic City was that feminists were disgruntled because they simply could not compete.

The implication that feminists were motivated primarily by envy, and that their critique of Miss America was directed at contestants themselves rather than at the sexist system that had created the pageant, was buttressed by some of the tactics of the protesters. Carol Hanisch (1970) would shortly pen a critique of the action in which her primary objection was that "a definite strain of anti-womanism was presented to the public to the detriment of the action" because "Miss America and all beautiful women came off as our enemy instead of as our sisters who suffer with us" (p. 133). For example, according to Hanisch (1970), "crowning a live sheep Miss America sort of said that beautiful women *are* sheep," and such signs as "'Miss America Is a Big Falsie' hardly raised any woman's consciousness and really harmed the cause of sisterhood" (pp. 134, 133, emphasis in original). Hanisch was worried about the possibility of alienating potential movement members, a concern that seems unwarranted in retrospect, given the seismic effect the protest would have on the movement's growth. The more stubborn problem was the implication, created by various media accounts, that feminists hated beauty contestants because they could never be one, and that their damaged psyches were the source of their rage at the pageant.

Such a perspective depoliticized feminist protest by speculating about personal, psychological motivations and by refusing to engage with feminists' analysis of beauty politics *as a politics,* a system put in place by patriarchy that disempowered women by pitting them against each other. Later news coverage of the movement would replicate this "women vs. women" strategy in its insistence on pairing coverage of feminist ideas and activities with the reactions of women who voiced disdain or disinterest. Two years after the protest, when a *Times* reporter asked the incoming president of the National Council of Women her opinion about feminism, the president remarked that not only did she not believe that women faced discrimination, but that "so many of [the feminists] are just so unattractive" that "I wonder if they're completely well" (quoted in Fosburgh, 1970, p. 44). The implication was that protesting had become a way of getting the attention that ugly and/or "sick" women were otherwise denied. At the most basic level, the Miss America Pageant protestors were different from "ordinary women" because of their insistence on calling attention to themselves in public. In a culture in which (white, middle-class) women's lives were presumed to take place in the private sphere—cordoned off from the public, political realm—for women to take to the streets (or the boardwalk) was a prima facie assault on conventional femininity.

Conclusion

News reports on the 1968 Miss America Pageant protest provide an early illustration of many of the image problems that have plagued feminism ever since, but the event was undeniably a success in terms of energizing the radical wing of the second wave, and the media visibility of the action put tremendous pressure on NYRW. Almost two hundred women showed up for the next meeting of the group; formerly, its size had been around thirty-five participants (Morgan, 2001). In a 1989 interview, former NYRW member Rosalyn Baxandall recounted, "It was more exposure than we were prepared to deal with, organizationally. There were so many letters, hundreds of letters from all over the country supporting the protest. We just couldn't answer them all. We couldn't even open some of them. We threw hundreds out" (quoted in Kelly, 2000, p. 169). Membership in the group swelled, ideological schisms intensified (a central one concerned the utility of CR versus public action), and, by early 1969, NYRW had split into multiple groups, including W.I.T.C.H. (Women's International Terrorist Conspiracy from Hell, an action group) and Redstockings (which focused on CR and theory building) (Echols, 1989).[12]

As a zap action, the Miss America Pageant protest had achieved its purpose of gaining media attention, and a number of other such actions by W.I.T.C.H. followed, including a hex on Wall Street on Halloween 1968 that was designed to dramatize women's economic inequality. W.I.T.C.H. also cast a hex on the New York City Bridal Fair at Madison Square Garden in February 1969, disrupting the event by carrying signs, singing ("Here come the slaves, off to their graves"), and releasing a hundred white mice on the floor of the garden (Klemesrud, 1969, p. 39). In the words of W.I.T.C.H. member Robin Morgan, described again as a "former child actress" in the story, their aim was to protest "the commerciality of the Bridal Fair and the institution of marriage as it exists in this culture . . . to oppress women" (Klemesrud, 1969, p. 39). The story also noted Morgan's participation in the Miss America Pageant protest, but it implicitly called into question the integrity of her opposition to marriage by mentioning that she was married and expecting her first child.

These actions received some national press, although not network, coverage, with the exception of footage of earlier W.I.T.C.H. actions that would appear in network reports in 1970. In Judy Klemesrud's *Times* story about the Bridal Fair, for example, the W.I.T.C.H. demonstrators did not make the lead and received five paragraphs of coverage in a twenty-six–paragraph story that described the day's events. Echoing a theme in the press coverage of the Miss America Pageant protest, Klemesrud (1969) reported that the master of ceremonies "opened the events to cheers and applause when he said of the demonstrators, 'I think they're just a little teed off because nobody ever proposed to them'" (p. 39).

Klemesrud's story, undertaken for the Style section under the editorship of Charlotte Curtis, is another indicator of the *Times*'s central role in early coverage of women's liberation and of the complex role played by sympathetic, usually female, journalists in the mediated construction of the movement. Much of the media activism undertaken during the second wave rested on the implicit assumption that if more women had central roles in producing the news, the news would, in turn, be less sexist. Radical feminists' insistence on dealing with women reporters indicated their stake in this belief, and anecdotal evidence suggests that women reporters choose and advocate for stories that might not otherwise be captured by the news net, something that was undoubtedly true during the second wave (Mills, 1997; Tuchman, 1978a, 1978b). In fact, Bradley (2003) claims that "no reporter was more important to the second wave" than

Judy Klemesrud, and feminists viewed both Charlotte Curtis and Judy Klemesrud as sympathetic to their concerns (p. 82). Betty Friedan would call Klemesrud "one of our own," at the reporter's funeral in 1985 (Bradley, 2005, p. 239).

In her 2001 memoir, Robin Morgan told a surprising behind-the-scenes tale of Curtis's role in the Miss America Pageant protest. She recounted that Curtis not only rode in the bus from New York that the protestors had rented, "gamely warbling 'We Shall Overcome' with us," but that Curtis had met with Morgan days before to talk about the protest and had gently offered suggestions about toning down tactics that might "alienate" rather than persuade (Morgan, 2001, p. 262; see also Morgan, 1999). Morgan recalled leaving the meeting convinced that Curtis would attempt sympathetic coverage. Most remarkably, however, after several protestors were arrested for their disruptive tactics inside the pageant hall, Curtis put up their bail so that they might be released and asked Morgan to "keep it quiet" that she had done so, no doubt for fear that her objectivity would be called into question if the news got out (Morgan, 2001, p. 262).

Even so, Curtis's and Klemesrud's reports on the pageant and the protests are an example of the power of news practices—and of conventional wisdom about gender, race, and what counted as politics—to shape coverage of feminist activism regardless of the gender or political sympathies of the reporters. Empirical studies confirm that journalists work within powerful constraints created by the values of their news organizations, their professional communities, and the culture at large, and that "the individual characteristics of journalists do not correlate strongly with the kinds of news content they produce" (Weaver, 1997, pp. 38–39; see also Bradley, 2003). Judy Klemesrud herself, interviewed in 1975, remarked, "the hardest part of the job [of covering feminists] is not sounding like one of them. I have to be objective, a gadfly" (quoted in Tuchman, 1978a).

Even with its limitations, the national press coverage of the protest had a profound effect on the growth and visibility of the movement. Equally as important, it created long-standing legacies for the second wave in subsequent reporting and in cultural memory. Reporters would revisit the feminist critique in subsequent years' coverage of the annual event, in which references to feminist opposition became ritualistic (Dow, 2003). The 1969 feature stories on the emerging women's liberation movement in *Life* (Davidson, 1969) and the *New York Times Magazine* (Babcox, 1969) would both begin by recounting the events in Atlantic City in September 1968, cementing the protest's importance to the movement's development. Feminists were convinced that the impact of their action had been so overwhelming that it might not be long before the pageant was closed down entirely (Duffett, 1968). To the contrary, the Miss America Pageant has proven remarkably durable, surviving through many changes designed to stave off declining popularity and television ratings, although it enjoys considerably less cultural power than it once did (Dow, 2003; Banet-Weiser and Portwood-Stacer, 2006).

The cultural memory of bra burning has proven equally as durable. It took hold almost immediately, even in the *New York Times,* despite Curtis's accuracy in her original story on the protest. In a follow-up story a few weeks later on the arrests at the pageant, the *Times* would refer to "bra-burnings and other demonstrations at the pageant" ("The Price of Protest," 1968, p. 25). The following year, *Newsweek* described the 1968 Miss America Pageant demonstration as 150 women who "gathered in front of Convention Hall and burned their brassieres" (quoted in Douglas, 1994, p. 159), and *Time*'s 1969 story on the movement noted that "the angries" picketed the pageant and burned brassieres ("The New Feminists," 1969, p. 54). More than thirty years later, in a September 2000 item noting the marriage of Gloria Steinem, *Newsweek* described the wedding ceremony as follows: "The sunrise ceremony, held in Oklahoma, was part Cherokee, with 'a lot of burning stuff,' said bud-of-the-bride actress Kathy Najimy. Like those old bras, huh?" (Davis, 2000, p. 92). Gloria Steinem did not attend the 1968 protest, but the connection between all things feminist and bra burning has proven an obstinate one.

Certainly, the specter of bra burning trivialized women's liberation. But the obsessive repetition of the bra-burning trope has deeper implications that go to the heart of the problems of early news media constructions of second-wave feminism. Even if feminists only threw them away rather than burning them, the fact remains that bras were an issue. When they rejected bras, feminists were refusing particular social constructions of womanhood that insisted on their status as sexualized beings by requiring that their bodies be held in place in artificial ways (in fact, the "torpedo," "bullet," or "cone" bras of the time highlighted rather than hid women's cleavage). For leftist women, many of whom had given up bras, girdles, skirts, and heels long before the Miss America Pageant protest, the rejection of such trappings of femininity was a repudiation of their objectification as women and a claiming of their status as humans. It was a de-emphasizing of their gender difference that became precisely the opposite in mass media representations that insisted on that difference at almost every turn.

Gendered binaries—public versus private, masculine versus feminine, personal versus political—operated throughout movement coverage, and gender anxiety erupted over feminists' breaching of conventional boundaries. Women's association with the private and personal and their concomitant exclusion from the public and political were underscored by press accounts that insisted on understanding feminists' critique of beauty politics as the bitterness of "homely harpies" unable to catch a man (Rhode, 1995, p. 696). The personalizing of feminist grievances was a refusal to grant feminists status as experienced political actors, although their tactics and discourse at the Miss America Pageant protest clearly indicated the legacy of their prior experiences with radical politics. For instance, the crowning of a live sheep as Miss America recalled the Yippies's nomination of a pig for president at the 1968 Democratic National Convention.

On the other hand, for those feminists striving to establish an independent women's movement, more recognition of those links could have worked against their interests by positioning them as mere copycats trying to get in on the action (an unfortunate implication of Lindsy Van Gelder's analogy between the burning of draft cards and bras). Indeed, radical feminists' emphasis on sexual politics often looked inconsequential when compared to the issues—such as violent racism and U.S. imperialism—raised by other contemporaneous movements. The *Times*'s matter-of-fact recognition of the political nature of the Miss Black America Pageant and its refusal, in the face of feminist analysis, to give the same status to the Miss America Pageant illustrated tacit acceptance of this logic.

To put it another way, racism and its remedies had come to be understood within the philosophical frame of U.S. liberalism, in which public discrimination was recognized as a social problem and blacks qualified as an oppressed class. And liberalism was the source not only for the public-private divide but also for news values that demarcated what counted as legitimate public and/or political concerns, what did not, and how they should be discussed. Barker-Plummer (2010) has called news "an example of liberal epistemologies in action," noting that "the hard/soft news distinction, for example, is a clear reflection of the public-private divide, and the focus in news on personal stories, and on facticity, mirror quite well the individualist and rationalist tropes of liberalism" (pp. 193–194). Because these divisions are also gendered, they have proven particularly stubborn for feminist discourses that seek to challenge them; because they are rooted in raced and classed understandings of gender, they work against recognition of intersectionality.

Early news coverage of the second wave provides powerful evidence of the inflexibility of the gender binary and of cultural understanding of it as a zero-sum game; that is, if women discard their femininity, they must be acquiring masculinity instead, which means men must be losing it. Feminists *were* assaulting femininity (and its powerlessness) as well as masculinity (and its privileges). In attempting to make the personal political, they confronted "the ancient association of men and maleness with public life (politics and power) and women and femaleness with domesticity (personal life and subordination)" (Evans, 2003, p. 3). Cultural resistance to interrogating the stark demarcation between those realms is evident in the coverage discussed here; reactions and reports show attempts to claw the feminists back onto personal grounds and to question their credibility to make political claims. That questioning took myriad forms, all of which foreshadowed challenges that feminists would face during the wave of broadcast coverage in 1970. Did feminists attack femininity because they could not achieve it? Could feminist claims be believed if all women did not support those claims? Were not the differences between men and women rooted in nature, and, if so, were not feminists deviant, unnatural, and thus not to be taken seriously (or even feared)? And, last but not least, should sexism be taken as seriously as racism when its emblem was a burning bra rather than "protestors being hosed down or attacked by dogs?" (Douglas, 1994, p. 187).

Radical feminists, in particular, faced formidable obstacles as they pursued recognition and salience for their critique of sexism and patriarchy as political systems that did real damage to women. If such status could not be established, then feminists were airing personal pettiness rather than political analysis, and they were entitled to no more authority than the "ordinary" women who disavowed their claims. This conflict between personal and political understandings of women's lives, what Sara Evans (2003) has called "the most distinctive characteristic" (p. 3) of feminism between the 1960s and today, continued to play itself out in various ways when women's liberation finally made national broadcast network news in 1970.

CHAPTER 2

The Movement Makes the News

Network News Feature Stories
on Women's Liberation in 1970

Get out there and find an authority who'll say this is all a crock of shit.

—Male editor's comment to female reporter writing a story on
women's liberation (quoted in North, 1970, p. 106)

Get the bra burning and the karate up front.

—Male editor's comment to a writer preparing a news magazine story
on women's liberation (quoted in Brownmiller, 1970b, p. 27).

In a February 9, 1969, article in the *New York Times Magazine*, under the title "The Women of the Revolution, 1969," writer Peter Babcox opened with a vivid description of the 1968 Miss America Pageant protest. He also detailed reactions to the protest, including a letter received by Robin Morgan that read, "Dear Ugly: What right have you to disrupt the Miss America pageant? Just because you are a frustrated female who, because of her homely face, can never have a chance, doesn't give you the right to cause trouble. Only an insane person would do a thing like this" (Babcox, 1969, pp. 35–36). Noting that Morgan was far from homely, Babcox (1969) chalked up such reactions to the "durable cultural fantasy that feminine assertiveness—political, professional or sexual—is but a symptom of raging nymphomania or other grave psychic disorder" (p. 35). The largely sympathetic article contained lengthy profiles of Morgan and two other leftist women as well as a discussion of the chauvinism they all faced in "the movement," a term that broadly encompassed leftist activity. Babcox's recognition of the roots of women's liberation in the left distinguished his article from the

Time's coverage of the Miss America Pageant protest, and his was among the first in a wave of print features on the movement that began to proliferate by the end of the year, when *Life* magazine ran a lengthy story on feminism (Davidson, 1969), as did *Time* ("The New Feminists," 1969).

Feminism was emerging as a social trend story around this time, particularly in New York, the media hub of the country and the home of several radical feminist groups as well as the country's largest and most active chapter of NOW. The purpose of the trend story is to illuminate shifts in social behavior, and it "attains authority not through actual reporting, but through the power of repetition" when "a trend declared in one publication sets off a chain reaction, as the rest of the media scramble to get the story, too" (Faludi, 1991, p. 79). Or, as a *Newsweek* reporter later remarked about the explosion of national coverage of women's liberation, "it's New York groupthink. You can hear them all mooing like a herd of cattle when they are on to the same trend" (quoted in Freeman, 1975, p. 148). By early 1970, women's liberation was a trend story at its tipping point. In February and March, "the new feminism" or women's liberation was the subject of a cover story in *Saturday Review* (Komisar, 1970), a lengthy story in *Newsweek* (Dudar, 1970), and whole sections of *Mademoiselle* and *Atlantic Monthly*. Also in March, the *New York Times Magazine* ran another feature on women's liberation; this one, written by New York Radical Feminists (NYRF) member Susan Brownmiller, was subtitled "A Member of the Women's Liberation Movement Explains What It's All About" (1970b).[1]

Several of the articles in this wave of coverage were thoughtful and informative, and several were written by women, like Brownmiller, who were active in the movement. Magazines had the advantage of being able to draw on a pool of feminist journalists that could freelance such stories (Bradley, 2005). For example, Lucy Komisar (1970), who wrote *Saturday Review*'s cover story, was a vice president of NOW, *Atlantic Monthly*'s special section titled Women's Place included at least three stories written by self-identified feminists (Gerrity, 1970; Janeway, 1970; North, 1970), and Brownmiller authored one of the February *Mademoiselle* articles (1970a).

Thus, by the time network feature stories on women's liberation began to appear, elite print media already had established the movement as a legitimate topic. That network news followed rather than led the media stampede to what would quickly become "the story of the year" reflected television news' youth and lesser credibility relative to print media (Douglas, 1994, p. 166). Until 1963, the nightly newscasts on CBS and NBC were only fifteen minutes long, and ABC did not go to a half-hour nightly newscast until 1967. By 1970, however, television was becoming America's primary news source, a fact that demonstrates how quickly the medium penetrated American homes (more quickly than the telephone, for instance) (Hammond, 1981; Stephens, 1998). But network television news was still a sort of illegitimate stepchild of national journalism, driven by ratings and sponsor dollars in a way that print news supposedly was not, and it tended to follow the lead of major print venues like the *New York Times* (Gitlin, 1980). Feminists' escalating efforts to gain media attention played a role as well, as the cumulative effect of a "sequence of public events by feminists" that had received some print and local broadcast attention in prior months (various NOW pickets, the second Miss America Pageant protest in September 1969, public "hexes" by radical feminist action group W.I.T.C.H) made the movement ripe for network broadcast attention (Freeman, 1975, p. 149).

Beginning on March 9, CBS would offer the first network feature treatments of women's liberation, soon to be followed by NBC's six-part series. But CBS initially broke national television news' silence on feminism in January 1970 when it covered the Senate hearings on the birth control pill that were disrupted by members of D.C. Women's Liberation.[2] For the networks, the Senate's investigation into the pharmaceutical industry was newsworthy in itself, and CBS's first story, on January 15, mentioned the feminist presence in the audience for the proceedings only as an aside. On January 23, however, the confrontational tactics of the feminists became the lead in stories on both CBS and ABC, which showed women shouting at the senators who would not allow them to speak at a hearing that featured an array of male medical and scientific experts but included no testimony from women who actually used the pill. Both network stories featured the same feminist's sound bite ("You are murdering us for your profit and convenience!") and showcased Chairman Senator Gaylord Nelson's obvious frustration with the interruption. These event-centered stories did little more than establish the feminists as angry and loud, and likely to be understood as unreasonably so, since no information was provided about their grievances.[3] For example, ABC's story began by stating that the hearings were "shrilly disrupted by women's liberation ladies," and, after noting that Nelson recessed the hearings briefly to reestablish order, it closed with the observation that "the public, and its virago elements, were not welcomed back" into the reconvened proceedings.

NBC's January 23 story, in contrast, focused on information rather than behavior. It began with a lengthy interview with the new Food and Drug Administration chairman, who spoke thoughtfully about the credibility problems of the agency (under scrutiny for lax regulation generally) and acknowledged the legitimacy of concerns about the pill. This story also noted the feminists' interruption of the hearings and Nelson's closing of the hearings in response, although reporter Ron Nessen concluded by observing that Nelson had pledged to meet with the women and hear their objections. NBC's January 29 follow-up story covered the feminist delegation's meeting with Nelson, depicting the women as orderly and smiling, shaking hands with the senator as they filed into his office. The story closed with lengthy footage of a member of the delegation calmly reading a prepared statement that detailed the group's intent to hold their own hearing to investigate a series of issues related to the safety and marketing of the pill (the hearing would take place on March 7, 1970 [Ward, 1970]).

NBC's more judicious depiction of the feminists, coupled with contextualization of their grievances and attention to the protest's outcome, diverged sharply from that of the other networks. By focusing on the disruption itself and by offering no justification for the behavior that they described so censoriously, CBS and ABC amplified the impression (created by the visuals) that the feminists were making trouble for no good reason. These stories also positioned the feminists and hearings chairman Gaylord Nelson as adversaries, but Nelson was well intentioned and shared feminists' skepticism about the safety of the pill. He had decided to include it as a focus of the committee's investigation after reading journalist (and later women's health activist) Barbara Seaman's 1969 book, *The Doctor's Case against the Pill* (Kline, 2010). NBC made it clear that Nelson took their objections seriously and hinted at the success that feminist intervention in the hearings would turn out to be. The ultimate outcome was an early victory for the nascent women's health movement and its advocacy for informed consent. When the Food and Drug Administration required that every package of the pill include information about side effects, it was the first such requirement for any prescription drug (May, 2010).

The January 1970 stories on the birth control hearings are a useful introduction to the networks' treatment of women's liberation because they indicate the ways that some negative constructions of feminists (as shrill viragos, for instance) emerged very early in television coverage of the movement. At the same time, the NBC stories indicate that network coverage was not uniformly negative in terms of its depictions of feminist grievances and behavior. Similarly, the network news feature stories broadcast several weeks later make clear that generalizations about prejudicial news treatment of women's liberation simply do not apply in all instances. Although the CBS and NBC series had some noteworthy parallels, their televised narratives about the movement diverged along three important lines: their characterizations of the movement itself (particularly the relationship between liberals and radicals), their use of images in their treatment of the movement's issues, and the imagined audiences that their reports addressed.

The CBS stories, all reported by one male correspondent, offered a narrative about the movement itself, with a primary focus on the players and their tactics but a much less fleshed-out portrait of the issues. In particular, radicals and the issues they raised were subjected to the belittling representational strategies that had already taken hold in some print coverage. The NBC stories, reported by four different women, constructed a narrative that was primarily about the movement's issues—sexism and discrimination—presenting them as troubling social problems while barely mentioning women's liberation in three of the six reports.[4] In short, the NBC stories exnominated, in Roland Barthes's (1972) sense, the gender bias that motivated the movement. Rather than reporting on sexism as a feminist claim, as the CBS reports did, they presented it as objective reality, as the background of women's lives, as "that-which-cannot-be-challenged" (Fiske, 1987, p. 292).

Although both series ultimately emphasized the easily understood policy demands of liberal feminism and, relatedly, foregrounded working women as ideal feminist subjects, they did so using noticeably different strategies. The CBS stories' approval of liberal feminist workplace equality demands came at the expense of radical feminism, which was portrayed as the extremist "other" in contrast to the reasonable moderates. NBC's discussion of the movement, rather than marginalizing the radicals, assimilated them into a broad and unified vision of women's liberation in which the sexual politics central to radical feminist critique were treated as a foundational factor in women's public inequality that could be addressed through policy measures like the ERA.

The networks' different utilization of television's visual capabilities was crucial to their contrasting narratives and was most evident in the relationship between words and images in their series. The CBS stories often used images as an end in themselves, as decontextualized devices with little information value or sense-making narration, depicting feminism as a kind of spectacle that fostered the "pleasure of looking" rather than the construction of meaning and thus distanced viewers from the transgression that the radicals, in particular, represented (Fiske, 1987, p. 246). Represented through images of protest and confrontation, radicals were often shot at an extreme close-up angle that made them appear wild-eyed and eccentric. Liberal feminists, in contrast, were illustrated by footage of meetings and talking heads in medium shots, and generic footage of anonymous women going about their low-status and poorly paid jobs accompanied narration of liberal feminist complaints about workplace discrimination.

The NBC series also deployed images of moderation to illustrate liberal feminism, but it forwent the exploitation of radical feminism's capacity for producing shocking visuals. Instead, NBC's reports exploited the capacity of visuals to make ideas concrete and relatable, using images to make the pervasiveness of sexism, rather than the excesses of feminism, the ultimate focus for viewers. They verified feminist claims by visually illustrating the sexism being verbally described, or, in other cases, by accompanying a sexist claim with an image that contradicted it.

In NBC's reports, those viewers were often presumed to be women themselves, who, the stories suggested, could benefit from some hard information about the existence of sexism and its potential remedies. In contrast, CBS reporter David Culhane's tone of bemusement and skepticism in his stories, as well as the shockingly sexist camera work they contained, indicated that he presumed he was describing the movement to an audience of men who would find much of women's liberation both absurd and anxiety provoking.

The differences in their imagined audiences are especially evident in the two network series' treatment of abortion. Culhane integrated the issue into a discussion of radical feminists' desire to "transform the whole relationship between women and men," thus articulating it to the gender anxiety of a presumed male audience as well as to radical feminist extremism. NBC devoted an entire story to abortion, framing it as a logical response to the social problem of unwanted pregnancy, and reporter Catherine Mackin targeted an audience of women by including a virtual primer on how to obtain access to the procedure.

These differences in the audiences implied by the reports are linked to another prominent dissimilarity: the roles and responsibilities the two series' narratives assigned to "ordinary" men and women. Straightforward in their recognition that men were the culprits behind and the beneficiaries of sexism and discrimination, the NBC reports used testimony from men themselves to make the case; similarly, they used testimony from "ordinary" women to show the damage done by sexism. Yet the CBS stories presented women's indifference to the movement as, in the words of David Culhane, feminism's "one fundamental problem," a claim that cast male resistance as "a completely insignificant barrier to change" (Douglas, 1994, p. 175).

The CBS and NBC series were the networks' first efforts to create some coherence out of the movement's complexity in 1970 and to illuminate its implications for a national television audience. A close reading of the narratives each produced makes clear that, even within the broad constraints of news as a genre and as an "ideology in action," rhetorical choices operated in large and small ways at every turn (Tuchman, 1978b, p. 155). If the CBS series is the exemplar of negative television reporting on women's liberation, the NBC series is arguably the exemplar of the opposite. These two polarized portraits of the women's movement, appearing in short succession in early 1970, were the networks' opening salvos in the televised struggle over feminism's image politics.

Representing the Movement

The first stories in the CBS and NBC series functioned as scene-setting overviews of the movement, introducing themes and strategies that would be developed in the reports that followed. Despite a couple of similarities—the most evident of which was their recitation of women's employment and pay statistics that motivated liberal feminist activism—they offered markedly different visions of women's liberation. Initiating a strategy that would thread throughout his three reports, David Culhane's first story worked to *separate* liberal and radical tactics and ideas, representing the former as sensible and defensible while depicting the latter as irrational and threatening. Aline Saarinen's first story for NBC would emphasize and legitimate the factors *unifying* feminist discontent, offering a first picture of the movement that highlighted issues rather than activism, a focus that persisted in the stories that followed.

CBS: DEMARCATING LIBERALS AND RADICALS

CBS's March 9 story opened with archival footage of suffragists marching in New York City in 1920 as the viewer heard background strains of the "Battle Hymn of the Republic." In voiceover, David Culhane noted that women "won the franchise fifty years ago, and now, in the minds of many people," they "are better off than ever before in history." The suffrage footage faded into an image of a group of four present-day feminists on a stage singing a parody of "The Battle Hymn of the Republic" that included the line "We will vote ourselves in power with our own majority."[5] Images of suffragists marching, followed by images of contemporary feminists on a stage singing about voting, created a clever connection between the first and second waves, but these images functioned as entertaining, even trivializing, spectacle and told the viewer almost nothing about what feminists wanted. This was the first of several times that the series would feature footage of feminist theater; each time, it was presented as a kind of amusing diversion dropped into the report's narrative and unaccompanied by explication from Culhane or the participants. The upshot of this opening segment was clear: by noting that "many" considered women better off than at any time in history, Culhane placed the burden on feminists to prove that women actually had any problems worth complaining about.

Yet, as the story continued with a visual of rows of women typing at desks, he legitimated feminist complaints, pointing out that there were 30 million working women, yet "very few are in executive positions," and that the average man made almost twice as much as the average woman. Over images of women nurses and women teachers going about their jobs, he detailed the dearth of women doctors and college professors, following up with a statement from Betty

Friedan, identified as the founder and president of NOW. Framed in a medium shot, seated in a chair, Friedan pointed out women's underrepresentation in leadership positions of all kinds, from business to politics. She concluded, "In the big decisions—of war and peace, of crisis in the cities, even the decisions as to what happens to women's . . . own bodies and the self-determination of their own lives . . . women's voice has not been heard." Footage that followed, of an apparently liberal feminist group (conservatively dressed and coiffed, mostly middle-aged and seemingly middle-class) gathered in a suburban living room in Northridge, California, offered a clear justification for feminist frustration as one of the women spoke: "Most women are at some time in their life going to have to work as head of household to support an entire household and taxed the same as the man and paid a third as much for identical work. How do we make the public understand that this woman can't compete, even if she has no man at all? She can't compete in the labor market enough to feed her children."

The first story offered a coherent rationale for liberal feminism: women were underpaid and underrepresented in many arenas—importantly, Culhane provided those statistics himself—and this discrimination made it difficult for women to support their children. Verbally linking equality demands to women's roles as breadwinners for their families, the story depicted them as pragmatic rather than ideological. The mundane visual elements—stock footage, a talking head interview, calm group discussion—functioned as background for the verbal content, amplifying the impact of the latter. Because Culhane opened the story with a comparison of the first and second waves, one could read these early segments in the story as his confirmation that, just as first-wave feminists had made a reasonable and ultimately successful demand for the vote, some second-wave feminists were making reasonable demands for equal pay and equal opportunity.

In a stark reversal, when Culhane turned his attention to what he termed the "militant" faction in the movement, visuals were foregrounded and verbal

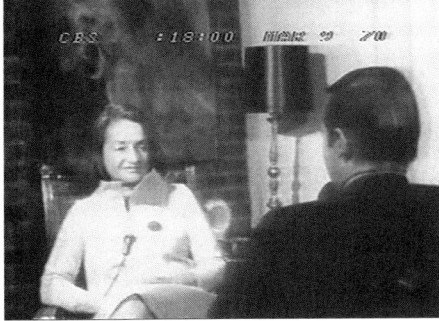

Figure 4. Betty Friedan, in medium shot, being interviewed on CBS.

affirmation of feminist grievances diminished. The next segment was dominated by vivid images of public protest that were largely unaccompanied by a verbalized explanation; thus the most evident difference between the liberals and the militants in this first story had to do with their *demeanor* rather than their politics: those who rationally discussed their issues were contrasted to those who acted out, and no justification was given for the behavior of the latter. The segment opened with footage from the birth control pill hearings, including the same "murdering us for your profit and convenience" line featured in CBS's January story. As though drawing a conclusion from evidence just presented, Culhane then said, "Some women, especially among the young, are becoming more militant. . . . On several occasions they disrupted hearings on birth control pills. They left no doubt they think the pill is unsafe and should be taken off the market." As in the January story, viewers received no further information on the reasoning behind feminists' concerns, and the images in this segment of the story functioned as "symbolic-only representations of angry women," displacing the issue motivating the behavior by focusing on the behavior itself (Bradley, 2003, p. 75). The segment's inclusion of an exasperated Senator Gaylord Nelson asking the women to sit down or be removed underscored the feminists' disorderliness and disrespect as the central point of the footage.

Culhane's lumping of feminist protestors under the militant label based on their behavior rather than their beliefs was most evident in the way he equated what *was* a radical feminist action—disruption of the birth control hearings—with the other protest featured in this first story: a sit-in dramatizing public discrimination at Chicago's Berghoff restaurant, which enforced a "men only" section in its bar. Yet Culhane failed to mention that this particular protest was not, in fact, spearheaded by militant feminists but by NOW, which had led several such protests at bars that excluded women.[6] The white women demonstrators seen in the footage were middle-aged and more conservative in appearance than were the women at the Senate hearings; one elderly woman among them was shown in several camera shots (a featuring of deviance akin to Charlotte Curtis's focus on grandmothers at the Miss America Pageant protest). Culhane noted that the majority of the restaurant was gender-integrated, but "a small part of it is set aside for men who want to have a quick lunch by themselves" (implying that having little space and using it for little time—and only at lunch—made the discrimination unremarkable). On the screen, the women confronted the bar owner with accusations of discrimination using a sex-race analogy, a favorite tactic for NOW: "Now we fought the public accommodations fight ten years ago with the blacks. Are we going to have to start all over again with women? How would you like a sign up there that said 'Blacks only' or 'Whites only?' It's the same principle." Culhane narrated that, after the CBS cameras left, "a scuffle at the bar between a man and a woman demonstrator" ensued, although no one was injured or arrested.

Despite their explicit invocation, on camera, of the parallel to the nonviolent civil rights movement—as well as their emulation of its tactics—Culhane classified the NOW members as militants, underscoring this categorization when he used their reaction to being physically attacked by a bar patron as his segue to a discussion of "militant feminist" interest in judo and karate. As the story cut to an image of a woman and a man in martial arts garb on a mat, he observed, "The woman being thrown by a fellow student at the University of Chicago is a militant feminist. Many of them are learning judo and karate and they say it's a splendid equalizer." The woman circled the man, threw him over her shoulder, and pinned him to the mat, as a group of watching women cheered and Culhane opined, "Many feminists think this is an apt symbol of equal rights, that as more women come to know their oppression, the symbol could become a reality." The implication was clear: Martial arts were an outlet for women's wrath, and women were willing to use violence in their quest for equality. In the report's final image, the young woman threw the man to the ground yet again and brought her leg down on his neck as he grunted in pain.

In a masterpiece of associative logic held together by images, a narrative that began with footage of "militant" public protest proceeded to connect that militancy to feminists' pursuit of martial arts and climaxed with a visual of a woman physically besting a man. Militancy was the uniting thread, but, with the exception of the judo segment, the activities depicted were merely verbally aggressive, illustrating news media's proclivity for using militancy "interchangeably with 'stridency'" in accounts of feminist activity (Bradley, 2003, p. 60). For feminists to practice aggression even through speech—and through their unwanted presence—was a shocking violation of expectations that merited ample airtime. Many radicals no doubt understood this, and wariness about participating in news coverage was partially linked to their fear that "it would drive women away" (Douglas, 1994, p. 158). For instance, one of the CR groups within NYRF had been solicited to appear in the CBS series and had declined after discussing the issue (Brownmiller, 1970b). The CBS reports gave credence to such reluctance by positioning radical feminism as profoundly transgressive in its aims and execution, a tendency even more pronounced in the series' third story, which focused specifically on the radical faction in the movement.

Walter Cronkite's lead-in to the third story, broadcast March 13, referenced the "battle of the sexes" and noted, "some women have declared war on traditional feminine roles and . . . are urging others to join the fight." As the screen showed footage of feminists throwing bras into a trash can at the 1968 Miss America Pageant protest, Culhane asked, "What are they liberating themselves from? Brassieres and high heels, female appurtenances that they think mark them as women who accept an ideal of femininity dictated by men, an ideal that somehow makes them 'slaves.'"[7] Extending Cronkite's theme that a central task of the movement was to recruit women to "join the fight," the report then moved to footage of a feminist singing as Culhane introduced "the Feminist Repertory Theater in New York, a kind of political cabaret designed to show women the reality of their condition."

Given that the feminist's song was about the tedium of baking cookies, Culhane's description became ironic and the issues animating radical activity looked frivolous. Feminist theater—like the New Feminist Repertory Theater mentioned in this report—was a major component of second-wave feminist activity that did powerful consciousness-raising work for its participants and its audiences (Case, 1988; Hole and Levine, 1971). Yet the centrality of CR to radical feminism went unmentioned and unexplained in this story, replaced by the insinuation that radical tactics such as feminist theater spread feminism "'by contagion' as women's libbers indoctrinated previously happy women" who presumably did not mind wearing bras and high heels or baking cookies (Douglas, 1994, p. 184).

Indeed, the radical feminist group on which Culhane would focus in this story was perhaps the most politically doctrinaire to be found in New York in 1970. A central aspect of the radicalism of The Feminists, as the group was known, was its stringent policing of its members' personal behavior. Introducing the group, Culhane referred to one of the most controversial of its rules, the stipulation that only a third of its members at any given time were allowed to be married to or living with a man. Founded by former New York NOW president Ti-Grace Atkinson in 1969, the group identified as a vanguard committed to the development and dissemination of political theory that could be used to forward the feminist revolution; unlike most radical groups, they did not practice CR (Echols, 1989). Because their central tenet was that "the pathology of oppression can only be fully comprehended in its primary development: the male-female division," The Feminists provided a great deal of fodder for the story's focus on radical feminists' disdain for women's traditional roles (The Feminists, 1969/1973, p. 370).[8]

The wide shot that first captured The Feminists also featured the only appearance of a woman reporter in the CBS series, Ponchitta Pierce.[9] Given radicals' refusal to deal with male reporters, Pierce's presence was necessary, but she was seen only briefly and her sole function in the story was to ask questions; Culhane retained all narrative control. Conservatively coiffed and suited, seated primly in a chair with legs crossed, Pierce provided a strong contrast with her subjects, who were young, dressed casually, sans cosmetics and hairstyling, and sitting on the floor (also a contrast with the groomed and professional looks of the Northridge group pictured in the first CBS story).

The rejection of men and heterosexuality that Culhane had foreshadowed with his reference to The Feminists's membership rules emerged as the theme of Pierce's interviews. The screen narrowed to a close-up of Feminist Barbara Mehrhof, who claimed, "Men are the oppressors, they're powerful, women are the oppressed, they're powerless. . . . Women are property exchanged among men, who marry certain women." After Culhane's voiceover noted that The Feminists's position that "the institution of marriage must go" was shared by other radical feminists, the story moved to Pierce's interview with Anselma dell'Olio. In an exchange that would raise the specter of lesbianism, Pierce asked her what would replace marriage, to which dell'Olio, framed in an extreme close-up angle, responded that sisterhood would replace marriage and that "women would discover each other as human beings." When Pierce then asked, "Will they turn to women instead of men?," dell'Olio paused before replying: "As friends, as sisters, as rebels, as fighters in a revolution in which they all share." Pierce then parried with "But what if they want love?" Still refusing to take the bait, dell'Olio replied, "we don't know what love means—it's just a phony word" that will be redefined "after the revolution."

On the one hand, dell'Olio might have sidestepped Pierce's implication because she did not want to feed mass media linkage of feminism to lesbianism. On the other hand, radical feminists' positions on lesbianism were complicated and difficult to communicate within the constraints of a news story. For example, in 1969, shortly after founding The Feminists, Ti-Grace Atkinson (1974) had declared that love was "the psychological pivot in the persecution of women," a fantasy state that reconciled women to their oppression by men (p. 43), a position with which dell'Olio's statements seem to cohere (e.g., love is "just a phony word").[10] Led by Atkinson, The Feminists advocated political lesbianism, in which women eschewed relationships with men and allied themselves completely with other women for political purposes. Such identification need not include sexual expression; in fact, Atkinson (1974) distinguished political lesbianism from sexual lesbianism, viewing the latter as not necessarily political, or, at worst, as an extension of a heterosexual system that prioritized genital sex. In her view, belief in love and sex as primary human needs was a creation of patriarchy and its investment in the institution of heterosexual intercourse. Thus sex itself, of any variety, was basically antifeminist.

As in all featuring of radicals in the series, explication of ideology was absent, and the uses of Mehrhof and dell'Olio were little more than decontextualized sound bites—akin to what Douglas (1994) has termed "disembodied quotations"—that functioned primarily to establish their deviance (p. 175). This effect was amplified when Pierce briefly interviewed Ti-Grace Atkinson, who asserted, "if you had equality between men and women, you couldn't have marriage." Using provocative analogies that were typical for her, Atkinson went on to compare marriage with slavery and cancer; her reply to Pierce's query about what could take the place of marriage was "What would you substitute for cancer?"

Atkinson had an unusual amount of visibility for a radical feminist because of her time as president of New York NOW, when she regularly made the papers. She had an active career as a public speaker and media personality, and her notoriety continued when she became a major voice for The Feminists, a phenomenon attributable to her extremist views (even within the context of radical feminism) about marriage and sex.[11] Atkinson's appetite for media exposure presented such a problem within the antihierarchy philosophy of The Feminists that she would leave the group shortly after her appearance in the CBS series (Hole and Levine, 1971).

Despite their somewhat anomalous position among radical groups, as well as their relatively small size (in comparison to, for example, the much larger NYRF), The Feminists were mentioned more than any other radical group in network news treatments of women's liberation in 1970. In addition to their presence in the CBS series, they would appear in Marlene Sanders's ABC documentary in May. Their relative prominence in the news in 1970 was partially a product of their self-styled function as an elite vanguard; as a result, they were simply more accessible to news workers in search of radical voices to speak for the movement. Other radicals who refused to appear in network stories because of their wariness of the problems of mainstream media representation ceded ground to those who had no such qualms, a category that included not only liberal leaders like Betty Friedan but radicals like Atkinson.

Culhane's series closed with the same visual that had opened it: the four women singing their "Battle Hymn of the Republic" parody. Following the trajectory of the reports themselves, which had traveled from affirmation of liberal positions to marginalization of radical ones, the lyrics in this final segment were more antagonistic than the verse about voting heard in the first story:

> There'll be men upon their knees to us and begging for their lives,
> And some we'll spare and some we'll not, for justice is our right,
> There'll be judo and karate and a rifle for each wife,
> For it's liberation time.

The CBS series' oscillation between depicting radical feminists as, alternately, inconsequential or dangerous was, at one level, about the gender anxiety provoked by radicals' position that the revolution would bring the end of male privilege, both sexually and socially. Ridiculing the radicals was one way to keep that anxiety at bay; another was using their own claims to make them look preposterous. Radical feminists' intellectual insights, transformative for the movement itself, were lost in translation to television news norms within which it was easier to simply exploit their confrontational, disorderly behavior and their seemingly bizarre ideas, all of which were presented without context and in little detail.

The complexity and creativity of radical feminist ideology collided with network news' demands for telling stories "visually, quickly, and in uncomplicated ways" (Bradley, 2003, p. 78). Economic discrimination, and its violation of American liberal principles of equality and fairness, was easy for reporters—and audiences—to understand and to recognize as a problem. Beauty contests, on the other hand, seemed harmless, while attacking marriage, a basic unit of social organization, was bona fide evidence of extremism. Radical critiques of such institutions were extensive and intricate, grounded in the insights of CR as well as those of traditional social theory, like Marxism (recall Mehrhof's designation of women as property), and they were virtually impossible to reduce to a sound bite that would sound anything but outrageous. In addition, unlike NOW, the radicals' audience was not opinion leaders, judges, and politicians, but women themselves, whom they tried to reach through CR groups and through public versions of CR in feminist publications, protest, and performance. Yet such activities were hard to represent (in the case of CR groups) or easy to sensationalize, as the CBS stories so clearly illustrate.

NBC: ASSIMILATING THE RADICALS

A key outcome of CBS's narrative about women's liberation was the "carving up of the women's movement into legitimate feminism and illegitimate feminism," but NBC's series was distinguished by the opposite tactic (Douglas, 1994, p. 186). It assimilated rather than marginalized the radicals, a strategy initiated in the first of reporter Aline Saarinen's two stories on the movement. Rather than separating radical feminists' concerns with cultural or symbolic forms of sexism and liberal feminists' concerns with equality and employment discrimination, Saarinen would subsume the former within the latter, linking the gender stereotypes afflicting women to the discrimination they faced in the workplace.

On March 30, Saarinen opened the first story in the series with a montage of images of women (all white) protesting, including footage of suffrage parades from the early twentieth century, and images of women (all white) from advertising, including an example of the infamous series of Virginia Slims ads that equated liberation and smoking. Her narration began with a feminism–civil rights analogy: "It's to women what the civil rights movement was to blacks—an increasingly vocal and active protest against discrimination. A demand for equal jobs, equal pay, equal opportunity, places at the top, freedom of choice, and an end to degrading stereotypes and traditional roles." Saarinen continued by verbally listing the stereotypes that afflicted women ("creatures of inferior intellect, child-like, hysterical, defenseless," and "sexual playthings") and constrained their social roles (wives, mothers, and housekeepers "by divine decree"), making the point that feminists believed that the attitudes that resulted from such stereotypes "account for the serious economic discrimination against women."

After reciting familiar statistics about bad pay and limited opportunity, she concluded that "prejudice and gentlemen's agreements have made this so," early articulation of a theme—male responsibility for sexism—that would receive extensive attention later in the series. As Culhane had, Saarinen also made the point that "forty-two percent of the women who work *have* to work. They're breadwinners, it's not for pin money," thus making the consequences of employment discrimination intelligible through a focus on the problems of working women struggling to support their children, a portent of the NBC series' promotion of such women as the movement's ideal beneficiaries.

The feminism–civil rights analogy that Saarinen used at the beginning of her first story was another of the series' intelligibility devices; she also closed the report with the observation that "the success of the civil rights movement has given all groups who feel put upon an impetus and a model for action." In fact, the civil rights comparison was part of the genesis of NBC's decision to prepare a series of stories on the women's movement. Nightly news executive producer Wallace Westfeldt had spent time as a reporter covering civil rights, and Jo Freeman (1975) quotes him as saying that it was "easy to see the similarities" between that movement and women's liberation (p. 149). The connection between feminism and civil rights was verbally articulated several times in the series, serving each time as a legitimation device that underscored the ways that women's grievances, regarding both image politics and discrimination, were similar to those raised by blacks. It also functioned to present women and blacks as two separate groups, as it did in Saarinen's story, despite the fact that her statistic about the 42 percent of women who were breadwinners probably included large numbers of women of color, who were more likely to work for wages than white women were (Coontz, 1992). The impression that women's liberation was a largely white affair was additionally bolstered by the report's use of exclusively white images and by the stereotypes Saarinen listed, all of which were primarily applicable to white, middle-class women (e.g., hysterical, defenseless, home-bound).

Saarinen's were the only stories in the NBC series that focused on describing the movement itself. After her initial story introducing the series, none of the three stories that followed would mention the movement, only the issues it had raised. Saarinen's second story on April 3, the fifth in the series, returned to a focus on the movement and was billed by anchor Chet Huntley as focusing on the "routes by which women seek equality, the organizations to which they belong, and the things they say and do." Like her previous one, this report was characterized by an emphasis on the movement's coherence around, in Saarinen's words, "fighting the roots and the results of discrimination." She began by observing that women's liberation included "women who had belonged to the freedom movement . . . until they found they were expected to make coffee, not policy." Narrating over footage of police in riot gear escorting protestors into police wagons (taken from coverage of the 1969 "days of rage" protest by the Weatherman faction of Students for a Democratic Society during the trial of the Chicago Seven), she observed that the women who formed feminist groups "have adapted the strategy . . . of confrontation" to women's liberation.

Saarinen's mention of women's participation in other radical movements was a rare instance in which a network story on women's liberation recognized feminists' previous political experience. Equally as noteworthy was Saarinen's mention of CR. Calling them "consciousness-arousing sessions, sort of female encounter groups" in which "miseries are shared, hostilities are aired, and female pride is prodded," she made the practice sound more like a support group than a political activity, but her report was the only time in 1970 that CR was even mentioned on national television news.[12]

Like Culhane, Saarinen used visual material to contrast radical and liberal feminism: the former was illustrated with images of protest, while the latter was exemplified by footage of women in a meeting. Yet her accompanying narration was, by and large, judicious. As the screen showed images of a W.I.T.C.H. hex on Wall Street on Halloween 1969, featuring feminists in black cloaks and tall witch hats moving in a phalanx down the street, Saarinen described the group as "uniquely satirical and witty." Visuals from Atlantic City in 1968 followed, and Saarinen described their protest of the pageant as "a symbol of society's exploitation of women as sex objects," thus accurately capturing the distinction between targeting the pageant and targeting Miss America herself. She continued by naming several of the "cells, brigades and associations" (e.g., Redstockings, Bread and Roses [a Boston socialist feminist group], and OWL [Older Women's Liberation]) of which the women's liberation movement was composed, noting that "there are groups that hate men and marriage and think all babies ought to be born out of test tubes," but the "largest, best organized, and best known" was NOW.

As the report cut to images of professionally attired women gathered in a meeting, Saarinen described their tone as "moderate" and their composition as "mostly business and professional women, mostly middle-class, many married or once-married." This description of NOW concluded, "the meetings look interchangeable with the PTA. They aren't. They discuss how to liberate a men's bar and grill and how to get Title VII of the Civil Rights Act fully enforced." This moment in the story was the closest Saarinen came to the sharp demarcation between liberals and radicals that had characterized Culhane's reports. She juxtaposed the most extreme aspects of radical feminism with NOW's moderation, and she diminished the importance of the former by noting the greater size of the latter. Yet rather than overtly dismissing the radicals, she used them as evidence of the movement's breadth; moreover, she implied that NOW's goals were less moderate than its appearance.

Ultimately, Saarinen's report created the impression that the movement was composed of a variety of women who used varying means toward the same ends, a point made both implicitly and explicitly. After she had contrasted them, the next segment in the report wove radicals and liberals back together, featuring a series of sound bites presented in succession without narration. Viewers first saw Congresswoman Shirley Chisholm, who claimed to an audience that "racism and anti-feminism are two of the prime traditions of this country," an implicit refutation of Culhane's rejection of Chisholm's intersectionality. Chisholm was followed by a young, white woman speaking of the need for solidarity among women, who should be "loyal to yourselves and to your sisters, and not sell them out for men's favor." Chisholm reappeared, saying, "when we ask the question 'do women dare,'" we are "asking if they are capable of bearing with the sanctions that will be placed upon them." In a seeming follow-up to Chisholm's point, the first young woman appeared again, speaking of the need for women's courage "to take the abuse which questions your sanity and your sexuality," an allusion to the habitual labeling of women's liberationists as lesbians. With ironic timing, given her history with lesbians in the movement, a shot of Betty Friedan followed, who maintained that the movement should steer clear of sexual politics: "it is not, as I have said, . . . a war to be fought in the bedroom, but in the city, in the political arena."

This series of statements by different women, well-known and unknown, younger and older, liberal and radical (the young woman, long-haired and casually dressed, was likely to be categorized as the latter), yet all seemingly in agreement, was the penultimate example of Saarinen's strategy of presenting women's liberation as a phenomenon involving disparate participants with much in common, including recognition of the strong resistance to their goals. She closed the segment with verbal affirmation of this perspective, noting simply "there's a group for every taste . . . from militant man-haters and lesbians to the happily mated," but their "strength lies in what they have in common: their fight against the roots and the results of discrimination, the demand for different but equal identities with men. Two things are true: discrimination against women is a fact, and each day more and more women are agitating about it." In contrast to David Culhane's closing line in his first CBS story, in which he claimed that that feminism's central challenge was convincing "the majority of American women that there is something basically wrong with their position in life," both of Saarinen's reports operated from the premise that the problems feminists were decrying were real.

Despite her refusal to exploit radical feminism's excesses, Saarinen's second story ultimately presented a liberal policy goal, the ERA, as the solution to feminist grievances. Her assimilation strategy hit its zenith when she asserted that the movement as a whole supported the ERA, marking the first time that the amendment would be mentioned on the national news in connection to the second wave. Saarinen's featuring of references to the ERA at the beginning and ending of her second story on the movement is a compelling example of mainstream news' tendency to promote social stability and the impression that "whatever is wrong in the world, it can be put right by authoritative (almost always official) agencies" (Gitlin, 1980, p. 266). Within such a worldview, the ERA would seem a commonsensical legislative solution to the social problems explicated by NBC's series of stories.

The relative importance that Saarinen's story gave to the ERA was underscored by two factors. First, it was the only policy goal of the movement—really, the only goal period—to which she gave more than cursory attention in her two stories. Second, her discussion of the amendment was the only time in the entire NBC series—not just her own two reports—that a feminist was interviewed. The appearance of eighty-five-year-old Alice Paul, a central figure in the battle for woman suffrage waged by first-wave feminists and the author of the original version of the ERA that was first introduced to Congress in 1923, was clearly designed to give credibility to the issue.

The elderly Paul was tough to categorize as extremist (particularly for an audience that likely knew nothing of her history as a self-styled militant suffragist) and she served as a living link between the uncontroversial (in retrospect) goals of the first wave and what Saarinen presented as a central and equally uncontroversial goal of the second wave. Paul's was the first image to appear in Saarinen's second story, and she was identified as the founder of the National Woman's Party as she spoke of her "hope that this fiftieth anniversary of the winning of the vote" would mark the passage of the ERA, legislation that, in Saarinen's words, "would make women people, in a legal sense, for the first time." Seen seated in a medium shot, Paul claimed that there were "10 million women who've united through their organizations" to support the amendment.

The persuasive power of this segment is difficult to overstate. Much as the Nineteenth Amendment had given women political rights, the ERA would give them legal ones, and the amendment's support by an elderly first-waver and millions of other women made clear that this was no fringe issue. What followed, however, was an astonishing rhetorical sleight of hand. As Saarinen segued from the Alice Paul segment to discussion of the larger movement, she claimed that 1 percent of those 10 million women supporting the ERA were members of women's liberation, and that they "range from reformers to revolutionaries," thus implying that support for the amendment was a goal shared by all movement members.

In fact, although NOW was firmly behind the ERA, many radical groups saw the amendment as a reformist copout that merely appended certain women to the ruling structure and would do little to undermine patriarchy. When members of a Washington, D.C., radical group were invited to testify at the Senate hearings on the ERA in May 1970, they dismissed the amendment as a "paper offering" designed to co-opt the movement. Later that year, The Feminists would publicly warn against "squandering invaluable time and energy on it" (Echols, 2002, p. 88). During NOW's planning of the Women's Strike for Equality, they were able to keep radical groups in the strike coalition by agreeing to omit the ERA as one of the action's three central demands. Consistent with her evident commitment to underplaying differences among feminist groups, Saarinen simply neglected to acknowledge such discord.

At the close of the story, Saarinen returned to the connections she had forged at its outset. Standing in the entrance hall of the National Woman's Party headquarters in Washington, surrounded by statues of prominent women activists of the past, she made the claim that discrimination against women was a reality and that women were asking, "as their active sisters did more than 50 years ago: 'Mr. President, how long must women wait for liberty?'" This question was delivered to the camera by Alice Paul herself, as her face filled the screen.[13] As the story closed, the screen's final image was of a statue of suffragist Susan B. Anthony. The verbal and visual connections Saarinen made in this story (and in her first one, which also included images of suffragists) to the first wave of feminism offered the implication that contemporary feminists were engaged in a campaign with a long history, that the achievement of woman suffrage had not produced what Alice Paul called "the emancipation of women," and that the agitation of women's liberation was, therefore, warranted. David Culhane's mention of the first wave in his initial CBS story had worked in precisely the opposite direction: when he noted that women had had the vote for fifty years, he implied that most problems that remained were feminist exaggerations.

Representing the Issues

The patterns established in the CBS and NBC series' representation of women's liberationists continued in those stories that focused specifically on the movement's issues. Just as both networks favored feminism's liberal goals in their discussions of the movement while diverging in their treatment of radicals, their presentation of the movement's issues would share a strategy of presenting working women—particularly divorced working women with children—as deserving feminist subjects while employing very different approaches in other ways. Similar to his first CBS story, Culhane's second report relied on an implicit comparison-contrast strategy in which a frivolous issue raised by radicals—sexual objectification—served as the negative contrast to a worthy issue raised by liberals—low pay and lack of affordable child care. Visual strategies were crucial to this effect: the CBS series' employment of visual techniques of spectacle was at its height in the second story, throwing into sharp relief NBC's matter-of-fact use of visuals to illustrate sexism in two stories on workplace discrimination. Importantly, those two stories expanded the definition of the worthy feminist subject by incorporating working-class women and women of color as potential beneficiaries of women's liberation.

CBS: RADICAL FEMINIST SPECTACLE AND LIBERAL FEMINIST SUBJECTS

David Culhane's second story, broadcast on March 11, was previewed by Walter Cronkite as exploring feminists' "questioning . . . of traditional roles." Over footage of Miss America contestants walking down the runway in Atlantic City, Culhane narrated that many Americans considered Miss America "the standard for an ideal woman." Feminists, on the other hand, considered her a "reduction of woman to a kind of domesticated sex object," a statement accompanied by footage of feminist protestors outside the pageant. Juxtaposing images of feminist protest with images of beauty contestants made the contrast clear: calm, smiling, *silent*, conventionally attractive women walked down a runway to applause while angry, unglamorous feminist protestors shouted, marched, and made a spectacle of themselves in front of a jeering crowd of onlookers. Feminists claimed that Miss America was a dangerous symbol of misguided ideals of femininity, but these visuals suggested that the feminists were the dangerous ones. And the targets of their wrath? The beautiful and traditionally feminine Miss America contestants themselves. Culhane's focus on feminist opposition to the Miss America Pageant in two of his three reports illustrates the powerful role the 1968 protest played in developing public narratives of the movement, as well as how quickly the "ugly feminists hate pretty women" canard transferred from print to television treatment of the movement.

Even while noting the feminists' objections to the positioning of women as sex objects, much of the camera work in the story's first segment reified that positioning, a tactic that became increasingly evident as the report moved on to a Playboy Club. An invisible narrator earlier in the story, Culhane planted himself squarely in the camera's frame in front of a room of professionally dressed white men being served drinks by Playboy Bunnies and offered the following commentary:

> Another place, and, the new feminists say, another symbol of the oppression of women. One of the Playboy Clubs, where men come to eat, to drink, and, incidentally, to observe some remarkable displays of feminine pulchritude. The woman's liberation movement despises the "Playboy" concept of women, who they say may have been liberated from a good deal of clothing but little else. So Miss America and the Playboy Bunny—nothing but sex objects—have got to go.

By terming the voyeurism practiced by Playboy Club patrons incidental, Culhane suggested that it "was, in fact, harmless" (Douglas, 1994, p. 173), an impression furthered by the ensuing camera work that made male viewers into voyeurs as well. As Culhane spoke, the camera traveled up and down a Bunny's body, then followed another Bunny's derriere as she traveled across the room, and, finally, shifted to a higher angle that allowed the viewer to see down the front of another Bunny's décolletage from above. The footage ended with the image of a smiling Bunny walking toward the camera.

In this segment, the camera's eye functioned, in the most conventional sense, as an extension of the masculine gaze; at the same moment that Culhane verbally recounted feminist objections, the camera work offered a different message: "Look at these gorgeous, happy women. No problem here." The visual images of the Bunnies did not add any information value to the story; rather, they functioned as spectacle in terms that film theorist Laura Mulvey (1975/1999) has described when she writes that the camera's focus on women's "visual presence tends to work against the development of a story line, to freeze the flow of action in moments of erotic contemplation" (p. 63). All Culhane told the viewer was that feminists did not like Playboy Bunnies; there was so little substance to the verbal report that it was easily overwhelmed by the visual content, and the rhetorical effect of the segment was the dismissal of feminists' concerns accompanied by some gratuitous titillation for the implied male viewer.[14]

This segment on sexual exploitation introduced a visual variation on an oft-noted strategy in second-wave news coverage: the near invisibility of men's opposition to feminism accompanied by the foregrounding of women's opposition (or sometimes their simple disinterest). Typically invoked verbally—by asking ordinary women what they thought of the movement—it was skillfully accomplished here through visual discourse in which images of smiling and happy Miss America contestants and Playboy Bunnies constituted an implicit refutation of feminists' claims that women suffered from beauty standards or sexual objectification. The only men featured during the segment on Playboy Bunnies simply aspired to "eat, drink, and observe," which hardly seemed oppressive. In fact, no men articulated opposition to the movement throughout the entire CBS series, making it even more likely that radical feminists, in particular, would be seen as troublemakers who were only trying to sow discontent where none existed and who were fighting an enemy that only they recognized.

Culhane's exploitation of images of attractive women persisted in the report's next segment, an interview with Alice Denham, described as "a novelist, former model, and once the *Playboy* Girl of the Month," now an "active feminist" who "doesn't think much of the image of women presented by *Playboy* and other men's magazines." A rapid series of images from Denham's modeling career flashed across the screen, showing her face and body in various suggestive poses (reclining, mouth open, arms over her head, smiling provocatively). Denham was a member of New York NOW who had participated in a number of public actions led by the group (and she would join the *Ladies' Home Journal* protest on March 18). Her activist credentials were far outweighed, in this segment, by her glamorous past as a model, as Culhane made clear: "For some of the feminists who feel this way, it isn't just sour grapes; they can and have won beauty contests." This observation implied that, for many or most feminists, the critique of beauty politics *was* about sour grapes and that few of them could qualify for a beauty contest, a bit of logic that harkened back to reactions to the 1968 Miss America protest.

The framing of Denham insinuated that it was "newsworthy—and shocking" that "a feminist would be anything but hideously ugly," and her commentary was shot in close-up, her face completely filling the screen, as if to further the point (Douglas, 1994, p. 174). The camera angle was not flattering, and Denham (2006) herself later remarked that it made her look like "a witch" (p. 300). It also implied what Torres (2003), remarking on a similar angle in network interviews with segregationist whites during the 1960s, terms "a lack of perspective, an over-proximity to the camera and to their own self-serving desires" (p. 41). Importantly, the angle used for Denham was quite different from the first CBS story's framing of Betty Friedan in a medium shot that suggested "a seemly perspective on the matters at hand" (Torres, 2003, p. 119).

Denham's (2006) own recollection of the interview intimates that Culhane did see her conversion to feminism as a form of sour grapes, and that he asked her, "Didn't you *really* become a feminist because you were too old for nude modeling?" (she had been in *Playboy* in 1956; in 1970, she was thirty-seven) (p. 300, emphasis in original). This question, and Denham's (2006) self-reported reply ("I became a feminist to fight for women's rights" [p. 300]) did not make the final story, but they perhaps explain the camera angle. Her analysis of *Playboy* magazine that the story ultimately included was brief:

> Well, it's sort of woman as mechanical doll. In other words, the magazine seems to assume that women drop dead of old age at twenty-five. A sex object orientation toward women in which they are only sort of bodies, nubile forms to give pleasure to the male. I think it's really sort of an urban male fantasy—it doesn't have a great deal to do with reality.

Ironically, Denham's analysis of objectification was a succinct articulation of the logic that had undergirded much of the camera work in the story thus far.

Somewhat abruptly, the story's focus then turned to the issue of child care, offering a poignant portrayal of Jean Temple, a college graduate and divorced mother of four who worked as a secretary, could not afford child care, and was forced to leave her children alone each day. As a result, according to Culhane, "two years ago she joined the feminist movement to agitate for child care centers so that she and other women like her could survive." After Culhane narrated statistics about the lack of child care, the segment closed with Temple's description of the worry and fear she faced each day when she had to leave her children at home alone, accompanied by footage of her children making their own breakfast, of Temple checking on them while at work, and finally arriving home relieved to find them unharmed. This segment, like the segment on the Northridge group in the first CBS story, underscored the legitimacy of feminism for women who presumably had been deserted by men and were left to find a way to provide for their children, an interpretation given explicit credence when the report returned to Alice Denham. Again in close-up, she spoke to the camera about the breakdown of marriage, claiming that it was becoming common for men to leave their wives for younger women, or, as she put it, "to turn in a forty for a twenty."

By this point, the unexplained transition from Denham's critique of sexual objectification to the segment on Temple and child care made more sense, and the combined segments offered the following logic: Inspired by the allure of the "urban male fantasy" of *Playboy*, men were abandoning their wives and children, and their wives were turning to feminism for a remedy. This logic had a basis in reality. As Barbara Ehrenreich (1987) has argued, *Playboy*'s "real message was not eroticism but escape—literal escape, from the bondage of breadwinning. ... In every issue, every month, there was a Playmate to prove that a playboy didn't have to be a husband to be a man" (p. 51). She maintains that the rise in divorce rates in the 1960s and 1970s, while often attributed to feminism, was equally traceable to men's growing frustration with and desertion of their traditional roles as breadwinners. To some degree, then, Culhane's story seemed to validate critiques of sexual objectification, but only because they could lead to the suffering of "good women" like Jean Temple.

Certainly, feminists themselves had offered the rationale that women deserved equal opportunity and pay because they could not always count on men to support them. Yet such an argument, based in need rather than desire to work, or in pragmatism rather than justice, had limitations. It positioned feminism as a back-up plan for woman who could not find a husband or could not keep him, but it left the logic of patriarchy intact: If men would only play their assigned part, feminism would not be necessary. This perspective not only failed to account for women who, whatever their circumstances, might choose to work for their own reasons, but it also discounted the ways that race and class discrimination made the "family wage" unattainable for some men. For example, none of the working women depicted in any of the network feature stories were married, when, in fact, most working women were. Lurking behind Culhane's implicit scolding of American men for their perfidy toward their families was a type of nostalgia for "the way things used to be," that Stephanie Coontz (1992) has ably deconstructed as "the way we never were."[15]

Culhane's depiction of white, middle-class, working women as credible subjects with the most legitimate claim to feminist grievances continued in the final segment of the second CBS story, noteworthy as the only moment in the series in which race was explicitly mentioned and/or visually represented. Opening the segment with footage of a racially mixed crowd of conservatively dressed, professional-looking women at a NOW meeting in Chicago, Culhane's voiceover described NOW as the nation's largest feminist organization and then introduced Shirley Chisholm, the first black woman to be elected to the U.S. Congress. Chisholm spoke to the meeting about the need for women to "acquire our unequivocal place in the American society" just as blacks were doing. Culhane went on to describe Chisholm as someone who claimed to have "suffered more discrimination from being a woman than from being black." He concluded, incredibly, that "she speaks not as a black but as a woman," thus functionally folding her into the category of white liberal feminist subjects constructed by his reports. Chisholm (1970, 1973) had indeed observed that, in her political life, she had faced more sex than race discrimination, a claim related to the campaign for her Brooklyn seat in 1968, in which she ran against well-known black civil rights activist and former Congress of Racial Equality chairman James Farmer Jr. Her appearance in this story was the only time Culhane raised the topic of race, either visually or verbally, only to dismiss it, displaying the media tendency to deny intersections between the interests of white women and women of color.

By this point, the CBS reports had firmly established the rationality of certain feminist goals related to equal opportunity and pay, all of which fit easily within American liberalism. At the same time, radical feminism's focus on sex role stereotypes was presented as insignificant in contrast, particularly given that women were visually presented as freely participating in those stereotypical roles. Indeed, visual elements were essential to the contrast Culhane drew. Liberal feminism's spokespersons—Betty Friedan and Shirley Chisholm, Jean Temple and the Northridge group—were all presented as calm and thoughtful while visually enacting a kind of respectable, middle-class womanhood. Conversely, as was true in the other stories in the series, the depiction of radical feminist grievances in the second was characterized by the dominance of visual spectacle (of both feminists and Playboy Bunnies) over political analysis.

NBC: VISUALIZING SEXISM AS A SOCIAL PROBLEM

If spectacle was a dominant visual strategy in the CBS reports, its counterpart in the NBC series was the use of visual argument, or, more specifically, visual refutation of sexist claims. The use of images in service of argument ran throughout NBC's three social problem stories—two on workplace discrimination and one on gender socialization and sexism—that were bracketed by Aline Saarinen's reports on the movement itself. Catherine Mackin's April 1 report on workplace discrimination and the Equal Employment Opportunity Commission (EEOC) embedded the strategy within a human-interest frame, presenting sympathy-inducing portraits of two divorced white women, sole providers for multiple children, who were involved in EEOC complaints. Like David Culhane's treatment of Jean Temple, Mackin presented these women as "individualized worthy victims," who were hindered by discrimination from providing for and protecting their children, a tactic with clear rhetorical appeal (Bodroghkozy, 2012, p. 57).

The treatment of the plight of working women in the two network series was distinctive in other ways, however. Unlike Culhane's emphasis on the discrimination faced by white college-educated and professional women, Mackin's report focused on working-class women, reflecting the fact that several early sex discrimination cases championed by the EEOC dealt with women's access to blue-collar, unionized jobs (Mayeri, 2011). These cases were linked to Title VII of the Civil Rights Act of 1964, which prohibited race- and sex-based employment discrimination. The EEOC was created in 1965 to enforce Title VII, but it initially focused almost entirely on discrimination against black men, virtually ignoring the sex discrimination complaints that constituted a quarter of all those received by the agency in its first two years (Davis, 1991).[16] Some EEOC grievances were filed by women of color, which made them sex- *and* race-discrimination complaints, but EEOC commissioners found intersectionality difficult to grasp. The agency's failure to pursue sex discrimination was a motivating factor in the creation of NOW, and the organization put pressuring the EEOC at the top of its agenda, with swift results (Rhode, 1989).

Mackin's story on Title VII enforcement omitted NOW's role in forcing the EEOC to take action on women's complaints, relying instead on a human interest format that told the stories of two women who were plaintiffs in sex-discrimination lawsuits. This strategy echoed network reports on civil rights that "seemed particularly comfortable with black seekers of desegregation" who were not "closely aligned or affiliated with a black civil rights organization or activist group," and it reflected journalists' attraction to telling the stories of individual struggles (Bodroghkozy, 2012, p. 56). The human-interest focus not only made the two women who had filed suits heroic figures for identification by viewers, it also indicated Mackin's targeting of an audience of women, who are generally assumed to be attracted to the softer elements of such narratives (Rakow and Kranich, 1991). The compelling visuals that supported the women's claims were key elements in this strategy, as was the plainspoken testimony they offered to the camera.

Mackin opened her discussion of the two EEOC cases by introducing the protagonists: Leah Rosenfeld, who had successfully sued for a promotion to railroad station agent in California, and Ida Phillips, a waitress in Florida who was suing Martin Marietta, a company that refused to hire her because she had a pre-school-aged child. Phillips's case awaited Supreme Court consideration over whether it was a violation of the Civil Rights Act of 1964 that, Mackin helpfully explained, prohibited employment discrimination on the basis of "race, creed, national origin, or sex."[17] Viewers next saw a visual of the EEOC office in Washington, where a black woman, presumably a receptionist or secretary, answered the phone, an image accompanied by Mackin's claim that "a woman who thinks she has been discriminated against can go to the EEOC and expect results."

In her telling of the story of Rosenfeld's case, Mackin's clear message was that Rosenfeld's treatment by the railroad was unfair, both because she was fully capable of the job she sought and because she was the sole breadwinner for a dozen children. Rosenfeld had gone to the EEOC in 1966 because the Southern Pacific Railroad refused to promote her from clerk to station agent, citing a California state law prohibiting women from working overtime or lifting more than twenty-five pounds.[18] As Mackin gave these details, the screen showed Rosenfeld lifting a large box, registering at *thirty-five* pounds, onto a scale in the railroad station office. At another point, Rosenfeld was seen climbing to the top of a tall pole next to the railroad tracks (in a dress!) to leave a signal for an oncoming train. The genius of these images was that viewers saw Rosenfeld ably performing the job that the California law presumed women were unable to do, even as Mackin noted that the railroad and the state were appealing the federal court's ruling in Rosenfeld's favor (it would be upheld in 1971). As the segment concluded, Rosenfeld spoke to the camera from behind her desk at the railroad station, saying that "most women work because they have families to support and they need the money," and that she "hasn't noticed that the grocery stores give us any discount on food and yet we're expected to work at a lower wage. I don't think it's fair."

The visuals and narration in Ida Phillips's case were similar: an affecting story was accompanied by images refuting sexist claims. Phillips, thirty-six and divorced with seven children, went to the EEOC in 1966 after her application to a Martin Marietta training program was rejected because the company believed that her two-year-old "would keep Mrs. Phillips home from work too often." During footage of Phillips working as a waitress in a diner (including a shot in which she scraped a tip of a few coins off a table), Mackin told viewers that the Martin Marietta job paid six thousand dollars per year but Phillips currently worked fifty-six hours a week for two thousand dollars per year and lived on "four hours sleep a day so that she can be at home when the children are awake. But when they are asleep, she works, so they can eat." This narrative about the difficult conditions of Phillips's life not only established her as a sympathetic figure, it simultaneously highlighted her impressive work ethic and rebutted Martin Marietta's stereotyping of mothers of young children. As she had in the Rosenfeld segment, Mackin closed the report with testimony from Phillips herself: "If I win my case it would mean that I would have a job, that I would have regular hours in order to plan things with my family, it would mean that I could educate my children, . . . and it would also mean that all other mothers in my case would have the same thing happen to them, because when you're a mother you look out for the children, for their welfare and their wants."

Mackin's perspective that the discrimination against Rosenfeld and Phillips was prima facie unfair was underscored by the absence from her story of any discourse from representatives of the states, unions, or corporations that opposed their claims, even though the Phillips case had not yet been decided and Rosenfeld's was under appeal. Equally as noteworthy was the story's implicit assumption of a female audience and its potential function as a primer for that audience on what to do when faced with sex discrimination. Mackin not only recited the text of Title VII early in her report, she explicitly directed women with discrimination complaints to the EEOC. Ida Phillips's final remarks made the point that a positive outcome in her lawsuit meant that "all other mothers in my case" would have the same protection, enabling the report to bridge the divide between its individualistic human-interest elements and the collective empowerment of women that feminists sought to achieve through such lawsuits.

NOW's involvement in these cases (e.g., NOW's Legal Defense Fund filed an amicus brief in the Phillips case) and its influential role in pressuring the EEOC ran counter to the organization's reputation as one solely concerned with white, middle-class women's issues. Ida Phillips, for instance, received representation from the NAACP's Legal Defense Fund, and the organization's brief on her case claimed that the bona fide occupational qualification (BFOQ) at issue would have a disproportionately negative effect on black women, who were more likely to be primary wage earners for families. The briefs filed on Phillips's behalf by the EEOC, NOW, and the American Civil Liberties Union relied heavily on a race-sex analogy, arguing that an allowance for BFOQ's based on gender and/or maternal status would open the door to similar restrictions based on race (Mayeri, 2011).[19] Although Mackin did not feature such connections, the story's emphasis on bread-and-butter issues faced by female heads of households was likely to have resonance for many women of color and working-class women who otherwise saw few connections between their lives and the portrait of women's liberation offered by national news media.

NBC's expansion of the category of feminist subjects continued in its April 2 story, introduced by Chet Huntley as one that examined the "opportunities and prejudices facing women who work for pay." As in David Culhane's first story, NBC reporter Norma Quarles detailed the familiar statistics on women's low pay and limited opportunities while the screen showed generic footage of women doing menial jobs. Yet there was an important difference: the images of working women contained several that featured women of color, a factor perhaps given more notice by viewers because Quarles herself was a rare woman of color on network news.[20] At various points in the story, viewers saw women of color working as bank tellers, computer operators, and secretaries, as well as in blue-collar jobs. Quarles never mentioned them verbally but simply included their images within the story's narrative. Atypical and noteworthy for both print and broadcast reporting, her story positioned women of color as victims of sexism (and as potential constituents for feminism) and did not explicitly or implicitly separate their concerns from those of white women.

In her first concrete example of discrimination, Quarles, as Mackin had, used images to demonstrate women's capabilities. Noting that there had been progress on expanding opportunities "in a few industries," Quarles focused on a white woman, Genevieve Glass, who had successfully "filed a sex discrimination complaint with the federal government" (presumably the EEOC) in 1966 after Ohio Bell had denied her a higher paying position that was classified as a man's job.[21] Glass was seen at her current job as an "apparatus man," wielding pliers as she stood before an enormous bundle of wires, alongside a black woman and two white men doing the same. The image of harmonious workplace diversity made the point clearly: Women could do this job right alongside men. Quarles's example of the telephone industry also indicated that she had done her homework: AT&T and its Bell subsidiaries were a prime target for Title VII lawsuits in the late 1960s. As the largest employer of women in the country, AT&T was targeted with more discrimination complaints than any other company, and a 1971 EEOC report would call it "the largest oppressor of women workers in the United States" (Herr, 2003, p. 66). Glass's victory was a harbinger of what was to come. In 1973, AT&T's long tangle with the EEOC would result in a company-wide affirmative action program, a milestone in women's workplace rights (Williams, 2008).

Moving on to the "white-collar level," Quarles observed that "women start slower and move up slower," and that "the executive ranks are virtually closed" to them, citing the statistic that "only 1 percent of the 31 million working women in the United States earn $10,000 a year or more." Yet, as the camera focused on a middle-aged white woman behind a desk, she named an exception, Edith Grimm, a vice president at a department store in Chicago, and claimed that Grimm had "made it in spite of men." Framed in a medium shot, Grimm offered this explanation of her success to the camera: "I find if you recognize certain primary facts, like the fact that the male has a big ego and it must be protected, it becomes sort of a conscious part of your operation. You don't have to think about it every second, but neither will you forget it." Together with the testimony from Rosenfeld and Phillips in Mackin's EEOC story, Grimm's interview discourse stood as the third example in the NBC reports in which women ostensibly unaffiliated with women's liberation made the case that they had experienced discrimination, thus offering refutation of David Culhane's claim that the movement's biggest problem was convincing women themselves that there was anything wrong with their lives. If Grimm's testimony did not sufficiently make the point that progress was hard won, Quarles drove the lesson home in her stand-up that followed: "So it can be done. A woman can be a success in the business world. But it takes an exceptional woman, and she'll be fighting men's prejudices all the way."

Quarles's report closed with additional evidence of men's resistance to women's equality, as viewers heard a series of male voices offering their evaluation of women's capabilities as workers. Each statement was paired with a visual; for example, one voice asserted, "most women, I think, have a problem with concentration," accompanied by footage of a row of black and white women typing assiduously at their desks. As the screen cut to an image of a white man driving a forklift, another voice declared, "women do not have the killer instinct that men have. A man is, by very nature, the hunter." In a variation on Mackin's visual refutation technique, the accompanying images contradicted each sexist claim and invited an opposing perspective. For example, did not the boring and tedious nature of the "women's work" pictured here actually require *more* concentration? Did a forklift operator need a killer instinct? These final seconds in Quarles's report both substantiated men's sexism *and* made it look ridiculous.

The two network series ultimately concurred in their approval of the liberal goals of women's liberation—equal opportunity, equal pay, child care, and, in NBC's case, the ERA—but that similarity was tempered by their substantive and salient differences. At every turn, Culhane bolstered the case for working women's grievances by verbally and visually juxtaposing the thoughtful moderation with which they were expressed with the intemperate discourse and disruptive tactics of radical feminists. In the end, with his affecting portrayal of Jean Temple, Culhane gave his strongest approval to a reform that was less warranted by fairness than by the need to preserve women's ability to fulfill their traditional roles as mothers. Some changes might be necessary to aid those women who had lost the protections of patriarchy, he implied, but complaints about other issues were hardly to be taken seriously.

NBC's stories, on the other hand, did not legitimate workplace discrimination complaints at the expense of less palatable radical ideology. Mackin's and Quarles's reports framed sex discrimination as a social problem that was finally receiving the attention it deserved from government agencies and the courts, and Mackin hailed a female audience by announcing that the EEOC was a solution for any "woman who thinks she has been discriminated against." Although Mackin's story on the EEOC featured women's roles as providers, it made fairness under the law its central issue, and Quarles stressed the same point with her example of the successful Ohio Bell complaint. Moreover, Quarles's inclusion of women of color in the visual background as she affirmed the reality of sex discrimination implicitly made the point that those women suffered from sexism alongside white women.

The ascendance of equal rights in the workplace as a central signifier for mass-mediated liberal feminism was a product of the issue's easy fit within media logics. Workplace inequality was a concrete goal of liberal feminist organizations, it was easily documented through statistics (used in both series), it had a relationship to public policy (made especially clear in the NBC reports), and its basic unfairness was a matter of social consensus, even more so when it was connected to women's role as providers for their children. By 1970, despite the persistence of gendered wage inequality (despite its persistence still), there was little abstract support for pay discrimination on the basis of sex; as early as 1962, 88 percent of survey respondents agreed when asked if they favored women receiving equal pay with men for the same job (Mansbridge, 1986).

In contrast, radical feminists in 1970 lacked a similar overarching and concrete public policy issue around which to orient their activism, and, did not make it a priority to create one, given that their aim was revolution, rather than reform. Important feminist issues originally raised by radicals (often through CR), such as rape and domestic violence, would eventually be mainstreamed as social problems, but these topics had not yet risen to public prominence in 1970, either within radical feminist activism or through attention in national media, although they shortly would (Bronstein, 2011; Cuklanz, 1995).

Representing the Audience: Reporting on Abortion

The issue that united liberal and radical feminism in 1970 was abortion rights; it would be one of the three goals, along with federally funded child care and equal opportunity in education and employment, agreed on by the diverse coalition of feminist groups that participated in the August 1970 Strike for Equality. Although liberals and radicals offered different rationales for women's unrestricted access to abortion, they agreed on its importance to the movement. Despite the issue's singular status as a radical-liberal meeting ground, David Culhane gave it only brief attention in the CBS series; moreover, although he noted that "even the moderates" favored liberalization of abortion laws, the mention of abortion was embedded within a segment focused on radicals' disdain for motherhood. NBC devoted the entirety of the final story in its series to abortion, and Catherine Mackin gave the topic the same kind of framing as she had previously given workplace discrimination: unwanted pregnancy was a social problem from which women suffered and for which abortion was the clear solution. From beginning to end, her story reflected an "everywoman" point of view, positioning abortion restrictions as a concern for women, not just feminists. In the process, she offered the report's implied female viewers helpful advice on how to go outside the law and obtain the procedure.

Both the NBC and CBS reports connected the desire for abortion rights to women's traditional roles, but with crucial distinctions. According to Mackin, *women* were asking if motherhood was always right for them, but Culhane attributed the raising of the issue to *feminists*, specifically radical feminists. Viewers had just heard Ti-Grace Atkinson compare marriage to slavery and cancer when Culhane segued to abortion by claiming that feminists supported abortion so that women would not be "in bondage with children they don't want." After a short scene from a feminist play about abortion, yet another decontextualized bit of feminist performance,[22] Culhane introduced Shulamith Firestone as "a member of another New York group called the Radical Feminists" who "argues that women should not have to bear the burden of pregnancy." Given radical feminists' eschewal of media stardom, Culhane's brief introduction is not surprising, although Firestone had the most extensive history in feminist organizing of anyone in New York in 1970. She had been instrumental in founding several important second-wave groups, including Chicago's Westside group (the first major radical feminist group in the country), New York Radical Women, Redstockings, and, finally, New York Radical Feminists, of which she was a member at the time of the CBS report.

More surprising is that Culhane did not mention Firestone's book, *The Dialectic of Sex,* which would become a best seller upon its publication in the fall of 1970 and was already the subject of considerable buzz in New York (Echols, 1989). In a close-up that visually emphasized her extremism, Firestone briefly articulated the central argument of the book, that women were oppressed by biology and that pregnancy was "barbaric," after which Culhane's final bit of narration summed up the argument: that true liberation would entail reproduction in the laboratory, what he termed "the so-called bottled baby."[23] Returning to his central strategy in which the fanaticism of the radicals functioned to legitimate liberal concerns, Culhane opined that Firestone's position "is one of the most radical versions of feminism. The moderates simply want equal pay and equal job opportunities as well as repeal of abortion laws and more day care centers."

This final segment in a report that was focused on feminists' challenge to women's "traditional roles"—as sex objects, wives, and mothers—folded abortion into a depiction of radicalism, despite the wide and deep support for abortion rights among feminists of all kinds. The rejection of men, marriage, and childbearing depicted in this story culminated in a vision of radical feminism as a "science project gone berserk" that was symptomatic of the gender anxiety provoked by radicals' critiques of patriarchal institutions and prerogatives (Douglas, 1994, p. 170). This depiction also underscored the series' overall racism

Figure 5. Shulamith Firestone, in close-up, being interviewed on CBS.

and classism evident in its exclusive focus on white women (and in Culhane's severance of Shirley Chisholm from her blackness). The reports' notions of how marriage was supposed to work (men should support their families so that their wives did not end up like Jean Temple) and of its problems (married women were slaves, children put women in bondage, pregnancy was barbaric) were derived from the experiences of white, middle-class women, particularly those who felt trapped in their roles as wives, mothers, and homemakers á la *The Feminine Mystique*. Such a narrowly drawn depiction was liable to alienate women of color who had been subjected to forced sterilization, who saw family as a refuge from the racism of public life, and who might have welcomed the chance to stay home with their children (hooks, 1984). Women of color disaffected by what they saw as the largely white and middle-class concerns of feminism were unlikely to find much solace in CBS's portrait of the movement.

On NBC, Catherine Mackin's much more extensive rationale for abortion law repeal represented the clearest possible contrast with Culhane's approach; most remarkably, the April 8 report contained the only explicit discussion of white and black women's different relationships to a feminist issue contained in a network report on the second wave in all of 1970. Anchor Chet Huntley's lead-in to the story framed abortion as a public policy concern as well as a movement issue by noting that the New York State Assembly was considering an abortion law. The report began with footage of a variety of pregnant women and women with children and strollers walking down the street as Mackin narrated: "Most women are raised to believe their true role is that of wife and mother." Yet, she continued, many women were asking, "Is this their true role? Do I have to get married? Do I have to get pregnant? Do I have a choice?"

As Mackin observed that the pill had offered millions of women "unprecedented freedom from unwanted pregnancies," viewers saw footage from the January pill hearings. She noted that the hearings included "many who said the pill can be dangerous" and that "of the first 18 people to testify at the hearings, none were women. But women went anyway." What followed was a much more extensive clip of feminist objections to the pill than had been included in the CBS series. Although the "murdering us for your profit and convenience" line was included, as it had been in all previous network coverage of the hearings, it was preceded by a feminist's mention of the pill's link to cancer of the breast and the uterus and was followed by the scene of police attempting to escort the women from the hearing room. Mackin closed the segment with the statistic that "almost 20 percent of the women taking the pill have stopped, and doctors predict that the rate of unwanted pregnancy will rise," thus segueing to her discussion of abortion.

Mackin's framing of unwanted pregnancy as a social problem put a depiction of feminist activism in the service of explaining an issue rather than making the event of the activism itself the point of the story. She established that the concerns about the pill's safety were shared by experts and feminists alike and made a point of noting the lack of women who testified, thus justifying the protest. In fact, she exnominated the protestors, never naming them as feminists or women's liberationists; rather, she simply presented them as motivated by their exclusion from discussion of an issue that affected them as women.

Ultimately, Mackin used agitation against the pill to set up the rationale for abortion law repeal. Linking the problems with the pill to the "question of what women will do about unwanted pregnancies," she presented the pursuit of abortion as a natural consequence of women's narrowed birth control options. Although "many women say they should have recourse to abortions," she continued, access was limited in most states, so "most women who want abortions must go around the law, and a million women in this country do that every year." As the screen showed a young white woman on the phone at a desk, Mackin stated that "in Illinois and a dozen other states where abortion is illegal," women could get help from a clergy counseling service "simply by calling on the telephone." Viewers then heard an answering service recording that advised the listener to wait for the names and numbers of the clergy on call for pregnancy counseling while the woman sat poised with a pad and pencil. Mackin concluded by explaining that "if, after consultation, an abortion is decided on, the clergyman will refer the woman to a qualified physician. The operation often has to be performed out of her state, sometimes out of the country."[24] This segment, clearly targeting a female audience, was practically a tutorial on how to find an abortion, and the story as a whole included no discourse opposing abortion.

The report's final segment opened with an image of a group of women, all white and young, on the floor in a circle in a room, introduced by Mackin's voiceover: "For many women, like those in the Chicago Women's Liberation Union" (CWLU), the issue is "the right of every woman to control her own body." The remaining unnarrated moments of the report depicted the women talking with each other about various issues related to reproductive politics. They began with access and cost, but moved on to a fairly extensive discussion (more than a minute long within a four-and-a-half minute report) of the plight of poor women, black women, and women on welfare who were sterilized against their will and/or who were threatened with removal of their children if they did not agree to sterilization. One woman commented, "the same hospital that wants to sterilize the black woman will not let a middle-class white woman be sterilized" without medical approval, thus creating the implication, if you were such a woman, that "you have to be crazy . . . you have to be sick" to not want more children. Another woman in the circle summarized the discussion, providing the last line of the story, by reiterating that the issue was "control," and "the right to have children if you want them or the right not to."

Although Mackin's foregrounding of women's questioning of their "true role" as wives and mothers in her introduction to the story elided the wide variety of raced and classed reasons women might seek abortion, the discussion of the class and race politics of reproductive rights that closed her report was surprisingly sophisticated. The Chicago feminists did not go so far as to describe abortion as genocide for African Americans, a position taken by various civil rights and Black Power groups in the 1960s (including the Student Non-Violent Coordinating Committee, the Southern Christian Leadership Conference, the NAACP, the Urban League, the Nation of Islam, and the Black Panther Party), but they did recognize the fraught relationship of the black community to abortion and the ways that the concepts of "choice" and "control" resonated differently for women occupying disparate social positions. Coerced sterilization was no paranoid fantasy; in 1970, black women were sterilized at more than twice the rate of white women, and a 1973 study found that nonwhite women (including blacks, Hispanics, and Native Americans), poor women, and women receiving public assistance were sterilized at higher rates than white women were. Forced sterilization had been an issue for civil rights activists throughout the 1960s and would become a central concern of black feminists in the 1970s (Nelson, 2003; Roberts, 1997).

Mackin's featuring of the CWLU was the only moment in the NBC series when a second-wave feminist group of any kind was more than a visual backdrop for narration. Rather than offering decontextualized sound bites, Mackin's report gave CWLU members a sustained amount of time to offer thoughtful discussion of an issue. The CWLU was a prominent socialist-feminist organization that had as many as five hundred members at its peak, and its members were committed to fighting class as well as gender oppression, as the sensitivity to class differences in their discussion of abortion illustrated (Echols, 1989). The group's appearance in Mackin's report was a rare moment of representation for socialist-feminists in mainstream news, although viewers likely understood them to be simply another radical group, given the ways that their appearance instantiated the familiar visual codes for radicals (longhaired, casually dressed, white women sitting on the floor). All of the women shown on screen were white, but their discussion was the singular example of feminist intersectional analysis to appear on network news in 1970.

Finally, as in her segment on the clergy counseling service, Mackin appeared to be drawing women viewers' attention to a group that could help them. The CWLU was distinctive among feminist groups for its commitment to actually providing access to illegal abortions. In 1969, members of the organization formed a collective called "Jane" that began to provide illegal abortion referrals; by mid-1971, members of Jane had trained themselves to perform the procedure, which they provided without regard to a woman's ability to pay. By the time legal abortion clinics opened in Chicago in 1973, members of Jane estimated that they had performed over eleven thousand abortions (Kaplan, 1995).

The report's commonsensical presentation of abortion as a logical solution to the social problem of unwanted pregnancies seems unusual in today's culture of contestation over abortion, but it reflected the momentum of the abortion decriminalization movement in 1970. In addition to feminists' adoption of abortion as a central issue, mainstream acceptance of the necessity of abortion law repeal also was spurred by the activism of clergy and doctors as well as by the organizational base provided by the formation of the National Association for the Repeal of Abortion Laws in 1969 (Davis, 1991). In fact, abortion reform had begun well before 1970; between 1967 and 1970, a dozen U.S. states passed laws allowing for abortion under certain circumstances, including rape, incest, risk of birth defects, and physical and mental health of the mother (Luker, 1985).

Such laws, while an improvement over complete criminalization, still took the decision out of women's hands. The dominant feminist position was that all laws restricting abortion should be repealed. The laws that began to be passed in 1970, such New York's, dramatically expanded access, although they still carried some restrictions that varied from state to state, such as a residency requirement (e.g., ninety days in Hawaii) or stipulation that the pregnancy could not have progressed past a certain point (e.g., twenty-four weeks in New York) (Davis, 1991; Hole and Levine, 1971). The need for liberalization of abortion laws was becoming a matter of elite media consensus in 1970, and the treatment of the topic by both networks reflected that the various religiously based interest groups who would make abortion a highly contested issue later in the decade had little presence in the public policy arena in 1970 (Condit, 1990; Luker, 1985). For example, when the August 1970 Women's Strike for Equality featured abortion rights as a central demand, none of the network coverage treated it as controversial.

Ultimately, the differences in the CBS and NBC treatment of abortion were consistent with the distinct rhetorical approaches of the two network series. Mackin's story exemplified NBC's tendency to assimilate radicalism under a cloak of liberalism; it presented choice and identity as the central concerns around abortion rights while not elaborating on the fundamental power imbalances that reproduction and its socially assigned responsibilities signified for radicals. For radicals like Shulamith Firestone (1968), abortion was a matter of freedom from biological factors and their social consequences that created a "dominant/submissive" relationship between men and women in all arenas: without abortion, women had no self-determination. Thus, Firestone's advocacy for abortion and her arguments for extrauterine reproduction in *The Dialectic of Sex* (1970) stemmed from the same rationale. Her appearance in the CBS report, however, made none of this apparent, and Culhane simply used Firestone as the climax of his narrative of radical deviance.

Representing Sexism: Men and the Movement

The focus on workplace discrimination that occupied much of the two networks' series and the sustained focus on abortion in NBC's reporting illustrate the tremendous advantage that liberal feminism possessed with regard to mass media representation. Their emphasis on public discrimination and policy concerns was easily translated into mainstream news vocabularies and was intelligible within cultural ideologies of fairness and equality that had renewed resonance from years of struggle over black civil rights. In fact, for many liberal activists, the battles for workplace equality and against abortion restrictions were two sides of the sex discrimination coin: A central argument in the liberal rationale for abortion law repeal was that, without control of their fertility, women were disadvantaged as workers (Luker, 1985). For radicals, however, the public discrimination women suffered could not be extricated from the private subordination, cultural stereotyping, and gender socialization that shaped their subjectivities, thus their first priority was to raise the consciousness of women themselves. Neither of the network series on women's liberation clearly communicated this defining characteristic of radical feminism and/or represented CR's centrality to the radical movement. Moreover, as CBS's stories exemplified, radicals' decontextualized claims about sexism and patriarchy sounded bizarre in a historical moment in which "sex roles" were widely understood as natural and biological and in which "gender" was still just a grammatical term.

Yet the second report in NBC's series, broadcast on March 31, was remarkable for its efforts to detail the depth and breadth of cultural sexism and to matter-of-factly present it as a social problem. While never mentioning CR, reporter Liz Trotta's story emphasized one of the practice's most common foci: the psychological impact of gender socialization on women. Her story, like Mackin's, camouflaged the radical implications of the topic by framing it in familiar liberal feminist terms, ultimately concluding that internalized sexism led young women to limit their career aspirations. Even so, Trotta established that men both participated in and benefited from sexism and discrimination. She did so while never mentioning women's liberation; rather, using a "fly on the wall" technique, she simply allowed men and women to speak for themselves.

NBC anchor Chet Huntley introduced the story as an examination of "male attitudes, both overt and hidden, in private and public life, at home and at work." Opening her report by claiming that "discrimination begins early in a girl's life, even before she is born," Trotta kept the focus on men that Huntley had previewed: As the screen showed a hospital maternity ward, three waiting fathers-to-be all acknowledged to the camera that they hoped for a boy. Viewers saw pink and blue name cards on hospital bassinets as Trotta's voice observed that girls were told they were "different" from boys "every day of their lives," urged to play with dolls instead of trucks, to sew instead of playing sports, and reminded that their "place is in the home." Girls' activities (exemplified by camera footage of synchronized swimming) stressed "the graceful, the attractive, the cooperative," while boys' (exemplified by images of a swimming race) emphasized "the tough, the energetic, the competitive." Trotta concluded this section with the following: "By the time a girl reaches high school, she has been brainwashed by parents and relatives into believing that her life must go in a direction that is different from that of her brother. She's a housewife in training. Rare is the girl who wants to be a doctor, an engineer, or a pilot."

Like the NBC stories that made social problems out of workplace discrimination and unwanted pregnancy, Trotta's story made a social problem out of cultural sexism, and these segments offered unqualified affirmation of the existence of gender stereotyping, supported by illustrative images. Particularly noteworthy is Trotta's use of the term "brainwashed," which carried the implications of indoctrination that, in Culhane's stories, had been reserved for feminism itself. Yet Trotta exnominated feminism as a source for claims about gender socialization, presenting her claims as objective reporting that was simply communicating the reality of women's lives.

This approach took an innovative tack in the story's longest segment, which focused on a high school classroom in Austin, Minnesota, where male and female white students were engaged in a discussion of gender roles. While Trotta remained unseen and unheard, the young men in the room articulated a variety of sexist sentiments, such as "girls go to college so they can get a man," "there's no reason for a girl to go to college," and "my mother went to college, and she got some dietary deal [a nutrition degree, perhaps?] and she doesn't know anything." The most generous comment from a male student was this: "We're superior and they're minor to us, but I think the women should have a chance today because I think they've kinda earned it."

Comments from the young women in the room were not as numerous, although one female student interjected that girls "go to college to get an education. It's a little expensive to go to college to get a boy." After the teacher asked the room why "something hasn't been done," a female student replied that after "thousands of years . . . of male domination, you come to accept it," succinctly reinforcing Trotta's earlier claims regarding gender socialization. To this, a male student replied that if girls get more rights, "it's gonna be an infraction on our rights. . . . We give you guys higher wages and put you on equal working basis with the men, and there goes our job opportunity." The segment concluded as the teacher observed, "it sounds very much like the whole question of black civil rights," and a young man agreed, saying "yeah, they [women] gotta work for their own rights, too." [25]

The teacher's comparison to the civil rights movement, like other uses of the analogy in the NBC series, was brief and functioned to give weight to feminist complaints about discrimination, as it had in Aline Saarinen's first story. In contrast to the racism-sexism analogy in coverage of the Miss America Pageant protest, the comparisons here functioned as a legitimation device that implicitly urged viewers to understand sexism, like racism, as a social problem linked to a struggle over power, privilege, and resources (for instance, young men in the story twice commented that women needed to somehow earn their rights, as though they themselves had already done so). This interpretation was bolstered by Trotta's strategic featuring of young men's articulation of bald sexism in front of the watching cameras with few cuts and no narration. By today's standards, the segment is tedious and overlong—it lasted three minutes, making up fully half of the six-minute story—but in 1970 it would not necessarily have seemed so, and the absence of any narration or obvious camera work in the segment only enhanced its aura of objectivity derived from "the myth of photographic naturalness" (Rosteck, 1994, p. 45).

Trotta's final segment repeated the unobtrusive observation technique to illustrate the impact of socialization on Austin's young women. Her voiceover observed that young women's fear of being "an old maid" meant that they were not inclined to enter "serious fields," believing their future to be "already charted." The camera cut back and forth between several young women seated at a coffee shop, each of whom spoke about her conventionally feminine aspirations after high school, which included waitressing, teaching, being an airline stewardess, working in an orphanage, and teaching dance. The final young woman to speak gave a short, rueful laugh and said, "I'll probably just get married or something." Trotta's concluding stand-up offered this depressing summary: "What's happening in Austin, Minnesota, is happening across the country. There are young girls here who are bright, enthusiastic, and full of hope. But, like most women, they'll go out into the world knowing their place. And that place is secondary to men." The story's unusual Midwestern locale brought the implication of small town authenticity to its narrative (Gans, 1979), contrasting strongly with the urban radicalism featured in the CBS series, but Trotta pointedly extended the import of her example to include "most women."

Trotta's story was the most compelling example of the NBC series' overall tendency to accept sexism and discrimination as givens, as simply the context within which women formed their identities. Like other NBC reports, it laid the responsibility for sexism—and thus for resistance to women's liberation—at men's door. From Saarinen's initial mention of "gentlemen's agreements" to Norma Quarles's reference to "men's prejudices" to Trotta's dispiriting demonstration of youthful sexism in the heartland, these stories made men's culpability clear. The CBS stories were not only generally skeptical about the warrant for women's liberation, they simply neglected to mention men's relationship to sexism or their opinions about the movement, thus giving more power to David Culhane's claim that the movement's central challenge was its failure to convince women themselves of the relevance of its issues.

Conclusion

The nine stories produced by CBS and NBC in the spring of 1970 comprised a total of approximately fifty-three minutes devoted to explaining women's liberation, more than double the twenty-four minutes of reporting that ABC's documentary—the third network effort to explain the movement—would contain in its May broadcast. The documentary's format would allow for a more coherent narrative—no small thing—but, taken together, the earlier network series represented the most sustained attention the movement would receive in 1970. In fact, ABC's Marlene Sanders later recounted that her primary mission when she produced the documentary was to refute misapprehensions about the movement that had been created by previous coverage (Sanders and Rock,

1988). Yet the ABC documentary would replicate the central similarity of the CBS and NBC series; that is, all three networks ultimately offered viewers visions of the movement that supported those elements of feminism consonant with American liberalism.

The CBS and NBC series' contributed to this evolving consensus about the meaning of the movement in markedly different ways, however, and close reading of their divergent verbal and visual narratives challenges sweeping claims that media coverage of women's liberation consistently demonized radical feminism or that it always eliminated women of color from its purview. David Culhane's reports rationalized liberal feminist demands by marginalizing radical actions and ideas, but the NBC series simply assimilated the radicals into its predominantly liberal vision of women's liberation, masking the acute ideological disagreements among feminists by presenting them as mere differences in tactics geared toward similar goals. Although neither series captured the complexities of radical feminist ideas, the NBC reports refused to participate, visually or verbally, in the construction of radicals as liberal feminism's scary and sensationalized other.

Moreover, despite the two series' adherence to a general tone of approval for reformist, mostly workplace-related, goals, the NBC features presented moments of excess that poked at the raced and classed boundaries of this dominant narrative and eluded its "strategies of containment" (Nichols, 1991, p. 143). First, these stories' implicit and explicit recognition of working-class women and women of color was a significant departure from previous print and broadcast media treatments of the movement (and from those that would follow). In particular, Norma Quarles's inclusion of images of such women in her story on employment discrimination was remarkable not only because it included them among those affected by workplace inequities—thus bringing them into the category of legitimate feminist subjects—but also because she did not, in fact, remark on it: the images of women of color were simply interspersed in footage depicting women going about their jobs. In contrast to Quarles's implication that white women and women of color shared a similar relationship to sexism, the inclusion of discourse about race and reproductive rights by the CWLU in Mackin's abortion story foregrounded the distinctive relationships that white women and black women had to a feminist issue. Although they did it in different ways, and while neither made race a controlling focus, both reports challenged the overwhelming whiteness that characterized network reports on the movement and that was assumed to characterize the audience for such reports as well.

Second, the NBC series' depiction of sexism as not just an item of common sense but as a genuine social problem, using the techniques common to such framing—human interest and utilization of images to support verbal claims—not only distinguished them from the CBS reports' more skeptical tone, but also signaled their inclusion of women as a principal audience. These reports spoke to viewers presumed to understand these social constraints as not only prevalent but also problematic. Certainly, such a characterization did not apply to *all* women viewers, which meant that the reports contained the potential not only for appealing to women who recognized sexism but for heightening the awareness of those who, as of yet, did not. If David Culhane assumed he was speaking to viewers much like himself, the same could be said of NBC's female reporters, who decidedly did *not* present their analyses of the prejudices women faced as though they were a matter of opinion, as though women happily chose to accede to them, or as though ordinary women did not find them problematic. They were hardly unaware of the gender bias of the industry in which they were among few women at their level, and their approach suggests that they sought to address women who, like themselves, lived with the everyday realities of sexism. Catherine Mackin, for example, would join the class action suit alleging sex discrimination that NOW and other women's groups would bring against NBC in 1971, and Quarles and Trotta would both later discuss the gender bias they faced in their careers (Bradley, 2003; Gelfman, 1976 Trotta, 1991).

Third, Catherine Mackin's stories went beyond simply addressing women to virtually instructing them. The pedagogical tone of her reports suggested an audience of women who could benefit from information about how to file a sex discrimination complaint or how to get an abortion referral. In each case, the recommended remedy was to go to the government or to a network of clergy, hardly options with radical associations.

Ultimately, that three of the six NBC reports failed to mention women's liberation at all can be viewed as a rhetorically shrewd move in their historical context. My reading of these reports is that they reveal a rhetorical purpose of seeking to make the movement's concerns relevant and reasonable to their viewers. Asserting such a purpose is not a claim to knowledge of news workers' intentions; rather, I base that assertion on my interpretation of the verbal and visual content of the stories. With that view of their purpose, for the reports to explicitly attach claims about sexism and discrimination to the movement had the potential for tainting them with the same connotations of contagion and indoctrination that Culhane's CBS stories had done. For example, rather than using radical feminists to make the case, Liz Trotta's story simply presented typically radical feminist arguments about sexism and socialization as a matter of social consensus, a designation that Culhane refused to give them.

In the end, both network series used standard representational resources of news but toward very different ends, demonstrating reporters' exercise of rhetorical freedom within the limits of new practices and cultural ideologies. Culhane, for instance, used conventional visual codes for deviance to marginalize radical feminists within his narrative about the movement, while the NBC reports used human-interest elements and a social problem format to justify feminist claims within their narrative about sexism and discrimination. In each case, "compliance with the norms and conventions governing a particular mode" of representation provided the "authority of a socially established and institutionally legitimated voice" that worked against the movement's interests in some instances and for them in others (Nichols, 1991, pp. 33–34). The two series' narratives also invoked ideologies of traditional femininity, which both drew on to vindicate feminist workplace grievances but CBS also used to highlight feminists' violation of acceptable feminine behavior.

The NBC series' skillful avoidance of the available negative frames for representing feminism—frames exemplified with dazzling clarity in the CBS stories—merits acknowledgment. Even so, like all representations of the movement, NBC's narrative was limited, partial, and laden with unspoken ideological commitments, particularly those attached to evolutionary liberalism's notion that the problems in the status quo could be solved through reformist adjustments (like enforcement of Title VII or passing the ERA) in its controlling structures. Linking the concerns of women's liberation to widely accepted values like fairness, equality under the law, and individual choice, the series largely sidestepped radical feminist analyses of power and patriarchy that could not be made compatible with social consensus. Partially because of the strong contrast effect created by the CBS series, this seems a remarkable accomplishment rather than simply another demonstration of commercial journalism's domestication of dissent.

From my perspective, the differences in these two portraits of women's liberation are not inconsequential, and they underscore that national news treatment of women's liberation should not be viewed as a monolith, that any attempt to understand it requires attention to its singularities as well as its sameness, and that all assessments must take into account what was and was not possible within the constraints of dominant news practices. The dissimilarities in these two series illustrate 1970's unique potential as a moment when impressions of women's liberation were at an inchoate stage and media frames specific to the movement were still forming. ABC's Marlene Sanders, a journalist with strong feminist sympathies, was watching these developments closely, and the case studies of her reporting in the next two chapters illustrate her highly deliberate and well-meaning attempts to intervene in the movement's problematic image politics.

CHAPTER 3

Magazines and the Marketing of the Movement

The March 1970 *Ladies' Home Journal* Protest

The point is: this is 1970. All peoples and all sexes are free to reexamine their roles. They are free to grow where they have been stunted, to move forward where they have been held back, to find dignity and self-fulfillment on their own. As a magazine that for 87 years has served as an emotional and intellectual forum for American women, we can do no less than devote part of one issue to an explanation of Women's Liberation.

—*Ladies' Home Journal* editor John Mack Carter,
in his introduction to the feminist-produced special section
in the magazine's August 1970 issue (1970b, p. 63)

On January 26, 1970, a coalition of leftist women staged a takeover of the underground New Left newspaper *RAT Subterranean News* in New York City. Founded in 1968, *RAT* was an important voice in radical politics in New York, but it was controlled by men and displayed an increasing emphasis on what *RAT* writer Robin Morgan called "'cultural nationalism' for young white males: rock music coverage, pornography articles, and sex-wanted ads" (1978, p. 115). Leftist women who wrote for the paper had grown weary of *RAT*'s sexist tone and content and with its treatment of women writers as second-class citizens. Their unrest peaked with the appearance of a late 1969 special issue on "sex and porn" that featured a pornographic cover (Hole and Levine, 1971, p. 273). The successful takeover constituted an important moment of recognition by leftist women of the need for a specifically feminist underground press, and, as Morgan wrote, "the action created ripples all over the Left, with women following suit in other cities and taking over their local underground media temporarily or permanently" (1978, p. 116; see also Flannery, 2005).

The events at *RAT* also demonstrated the extent to which many women were still struggling with dual allegiances to feminism and the male-dominated Left in 1970. Robin Morgan, who was not involved in the initial takeover but was delighted when she heard about it, published her scathing denunciation of sexism on the Left, the soon-to-be-classic "Goodbye to All That," in the first issue of the feminist-controlled *RAT* on February 7, 1970:

> We have met the enemy and he's our friend. And dangerous. What the hell, let the chicks do an issue; maybe it'll satisfy 'em for a while, it's a good controversy, and it'll maybe sell papers runs an unoverheard conversation that I'm sure took place at some point last week. . . . The good guys who think they know what Women's Lib, as they so chummily call it, is all about—who then proceed to degrade and destroy women by almost everything they say and do: The cover on the last issue of *RAT* (front *and* back). The token pussy power or clit militancy articles. The snide descriptions of women staffers on the masthead. The little jokes, the personal ads, the smile, the snarl. No more, brothers. No more well-meaning ignorance, no more cooptation, no more assuming that this thing we're all fighting for is the same; one revolution under *man*, with liberty and justice for all. No more. (1992, pp. 122–123)

The *RAT* action was a shot across the bow in feminists' battle with sexist media institutions—both leftist and mainstream—that would expand over the course of 1970 and that would involve members of women's liberation groups across the political spectrum.

Less than two months later, 1970's most visible and effective instance of media activism instigated by feminism's radical flank would occasion a story on ABC's nightly news, when Marlene Sanders reported on the March 18th sit-in by a diverse coalition of feminists at *Ladies' Home Journal*. Inspired by the *RAT* takeover, roughly two hundred feminists would ultimately occupy *LHJ* for eleven hours as they launched a wide-ranging critique of its editorial, advertising, and employment practices, an event that would have powerful immediate and long-term consequences. The feminists not only successfully negotiated for space to air their views in an upcoming issue of *LHJ*, but the protest's visibility would hasten larger shifts in major women's magazines, which subsequently begin to incorporate themes of women's liberation within their self-help and self-improvement format, often by hiring feminist writers. Yet, just as the *RAT* action laid bare the tensions between men and women on the Left, the aftermath of the *LHJ* protest would reveal fissures within feminism, as some participants decried these outcomes as little more than co-optation of the movement's radical aims.

Protest organizer Susan Brownmiller (1999) would later note that "a large-scale assault, in the flesh, on a giant American institution had not been attempted since the Miss America Protest," but, unlike the 1968 action, the *LHJ* events would be the focus of national broadcast news same-day coverage (p. 86). ABC's Marlene Sanders had been tipped off by Brownmiller and was the only network reporter on the scene from the beginning of the protest, thus making her exclusive on that night's broadcast the first to break the news. In addition to Sanders's story, elite print outlets would provide ample coverage that offered initial interpretations of the import of the protest, but the implications of the *LHJ* action would build over the course of the next several months (and into the next few years) as women's magazines—and the movement itself—responded to the lessons of the protest.

A close reading of the print and broadcast reports on the *LHJ* action illustrates key similarities and differences in their characterizations of the action. Sander's network story was more evenhanded than the print coverage would be, but all of the media accounts ultimately foregrounded the protest's claims regarding discrimination against women as media workers. This interpretation fit easily within news workers' preferred equality opportunity frame for representing feminism, but it was also given strength by a wave of employee-driven and movement-inspired media reform efforts that escalated throughout 1970 and that brought women's liberation increasingly close to home for media organizations.

Feminism, Media Reform, and the *Ladies' Home Journal* Protest

The timing of the March 18 *LHJ* protest could not have been more auspicious in terms of the movement's media visibility. The CBS series on the movement had aired the previous week, Susan Brownmiller's insider account of women's liberation had appeared in the *NYT Magazine* on March 15, and the issue of *Newsweek* that hit newsstands that Monday, March 16, had a cover story on the movement titled "Women in Revolt" (Dudar, 1970). With purposeful timing, a group of women who worked for *Newsweek* held a press conference that same day to announce that they had filed a sex discrimination complaint against the magazine, charging that it unfairly relegated women at the magazine to jobs as researchers rather than writers. At the time, only one of *Newsweek*'s fifty-two writers was female and only one of its thirty-five researchers was male (Bradley, 2003; Davis, 1991; Povich, 2012).

As 1970 proceeded, expanding media coverage of the movement would be accompanied by acceleration of protests against media organizations. In April, Robin Morgan led a sit-in at the office of Grove Press, the alternative publishing

Figure 6. *Newsweek*'s female employees at the press conference announcing their sex discrimination complaint on March 16, 1970. The March 23, 1970, issue of *Newsweek* titled "Women in Revolt" is in foreground. © 2013 Bettman/Corbis.

house where she was an editor, to protest the firing of employees for unionizing; the protest also charged the press with publishing pornographic materials that objectified women (Bronstein, 2011). Feminists protested at the *San Francisco Chronicle* as well as disrupted a CBS stockholders' meeting in May, the same month that female employees of Time, Inc. filed a sex discrimination complaint with the New York State Division of Human Rights and that women editorial employees of the *Washington Post* accused the paper of discrimination, a case they later took to the EEOC (Davis, 1991; Beasley and Gibbons, 1993; Bradley, 2003). NOW undertook a series of boycotts aimed at products with sexist advertising in 1970, and NOW Vice President Lucy Komisar discussed discrimination in advertising when she testified before Congress that summer (Craig, 2003). After a campaign by women reporters and their supporters that had lasted ten years or more, the National Press Club took its first vote on admitting women as members in June 1970. The resolution finally passed early in 1971 (Mills, 1990). In August, NOW joined with other women's groups and charged sex discrimination in a Petition to Deny the License Renewal of NBC's owned and operated WRC-TV in Washington, D.C., the suit in which reporter Catherine Mackin was one of the plaintiffs (Perlman, 2007).

The *LHJ* action would prove especially visible during this string of media reform efforts. Although the planners of the protest took pains to make it a surprise,

Susan Brownmiller's *NYT Magazine* article offered hints of what was to come. Brownmiller (1970b) acknowledged the growth in mass media interest in the movement—observing that "women's liberation is hot stuff this season"—as well as the movement's interest in media reform (p. 27). Opposite the first page of the article, photographs depicted current advertisements from Times Square that had been plastered with stickers that read This Ad Insults Women. The caption noted, "One target of the women's lib movement is advertising that feminists (and others) call offensive and exploitative.... One group—Media Women—sells the stickers that have been affixed to such billboards all around town."

Media Women was the incubator for the *LHJ* protest; the group's members had come together through their involvement in a larger activist, primarily underground, collective called Media Projects that included men and women concerned with mass media coverage of contemporary political issues. As was often the case in leftist groups, the women members felt that "they were cast into a 'ladies-auxiliary-but-occasionally-useful-as-a-political-issue' role" (Hole and Levine, 1971, p. 254), and they resolved to form their own group to dramatize the unique problems created by media industries' treatment of women. Once formed in the fall of 1969, Media Women found themselves facing internal dissent. Battles over ideology, political goals, voting rights—and even how to run the meetings—threatened to paralyze the group until someone suggested the idea of unifying members through the planning of a specific action. Journalist Sandie North proposed occupying *LHJ*, where she had been an employee and still had connections that would give them inside information useful in planning the protest (Brownmiller, 1999; Hole and Levine, 1971).

Among the oldest of the top women's magazines—dubbed the Seven Sisters in the industry—*LHJ* claimed some 14 million readers and touted itself as "the magazine women believe in," thus presenting a suitable target that would gain maximum visibility (Zuckerman, 1998).[1] That *LHJ* had a male editor and heavily male editorial and writing staff was a central grievance of Media Women, although these characteristics made it little different from its peer publications. The only major women's magazine with a woman at its helm was *McCall's,* which had appointed Shana Alexander its first female editor-in-chief in late 1969 (Zuckerman, 1998).

The *Ladies' Home Journal* Sit-In Steering Committee was chaired by a junior editor at Harper and Row, Signe Hammer, who, along with Susan Brownmiller, would read Media Women's list of demands in Editor-in-Chief John Mack Carter's office on the day of the protest. The group took months hammering out the list of demands and making connections to feminist groups in New York City to drum up numbers for the protest. In the end, the action included members of NYRF, Redstockings, NOW, The Feminists, the Gay Liberation Front (GLF), and

Older Women's Liberation, as well as members of Media Women unaffiliated with other feminist groups.[2] For various radical feminists who faced criticism from leftists that their dedication to CR made them "living room feminists," the protest was opportune (Brownmiller, 1999, p. 86). Those eager to demonstrate that they did more than talk and theorize signed up to participate in the sit-in, and Brownmiller began to believe that the numbers would be large enough to be taken seriously.

The diverse group of women involved in the short-lived Media Women produced an equally multifaceted critique of media industry practices to be leveled at *LHJ*. The list of demands, distributed in a press release as well as read at the protest, not only critiqued editorial content and advertising but also attacked employment practices and the magazine's lack of employee child care as well. The feminists stipulated a female editor-in-chief, an all-female editorial and writing staff, and the hiring of "non-white women at all levels in proportion to the population statistics" (Brownmiller, 1999, p. 85).[3] They called for higher salaries as well as for open editorial conferences so that "the magazine can benefit from everyone's experiences and views" (Brownmiller, 1999, p. 85). In terms of content, they demanded an end to the publication's sole focus on women's responsibility for home and family and the elimination of advertisements that degraded women or that were paid for by companies that exploited women in terms of low salaries and employment discrimination.

The list targeted almost every characteristic that defined women's magazines at the time, demanding also that celebrity articles and romantic fiction be eliminated, as well as all articles about the preservation of youth and those that were tied to advertising make-up, food, fashion, and appliances. They took particular aim at a popular series in *LHJ* titled Can This Marriage Be Saved? and the fact that the answer was always "yes." The final demands were for an issue of the magazine to be turned over to the women's liberation movement and for the movement to be given a monthly column (Brownmiller, 1999; Jay, 1999).[4]

These demands indicated the varied strains of movement ideology that percolated through the protest and its participants as well as Media Women's considerable knowledge about how women's magazines worked. For example, the attack on celebrity articles, as well as the demands for open editorial meetings, exhibited radical feminists' rejection of elitism and their privileging of women's experiences in tandem with their repudiation of the idea that famous women should serve as examples for other women (especially because such women were often well-known primarily because they had married powerful men, e.g., Jacqueline Kennedy Onassis). Similarly, their grievances about content showcased radical feminists' critique of traditional sex roles that defined women solely as mothers, wives, romantic-sexual objects, and consumers of products that served those roles, while also demonstrating their understanding of the incestuous relationship of editorial content and advertising in such magazines, within which articles were used to push the products of advertisers (Steinem, 1990). Finally, emphasis on discrimination in hiring and compensation, although clearly influenced by liberal feminist concerns with employment and pay equity, also reflected the experience of many of the journalists involved in Media Women who knew only too well how few good jobs there were for women and how poorly they paid.

In her retelling of the events, Susan Brownmiller (1999) admitted that once the women had crowded into John Mack Carter's office and had read their demands, they were not sure what else to do. Serendipitously, that was the moment when reporters arrived, asked Carter for his response, and provided an audience for which the feminists could further perform their critique of *LHJ*. They had come armed with a mock-up of the cover of their proposed alternative, the *Women's Liberated Journal,* showing a pregnant woman with a sign reading Unpaid Labor. They also proposed a list of the kinds of articles that *LHJ* should be publishing, such as "How to Get an Abortion," "How to Have an Orgasm," and "Must Your Child Keep You from a Career?," which they claimed were more in touch with the concerns of women (Brownmiller, 1999, p. 84). For several hours, as journalists and *LHJ* staffers watched, the group volleyed accusations

Figure 7. *Ladies' Home Journal* sit-in on March 18, 1970. John Mack Carter (with cigarette) and Lenore Hershey (in hat) are in back left sitting in front of the "Women's Liberated Journal" mock-up. © 2013 Associated Press/SJ.

at Carter, and he responded calmly, although his second-in-command, Lenore Hershey, the only woman among the magazine's senior editors, was reportedly more obviously disapproving and disgusted.[5]

The proceedings reached a climax of sorts when a frustrated Shulamith Firestone lunged at Carter, apparently intending to push him off the desk on which he was perched (although some participants later said that they feared she might push him through a plateglass window). She was restrained by GLF member Karla Jay (1999), who claimed in her memoir that this moment "transformed the entire tenor of the sit-in" such that Carter "suddenly agreed to negotiate" (p. 118). The negotiation produced an agreement that eight pages of *LHJ*'s August issue would be turned over to the feminists, who would collectively pen a group of articles on women's liberation for which they would be paid $10,000. The funds were later donated to a variety of women's causes in New York, including a day care center, an abortion project, a women's newspaper, a women's film collective, a bail fund, and the New York City Women's Center (Brownmiller, 1999).

Mediating the "Militants"

The challenge for journalists on the scene on March 18 was to find a way to make sense of an event that was somewhat amorphous. Its only apparent leaders were the two women—Susan Brownmiller and Signe Hammer—who read the demands. The collection of feminists at the protest, many of whom had not been part of the planning, had very different ideas of what they were there to do, and the day's events were not well scripted. The print reports adhered to a conflict frame, spending the majority of their column inches recounting the protestors' behavior—and the reactions to it by *LHJ* staff—rather than explaining their grievances. For example, the *New York Times* story included a typical disavowal of feminist claims by a female *LHJ* employee, who commented, "I like having men around. . . . I think most of their demands are ridiculous" (Lichtenstein, 1970a, p. 51).

The print stories gave more attention to feminist grievances related to employment issues than to those about content. The *Times,* for instance, listed the demands for a woman editor, an all-female staff, a day care center, and an editorial training program for low-level staffers, while not detailing demands about content, save a quotation from Brownmiller that called *LHJ* "one of the most demeaning magazines toward women" (Lichtenstein, 1970a, p. 51). The *Washington Post* (Meyer, 1970), *New York Times* (Lichtenstein, 1970a), and *Time* ("Woman-Power," 1970) stories about the protest all acknowledged that Lenore Hershey was the only woman among *LHJ*'s top editors, and these references to Hershey's singular status were the most consistent way in which the stories agreed with any of the feminists' accusations. Complaints about content, on the other hand, were matters of taste. As one employee of the magazine, quoted in at least two press accounts, put it, "'If you don't like the magazine, don't read it'" (Lichtenstein, 1970a, p. 51; "Woman-Power," 1970, p. 59).

Adding to the emphasis on employment discrimination, the *New York Times, Time,* and *Newsweek* reports all made a connection between the *LHJ* events and the sex discrimination complaint filed by women at *Newsweek* two days earlier; *Time,* for example, grouped them under what it called "the rebellious restlessness of women in journalism" ("Woman-Power," 1970, p. 59). *Newsweek*'s article pairing the two events was headlined "Woman Power," and the *New York Times* called the *LHJ* protest "the second attempt of the week by the women's liberation movement to make inroads at a major magazine" (Lichtenstein, 1970a, p. 51). The *Newsweek* women had not publicly affiliated themselves with women's liberation, but their claims and statistics regarding employment discrimination cohered with the *LHJ* protestors' contention that women should play a greater role as employees at the magazine.[6]

The event-centered print reports stressed what was novel about the day's happenings: a large group of vocal women forcing themselves into Carter's office as he went about his business and berating him for what they did not like about the magazine he edited. The *New York Times* called the protesters "militant feminists" (Lichtenstein, 1970a, p. 51), while the *Washington Post* called them an "angry army" that "invaded and occupied," making a "virtual prisoner" of John Mack Carter (Meyer, 1970, p. A3). *Newsweek* called them "militant feminists" who "stormed" into *LHJ*'s offices ("Woman Power," 1970, p. 61), and *Time* magazine labeled them "trouser-clad feminists" who "marched" to the scene of the protest ("Woman-Power," 1970, p. 59).[7] These martial metaphors were so consistent, and so consistently placed early in the stories, as to indicate a seemingly commonsensical conclusion that a group of women with a grievance was not just novel, but threatening, echoing David Culhane's use of militant in his CBS reports. With no weapons other than their demands and plans for an alternative vision of the magazine, the protesters were cast, nevertheless, as a group of soldiers with a battle plan, a characterization that implied that they were far more organized and united than they actually were.

An army generally has a leader, and the protestors lacked that as well. Yet, in the *New York Times* story, Susan Brownmiller was called a leader—probably because she read the list of demands and/or because she was friendly with *Times* reporter Grace Lichtenstein. *Newsweek,* on the other hand, named Ti-Grace Atkinson as a leader in their story, seemingly only for the purpose of mentioning that she had "egged on" the "young and aggressive militant" (Firestone) who tried to push John Mack Carter off his desk ("Woman Power," 1970, p. 61).

Atkinson, who had no role in the planning of the action but possessed a visible media profile, may simply have been the only feminist recognized by the *Newsweek* reporter. Finally, not noting the irony in any way, three of the press stories used the term "spokesman" to refer to a protest participant who had provided information. Members of the group likely refused to give their names when speaking to the press, thus maintaining their commitment to the collective, but mass media need for representative voices is so acute that anyone who provided information became a voice for the movement.

The aggressiveness and unruliness attributed to the feminist protestors was a sharp contrast with the reported demeanor of their target, *LHJ* editor John Mack Carter. He was described as striving "manfully to be good-humored as the women packed into his office showered him with reproaches," in the words of the *Washington Post*'s Karl Meyers (1970, p. A3). *Newsweek* described him as "listen[ing] sympathetically" ("Woman Power," 1970, p. 61), *Time* noted his "extraordinary patience" ("Woman-Power," 1970, p. 59), and the *New York Times* quoted Carter as saying that the day had been "educational" (Lichtenstein, 1970a, p. 51). The contrast between the feminists and their target was crystal clear: They were belligerent and disruptive while he was patient and good-humored, as if dealing with a pack of ill-mannered children (several of whom, as two accounts noted, helped themselves to his desktop humidor at one point and lit up his cigars) (Lichtenstein, 1970a; "Woman Power," 1970). As if to underscore this amused tone, each of the four major print stories noted the irony of the magazine's motto: "Never underestimate the power of a woman."

Generally, the print coverage of the *LHJ* action offered strong support for the maxim that "media tend to act as preservers of the status quo by providing unsympathetic coverage to those whose behavior threatens it" (Martindale, 1989, p. 964). These stories usefully illustrate the catch-22 radical activists face: To get attention, they have to act inappropriately, "finding some gimmick or act of disorder to force their way in" to the news web (Gamson and Wolfsfeld, 1993, p. 122). Once they do so, shifting the focus from the behavior to the message proves difficult. Susan Brownmiller was right to assume that the protest would not be worth covering unless a large number of feminists participated; on the other hand, two hundred women targeting one man as the root of all evil in women's magazines was easy to frame as an unfair fight.

Conventional wisdom would hold that the problems of print coverage would be exacerbated in broadcast coverage because the latter, given time limitations and orientation toward the visual, is apt to emphasize spectacle more while generally offering less hard information. In the case of the *LHJ* protest, however, Marlene Sanders's television story contained none of the negative characterizations of the event that the next day's print coverage would. Sanders's report offered an account of the day's events that focused on issues rather than behavior and that downplayed the action's antagonistic aspects. The report's editing was crucial to this effect: By cutting together statements of the feminists and *LHJ* editor John Mack Carter, Sanders was able to frame the interaction as a discussion rather than a confrontation. She managed to make the protestors look much more reasonable than the print coverage had, but she did so at the expense of forcing the events into a narrow equal rights–equal opportunity frame that, like the print coverage, pushed aside feminist issues with content.

ABC anchor Frank Reynolds placed the event within the context of recent movement activity while sounding unconvinced that feminist concerns were legitimate: "Women militants objecting to what they consider male supremacy have been making themselves heard rather widely recently. Today their target was the male editor of a magazine for women." Foreshadowing the martial language that would surface in the next day's print stories, Reynolds's words seemed to anticipate a "battle of the sexes" scenario. Yet Sander's report that followed featured no militancy. The first image was of John Mack Carter holding the cover mock-up of the proposed alternative magazine, the *Women's Liberation Journal,* while a feminist was heard saying, "You put out a magazine like this and I guarantee you that your circulation will quadruple." This was a rare moment in the story that referred to *LHJ*'s content rather than its employment practices.

Couched in the language of commerce rather than revolution, this opening moment presaged the atmosphere of reasonableness that Sanders's report created around the protest. In contrast to the print stories' description of a bellicose horde, Sanders called the assembled protestors "representatives of a cross section of women's liberation groups" and did not describe the proceedings at all beyond noting the number of women, the location, and calling it a sit-in. "Sit-in," the preferred label of protest organizers, brought to mind peaceful civil rights protest and was the least incendiary label that could be used, particularly in contrast to those accounts that called it an invasion or an occupation. One wide shot in the story showed Carter sitting with his back against the wall wearily surveying the crowd of feminists that crowded his office, offering an image that could contribute to the impression of the events as a siege in which he was unfairly outnumbered. But viewers had to draw this conclusion themselves, as Sanders's description of the proceedings was so restrained. In place of characterizing the protestors, Sanders used her narration to detail some of their demands, providing those demands with a coherence and centrality to the event that the print coverage would not. Giving almost no time to the critique of *LHJ* content and advertising, the story emphasized those demands that fit well within an equal opportunity frame: the demand that all advertising, sales, and editorial employees be women; control of one issue of the magazine; a regular column for the movement; and a day care center.

Like the print stories, the television footage communicated Carter's composed demeanor, but the crowd of protestors was depicted as an audience for the discussion rather than as an aggressive army. Most importantly, the editing of the images, and specifically the use of a shot–reverse shot technique, represented the events as a reasonable exchange in which the feminists made a demand and Carter answered it. For example, after showing a feminist reading the demand that "all sales and advertising personnel be women," the screen immediately cut to Carter, who replied, "I like the idea. I have no objection to women selling advertising in this magazine. All for it." The screen then showed another feminist stating the demand that "all editorial employees of the magazine be women," and cut back to Carter for a reply: "I think it would be ridiculous to have only women working for *Ladies' Home Journal*. That's not the only qualification required of an editor on this magazine." After these exchanges, all framed in conventional medium shots, the last feminist seen speaking in the story cemented the depiction of reasonableness, saying in a matter-of-fact tone: "We didn't come here to make a fuss and go home. We have certain things on paper, they're very clear, we'd like to reach some agreement." Just as this protestor used the equitable term "agreement," Sanders noted, "The women were prepared to stay all day until their demands were negotiated." Not until their demands were *met*, but until they were *negotiated*.

Sanders thought of herself as someone who was dedicated to simply providing "straightforward" (presumably meaning unbiased) coverage of women's liberation, in contrast to the "snide and hostile" coverage that she saw dominating news accounts of the early movement (Sanders and Rock, 1988, p. 117).[8] Yet, the *LHJ* protest story that ran on ABC required considerable labor on Sanders's part to cast the day's events in the most palatable light. She omitted the most controversial aspects of the critique of *LHJ*, such as those that lamented its focus on Kinder, Küche, & Kirche[9] or those that demanded an end to "advertisements that degrade women" or articles "oriented toward the preservation of youth (implying that age has no graces of its own)" (Brownmiller, 1999, p. 86). Not only did attacks on these characteristics strike at the heart of the mission and identity of *LHJ*, they also critiqued central aspects of traditional feminine identity and echoed a radical feminist critique of sex roles. Avoiding such issues, Sanders put employment discrimination front and center in her story. Given her belief that the movement needed to play up its kinship with the public discrimination claims of black civil rights activism (see Sanders and

Rock, 1988), she likely believed that her report worked to rescue the feminists from their own excesses.

In her closing stand-up, Sanders smiled and commented, "The *Ladies' Home Journal* has long called itself 'the magazine women believe in.' Obviously, they've taken too much for granted." Here, she was not only kinder to the protestors than the print reporters would be, with their amused use of the "never underestimate the power of a woman" motto, but her final statement could be read as generally sympathetic with the feminists' claims. *LHJ* would demonstrate some sympathy as well; not only did its editors respond with surprising alacrity to the feminists' challenge, but ripple effects were felt across the major women's magazines.

Raising Consciousness in *Ladies' Home Journal*

In his first mention of the protest in *LHJ*'s May 1970 issue, editor John Mack Carter initiated a pattern that would characterize the magazine's approach to women's liberation: the separation of the protestors' demands into reasonable (equal opportunity) and unreasonable (critique of sex roles) categories:

> Many of the demands made by the scattered but noisy feminist groups asking for "liberation" do not seem unreasonable. There *should* be equal pay for equal work; legal rights *should* apply to both sexes; educational and career opportunities for women *should* expand. . . . At the same time, we recognize that there is still a predominant bloc of intelligent women who enjoy centering their lives around a family, and don't consider domesticity demeaning. (Carter, 1970a, p. 10; emphasis in original)

In this same editor's column, Carter politely called the sit-in a "visit" from women's liberationists and promised that the magazine "will examine their points of view in future issues" (1970a, p. 10).

He kept that promise: In the August 1970 issue in which the agreed-upon feminist section appeared, a regular *LHJ* column titled "The Journal's Newsletter of Involvement," which had previously contained brief snippets of information and quotations about women's activism at various levels (e.g., the Girl Scouts, Earth Day, highway safety, drug addiction), was retitled "The Power of a Woman: The Journal's Newsletter of Involvement," and it focused solely on the Equal Rights Amendment. The page contained eight different quotations, all but one supportive of the amendment, taken from the testimony of persons (John Mack Carter among them) who had appeared at the ERA hearings held in May. One of those quotations was from Betty Friedan, and it provided some publicity for the upcoming Strike for Equality: "I've called for a general strike of women on Wednesday, August 26. If by (that date) you and your fellow Congressmen have not sent the Equal Rights Amendment to the states for ratification, we are going to track you down in your offices here, or on the beaches, or in the mountains . . . until this amendment is passed. Because we mean business" ("The Power of a Woman," 1970, p. 50).

On the front of the August *LHJ,* an awareness of the publicity value of the sit-in was evident in the cover-line trumpeting the presence of the section on feminism: "'Women's Liberation' and You: The Special Feminist Section Every-one's Been Talking About" (printed in bold, black type that contrasted with the bright pink of the magazine's title and the other cover-lines). Carter's (1970b) introduction to the section recounted memories of the March sit-in, mixing respect with reproof and maintaining a distinction between radical critique and equal opportunity demands in sentences such as "beneath the shrill accusations and the radical dialectic, our editors heard some convincing truths about the persistence of sexual discrimination in many areas of American life" (p. 63).

Carter (1970b) distanced the magazine from the section's subject matter, mak-ing clear that *LHJ* staff had not interfered with content and had used a light edito-rial hand "in order to permit these women to express in their own terms exactly how they feel" (p. 63). Perhaps still smarting from his treatment back in March, he concluded with a guarded prediction that "this new movement may have an impact far beyond its extremist eccentricities. It could even triumph over its man-hating bitterness and indeed win humanist gains for all women—and their men" (1970b, p. 63). The section itself, titled "The New Feminism" (1970), contained eight unsigned articles and ended with a list of women's liberation groups in the United States and Canada, as well as a list of movement publications.

The section combined equal opportunity rhetoric and radical feminist analy-ses of sexual politics, although the latter far outweighed the former. The first article, titled "Women and Work," contained plentiful statistics (including those comparing the pay of white and nonwhite women) and discussion of legal bar-riers, including a review of Ida Phillip's sex discrimination suit against Martin Marietta and an explanation of the problems of "protective" laws such as the one at issue in Leah Rosenfeld's case in California. This essay's primary place-ment reinforced the dominant meaning given the sit-in by news coverage, but the remaining seven articles overwhelmingly reflected the radical feminist ex-ploration of sex roles typical of CR, treating topics such as differences in girls' and boy's socialization and educational experiences; the alienation women experienced during medicalized childbirth; the lack of appreciation and pay for housework and child care; the pressure to conform to hegemonic, white beauty standards (and its negative effect on sisterhood); and a transcript of a conversation among five women titled "Women Talk about Love and Sex."

The most direct critique of *LHJ* itself in these pages was an article titled "*Should* This Marriage Be Saved," a slight but meaningful shift from the title of the popular *LHJ* feature *Can* This Marriage Be Saved? (my emphasis). Telling the story of Barbara, an unhappy thirty-three-year-old housewife and mother who felt stifled by her traditional marriage, the article hypothesized about what she might be told by one of the counselors used in the *LHJ* feature and contrasted that advice with the wisdom she gained from discussing her situation "with women like herself" in a women's liberation group ("The New Feminism," 1970, p. 68). The crucial difference between the feminists' approach and that taken in *LHJ*'s Can This Marriage Be Saved? feature was the former's emphasis on the importance of Barbara's desires and happiness rather than on the ultimate importance of preserving her marriage.

The last essay in the section, titled "How to Start Your Own Consciousness-Raising Group," was followed by a list of addresses for women's liberation groups in different cities. A list of addresses of movement publications around the country was included as well (significantly, NOW was not mentioned as a contact group nor were its publications listed). As a whole, the section emphasized the topics, tone, and analysis that characterized radical feminist CR groups. Each essay made the personal political in some fashion, all were heavy on anecdote and narrative, and most of the articles used a collective we (e.g., "we are so convinced that our work is worthless that we become fanatic housekeepers, trying to prove again and again our own human worth" ["The New Feminism," 1970, p. 67]) or were told in the first person, as was the case with "Babies Are Born, Not Delivered" and "How Appearance Divides Women." "Women Talk about Love and Sex" read like a transcript of a CR group, as women recounted personal experiences in answer to the question "How many times have you had to fake orgasm in order to please your man?" ("The New Feminism," 1970, p. 70).

The articles reflected the drawbacks of CR as well. CR was most effective when participants shared similar backgrounds, and the fact that most "consciousness-raising groups were composed of self-identified white middle class heterosexual women" meant that "the method risked insinuating white middle class heterosexual identity as a template for all women" (Dever, 2004, p. 29).[10] The material in the *LHJ* special section reflected the commonalities in the identities of the majority of its creators and did not include, for instance, a discussion of lesbianism, an issue that had already begun to divide movement members and that had been a visible source of tension at the Second Congress to Unite

Women held in New York in May.[11] GLF member Karla Jay initially participated in the editorial meetings about the special section, but she was disappointed that it would not deal with lesbianism and dropped out before it was completed. Moreover, despite some attention to race differences in Media Women's demands at the sit-in, the section presumed and reproduced a race- and class-specific homogeneity of experience that black women found off-putting about white women's CR groups. Except for the comparison of white and nonwhite women's wages in the "Women and Work" essay, only "How Appearance Divides Women" mentioned race, albeit very briefly, when the white author admitted that "growing up in a white racist society . . . I considered black women less attractive and therefore less valuable" ("The New Feminism," 1970, p. 69).

In particular, the analyses of marriage, child care, and housework in the section's articles relied on a problematic universalism regarding women's experiences as wives and mothers (although it also reflected the writers' recognition of the profile of the typical *LHJ* reader). The role of the family in women's oppression was a topic about which there was significant cleavage between black and white women: "Unlike white women, many of whom experienced family obligations as a primary locus of exploitation, most black women found that the family was the least oppressive institution in their lives and constituted a refuge from domination by white racist institutions outside" (Roth, 2003, p. 102; see also Polatnick, 1996). Many politically active black women were impatient with radical feminists' emphasis on cultural change (e.g., body image, women's competition with other women) at the expense of addressing economic oppression. They were drawn instead to the focus of liberal feminist groups on electoral politics, equal opportunity, pay equity, and workplace discrimination, a fact reflected in NOW's greater racial diversity when compared with radical feminist groups (Roth, 2003; Evans, 2003).

The *LHJ* protest was revisited in press coverage of the August issue of the magazine. The *New York Times* published a brief article at the end of July noting the appearance of the *LHJ* section ("Ladies' Journal Has 'Lib' Section," 1970), as did *Newsweek*, which reviewed the content of the special section in less than flattering terms, once again separating equal opportunity issues from the critique of sex roles: "the section includes the standard women's lib polemic on job discrimination and the inevitable group discussion of love and sex. The quality of the articles varies from a well-written exposition of women's education to a strangely paranoid first-person account of the dehumanizing experience of childbirth. Much of the writing is repetitive and uneven" ("Liberating the Journal," 1970, p. 44). The *Wall Street Journal* offered a front-page story in early August that opened with a recounting of the *LHJ* sit-in but went on to detail the battles of *LHJ* and *McCall's,* as the two top women's magazines, to respond to changing times while still attempting to satisfy their advertisers and their traditional audiences. The title of the article was a good indicator of its tone: "Keepers of the Faith: *Ladies' Home Journal, McCall's* Fight It out with Sugar and Spice. Both Skirt Controversy, Fill Pages with Lavish Photos, Irk Women's Lib Forces" (MacDougall, 1970).

In John Mack Carter's (1970b) introduction to the August *LHJ* special section, he asked readers to "let us know what you think" (p. 63), and the magazine published readers' responses in its November issue. A brief introduction to the page of letters noted that "our assessment thus far indicates 46 percent con, 34 percent pro, and 20 percent mixed (cheering equal pay, etc., but condemning 'far out antics')" ("Women's Lib and Me!," 1970, p. 69). The editors also noted that "there were about 25 subscription cancellations along with some 150 declarations from previous non-readers of their awakened interest in the magazine" ("Women's Lib and Me!," 1970, p. 69). The letters that the editors chose to print in the November issue ranged from completely dismissive to very supportive. They included those from women who defended their traditional choices ("Keep your cotton-pickin' hands off my shackles. I don't want to be liberated. I know a good thing when I see it, and I'm hanging onto it") as well as those from readers who claimed the special section "really just scratches the surface. . . . There's so much more . . . so much bitterness . . . so much frustration" ("Women's Lib and Me!," 1970, p. 69).

Consistent with the editors' pattern of separating equal opportunity demands from the radical critique of sex roles, several of the more positive letters echoed support for the expansion of choices for women in education and work. One wrote, "when you're a girl who gets straight A's and enjoys math and science, you learn about discrimination. Often it comes when you can't take a physics course because all girls are required to take home economics," while another noted that the bra-burning image is "scary," but that "the ideas of freedom of choice and equality of opportunity are very attractive to the other suburban mothers of Boston's North Shore to whom I've talked" ("Women's Lib and Me!," 1970, p. 69). A third observed that "some of the voices in the Women's Liberation movement seem a little strident" but nevertheless termed the "battle cries" for day care and equal pay and opportunity to "have much merit" ("Women's Lib and Me!," 1970, p. 69).

Despite their slant toward the less controversial equal opportunity facets of the special section, some of the printed letters indicated that the feminists' attempts to raise the consciousness of *LHJ* readers had hit fertile ground. One reader wrote of "the many quiet questionings of a way of life, the small searches for a neighbor to be honest with . . . [and] the thinking about one's situation" that occupied women who were not involved in the movement ("Women's Lib and Me!," 1970, p. 69). Her description was eerily similar to the way that movement members would describe their lives prior to joining a CR group (see DuPlessis and Snitow, 1998).

Even before November, however, the editorial content of *LHJ* began to show changes. In the second half of 1970, the magazine included unprecedented stories on topics such as sex, abortion, and how women could make extra money on the side. In the July issue, an article titled "Masters & Johnson: Their New Cures for Sex Problems" (Weber, 1970) discussed the work of the renowned sex researchers and focused primarily on barriers to women's sexual satisfaction, from premature ejaculation to difficulty achieving orgasm. Sex was discussed only within the context of marriage, but the article did contain some discussion of the problems of sex-role conditioning, noting that "guiding girls toward adulthood, determined to have them avoid promiscuity, unwanted pregnancy, and soiled reputations, many parents and other counselors have used fear techniques. And the 'well-trained' girl may carry her fears, often in subconscious form, right into her marriage" (Weber, 1970, p. 107). The same issue carried an article by Lawrence Ladner (1970), chairman of the National Association for the Repeal of Abortion Laws, titled "A National Guide to Legal Abortion," which contained a helpful chart of abortion laws in various states as well as a discussion of the progress of the repeal campaign across the country. The December *LHJ* included an article titled "Jesus and the Liberated Woman" by none other than Reverend Billy Graham (1970). Graham's argument that Christ truly intended women for home and hearth precipitated such an outpouring of response from *LHJ* readers, 60 percent of it negative according to the editors, that the magazine published two pages of the letters in its March 1971 issue ("Jesus & Women," 1971, p. 80).

The editors of *LHJ* clearly had concluded that continued attention to women's liberation was good business, an assessment encouraged by the movement's escalating visibility and growth over the course of 1970, and the magazine certainly would have begun addressing women's liberation sometime that year anyway. On the other hand, the content and valence of the magazine's attention to the movement might have been different absent the protest, and there is significantly less likelihood that *LHJ* would have given the kind of space to feminists that the special section provided. By 1972, *LHJ* had institutionalized a feminist voice, hiring one of the planners of the 1970 protest, Letty Cottin Pogrebin (who also would be one of the founding editors of *Ms.* magazine), to write a regular column titled "Working Woman" that would prove to be a skillful blend of feminist ideology and self-help (Dow, 1996).

The fact that *McCall's,* the only women's magazine with a higher circulation than *LHJ,* also began to devote editorial content to the movement was a sign that women's liberation was becoming a legitimate topic for women's magazines' editors who prided themselves on keeping up with the zeitgeist. *McCall's* editor Shana Alexander began her June editor's column with "Hard times, these, for women. Granny and teeny-bopper, bra-burner, working mother and happy housewife—all of us are caught up in the great wave of social change boiling up in America, and sometimes boiling over" (1970a, p. 12). In her July column, she obliquely addressed the sit-in by making the point that "19 of *McCall's* senior editors are women" and "65 percent of all *McCall's Magazine* employees, business as well as editorial, are female," neatly separating employment issues from critiques of magazine content, which she did not address (Alexander, 1970b, p. 8).

In that same issue, however, *McCall's* profiled "Five Passionate Feminists" (1970), among them Anne Koedt, a founder of NYRF and a participant in both the Miss America Pageant protest and the *LHJ* sit-in, and Ellen Willis, a founder of Redstockings. Its October 1970 issue carried an article by Gloria Steinem (1970d) titled "What 'Playboy' Doesn't Know about Women Could Fill a Book." By January 1971, *McCall's* was including a feature called "Right Now: A Monthly Newsletter for Women" that touched on issues raised by women's liberation, and the magazine soon gave Betty Friedan a regular column, Betty Friedan's Notebook. When Shana Alexander left the magazine in 1971, she was replaced by another woman, Pat Carbine, who would soon go on to be a cofounder and publisher of *Ms.* magazine, but not before Gloria Steinem had been named *McCall's* 1972 Woman of the Year (Zuckerman, 1998; "Woman of the Year: Gloria Steinem," 1972).

One less than predictable outcome at *LHJ* was the ascension of Lenore Hershey, John Mack Carter's second-in-command, to the editorship of the magazine upon Carter's departure. In her memoir, Hershey (1983) linked her decision to seek Carter's position to the "seismic effect" that the 1970 sit-in had on her (p. 82). In their accounts of the March action, participants variously described Hershey as an "Aunt Tom" who was "being used to divide the women" (Jay, 1970, p. 4), as a "tiger at the gate," as a "bear guarding her cub," (Brownmiller, 1999, p. 89), or as a "peach," who, by the end of the protest, "had undergone such a startling transformation that many of us would have been glad to see her get" Carter's job (Leone, 1993, p. 214). Hershey was clearly unenthusiastic at the day's beginning, plaintively asking "Why the *Journal*? Why us?" of the protestors (Jay, 1970, p. 4). By her own account, however, she eventually saw the protest's relevance for her own career choices. As she described it, when she was appointed as the magazine's representative to work with the feminists on the production of the August section, "for the first time in my life, I got the feel of what it was like to have control of a situation, to be in charge" (Hershey, 1983, p. 88). When Carter's job became available in 1973, she faced a choice: "I could either wait for another male to whom I could genuflect. Or I could strike out for the job myself" (Hershey, 1983, p. 91). In November 1973, Lenore Hershey was appointed as the sole editor-in-chief of *Ladies' Home Journal*, a position that had not been held by a woman in almost one hundred years.[12]

Aftermath: The *Ladies' Home Journal* Protest and the Movement

Some participants in the protest did not see the aforementioned outcomes as positive developments; indeed, some of them feared precisely what, to some extent, occurred: that their radical critique of content and employment practices would be ignored as *LHJ*'s management scrambled to redeem the magazine by hiring feminist writers. Certainly, the majority of Media Women's demands were not met, including the immediate replacement of Carter with a woman, and much of the magazine continued in its traditional patterns. Some participants who became detractors during and after the event detected a contradiction at the heart of the demands—were they about transforming the magazine or creating professional opportunities for the women involved in the protest?

The possibility that some feminists used movement activities to gain personal visibility or to enhance their own careers was a sore spot for radicals who believed that the movement's goal should be social transformation, not the improvement of the lives of individual women. As one participant, Ros Baxandall (1998), put it, "Our idea was to talk to the secretaries, try to get them to organize and confront their bosses about *Ladies' Home Journal*'s lack of relevance to women, including themselves. However, this demonstration was led by some of the new career types, who . . . didn't want to change *Ladies' Home Journal* in a major way; instead, they wanted to write feminist pieces for the magazine" (p. 222).

For many radicals, it was a sin to use the movement for personal gain, and they harshly censured women who were perceived to be using the movement to become "stars." Susan Brownmiller would become target of this charge at the Second Congress to Unite Women, held in early May, where she and another *LHJ* protest participant, Lucy Komisar, were denounced in a resolution that accused them of "seeking to rise to fame on the back of the women's movement by publishing articles in the establishment press" (Brownmiller, 1999, p. 98). A list of rules, designed to prevent the kind of personal visibility Brownmiller had achieved, was proposed for dealing with mass media. After discussion, the rules did not pass, but they revealed the intensity of feeling around the issue.

Among them were the following (quoted in Echols, 1989, p. 208): "No member of a group can appear as an independent feminist—whether for fame or money." "No individual or group can earn a living by writing or speaking about women's liberation." "Anyone who wants to write should write for the movement, not for the publishing industry." "Any individual who refuses collective discipline will be ostracized from the movement."

Such fallout from the *LHJ* action showed the fault lines lurking beneath the fragile coalition that had made the protest possible. For some radicals, any cooperation with mainstream media was selling out the collective, a stance that created an untenable position for feminists who worked as journalists and thought they could use their expertise to forward the movement while also making a living. The issue of personally profiting off the movement was raised repeatedly by the protest participants who discussed the *LHJ* sit-in in the feminist incarnation of *RAT* that had appeared after the January 1970 takeover. Karla Jay (1970) wrote, "We folded under the offer of a few goodies! Somewhere, despite all our good intentions, the action had become elitist. What good had we done? Aside from the publicity, which might succeed in awakening Middle Amerika to its hypocrisy and lies, we had succeeded only in getting Vassar girls higher paying jobs in publishing" (p. 22). Verna Tomasson (1970) was similarly disappointed, claiming that radicals like her had been used as a "back-up force to what had apparently turned into a group job interview," and she laid the fault at the feet of the leaders of Media Women, characterizing them as elitist and self-interested (p. 5).

Susan Brownmiller was generally cast as the overly ambitious villain by those who were unhappy with the outcome of the protest. While she specifically dismissed the accusation that she and other feminist journalists were job hunting during the sit-in, Brownmiller seemed ultimately pleased with the publicity that the events produced (especially because no one was arrested). In fact, the language she later used to describe her model for the action is telling: "From the lunch counters of Greensboro, 1960, to the occupation of Columbia, 1968, sit-ins had been an electrifying tactic in radical movements. I suggested we try one, knowing that we had a surefire story that would get major coverage if we pulled it off" (1999, p. 84). For Brownmiller, and presumably for other media-savvy working journalists in Media Women, the purpose was publicity, a chance to dramatically deliver their critique of *LHJ* not only to its editor-in chief but also to a collection of reporters. By her own account, she used her connections with New York–based reporters to make sure that elite media representatives would be there, and her desire for large numbers at the protest was about making sure it warranted coverage.

Some radicals who participated in the protest but who had not been active in the planning had a different vision of the goal for the action. Ros Baxandall, for example, claimed that she, Shulamith Firestone, and Ti-Grace Atkinson left the protest in disgust when they saw Media Women's leaders begin to negotiate with John Mack Carter for space in the magazine: "We had assumed the action would be a real takeover, just like the time we took over *RAT*. . . . We assumed that feminists would run the *Ladies' Home Journal* and change every aspect of the magazine. Our demand was for a new order, not for positions in the hierarchy" (1998, p. 222). Brownmiller (1999), in contrast, saw the defection of the three as a matter of personality, not politics, and later implied that Firestone and Atkinson, in particular, had left the protest because they failed to be the center of attention at a protest that they had not even planned.

In a striking understatement, Karla Jay (1999) would later observe, "the action highlighted some of the tensions and inconsistencies in the feminist community" (p. 119). Yet she also called the sit-in "without a doubt the most successful one-day action taken by the Women's Liberation Movement" (Jay, 1999, p. 120). Jay (1999) was quite astute about the costs and benefits of the protest, particularly in terms of the contradiction between its radical goals and its reformist tactics and results: "We started more and more to appeal to [Carter's] capitalist self-interest—how much money he would make on a women's liberation issue," and "we appealed to his bourgeois instincts instead of to our needs, demands, and revolutionary ideals" (p. 120).

Brownmiller and the other working journalists in Media Women, while they may well have been motivated by a desire to create opportunities for themselves as writers, were also no doubt realistic about the negligible chance that the feminists would actually be able to take over *LHJ*. As one protester later put it, *LHJ*'s agreement to publish the special section (not to mention paying $10,000 for it) was "a lot more victory than was strictly needed to get rid of us" (Leone, 1993, p. 216). In contrast, Ros Baxandall's analogy between the takeover of *RAT* and the *LHJ* action, while it serves as a revealing indicator of radical feminists' revolutionary fervor in 1970, seems naïve, given the differences between a tiny underground newspaper and a corporate-controlled commercial magazine with a circulation in the millions.

Had the feminists at the protest stuck to their guns and maintained an all-or-nothing approach to their demands, chances are that the day would have ended in a stalemate or that *LHJ* editors might have called the police to have them evicted. Instead, what eventually occurred can be seen as a textbook case of the radicals making the reformists seem reasonable, not only on the day of the protest, but in the changes in *LHJ* that followed.[13] Three accounts of the protest recount a moment, after Shulamith Firestone had to be restrained from top-pling John Mack Carter off his desk, that Ti-Grace Atkinson turned to Carter and said, "'If you don't deal with them [referring to the less confrontational demonstrators], you get us,'" and Karla Jay (1999) describes this as the moment that Carter began to negotiate (p. 119; see also Cohen, 1988, p. 193; Davis, 1991, p. 112). Moreover, not only did *LHJ*'s editors give a kind of imprimatur to equal opportunity demands in their discourse about the protest (selecting readers' letters that did the same), but the magazine would shortly contain articles that seemed directly inspired by the list of topics provided by the protesters. Thus, "at the same time that radical feminists and their often shocking pronouncements were marginalized, portions of their vision were folded into the mainstream, this reconfiguring what constituted the middle ground" (Douglas, 1994, p. 189). For some radicals, however, this was simply more evidence of the commercial co-optation of the movement.

Conclusion

By early 1971, *Newsweek* quoted John Mack Carter saying, "Some of the complaints about our magazines made by the women's lib types were right. There has been a lot of silliness cranked out to sell products and lifestyles to women, but it will never happen in this magazine again" ("Liberating the Magazines," 1971, p. 101). Women's liberation had indeed become hot stuff, and the considerable print and broadcast attention to the movement in the spring of 1970 set the stage for the success of the *LHJ* protest, dramatically increasing the odds that the magazine's editors, even while experiencing a very uncomfortable day on March 18, would recognize that they had more to gain than to lose from being the public target of feminist wrath. In purely financial terms, *LHJ* profited more than anyone else from the March 18 action, but the changes in the magazine—and others like it—that began to occur after the protest are difficult to dismiss as *only* co-optation, although they certainly were that. The editors of these magazines, while always cognizant of the limits imposed by their advertisers, and thus by what sells, also saw themselves as opinion leaders who took (a particular category of) women seriously as an audience, although they sometimes did so in visibly paternalistic ways. That characteristic alone makes these magazines different from other forms of mass media at the time.

Indeed, women's magazines ended up providing an outlet for feminist discourse that was not appearing elsewhere in mainstream mass media (Douglas and Michaels, 2005; Hunter, 1990). That *Ladies' Home Journal* and *McCall's* both gave regular columns to feminists by 1972 is one example of this outcome, and the August special section's dissemination of movement thinking to a new audience is another. Oddly enough, the list of contacts for feminist groups included in the section proved to be an unexpected aid to the U.S. government as well as a stimulus for movement membership. By late 1970, "the White House received an average of three letters a week from women who wanted to know how they could join a women's liberation group" (Freeman, 1975, p. 231). The requests were referred to the Women's Bureau, which used the list in the August 1970 *LHJ* as one resource for answering them. Finally, the attention that publications such as *LHJ* and *McCall's* gave to women's liberation helped to prove that feminist content could be used to sell magazines, thus smoothing the path for the creation of *Ms.* magazine in 1972.

The events of March 18 proved to have a far-reaching impact on mass media co-optation and commodification of the movement, but radicals who blamed that outcome on the motives and influence of particular feminists personalized a multidimensional and overdetermined phenomenon. Women's service magazines inevitably would have brought their self-help–self-improvement philosophy to bear on issues raised by women's liberation, although their efforts were accelerated by the *LHJ* protest. Most compelling to me are the ways that the timing of the protest, the emphases of its national print and broadcast coverage, and the response of *LHJ* itself functioned collectively to produce a set of meanings and implications for the events of March 18, 1970.

On the one hand, Marlene Sanders's ABC story achieved her goal of depicting feminists as thoughtful women with a reasonable grievance: Women were underrepresented as employees in a magazine that ostensibly was geared toward women's interests. Unlike the print stories, Sanders did not portray the protestors as militant or unruly, and her story was as much or more about the issues (at least those she selected to emphasize) as it was the event, an unusual outcome for national media treatment of feminist protest. On the other hand, Sanders's choice to highlight equal opportunity in employment as the sit-in's central issue elided many other issues raised by the protest—for example, the lack of black women at *LHJ* as well as the pointed critique of magazine content. In short, Sanders's solution to resolving the private-public and personal-political dichotomies that plagued media representations of the movement was to accede to dominant notions of what "counted" as sex discrimination—and thus as actionable issues—and to do so in the narrowest possible way.

Although Sanders might be faulted for limiting the import of the protest, she was not working alone on this front, and the *LHJ* case exemplifies the importance of context in understanding the rhetorical work done by media representations of the second wave. The print stories also gave credence to the employment focus, and, even within reports that stressed the protestors' deviance and dis-orderliness, women's underrepresentation and underemployment in media jobs were presented as fact. As the year wore on, and grievances by women employees of media industries continued to stack up and to get media attention, the equal opportunity frame would gain additional strength, aided by *LHJ*'s own approving treatment of workplace-related issues. Seen in such a context, the large amount of radical feminist discourse disseminated by the special section in the August *LHJ* should be understood as a somewhat remarkable intervention into this developing public narrative of feminism.

By the time the August *LHJ* appeared, Sanders's May documentary had given her another chance to offer her vision of the movement. In the longer format allowed by the documentary, she did not simply eliminate radical arguments, as she had in the March report; rather, she incorporated them into a carefully structured and strategic narrative that would both account for and then skillfully *dis*count the salience of radical feminist ideology. The *LHJ* report foreshadowed Sander's commitment to the equality narrative that would emerge with even greater force in the documentary, but the latter was a much more complex and considered rhetorical text that would feature the most expansive, most persua-sive, and most problematic deployment of the sex-race analogy that national broadcast media would offer in 1970.

CHAPTER 4

Fixing the Meaning of the Movement

ABC's May 1970 "Women's Liberation" Documentary

The most success for the movement will come in the areas where the
movement is making specific requests, such as legislation to end
discrimination in jobs and wages.

—Marlene Sanders, interviewed in the *Daily Tarheel*,
student newspaper at the University of North Carolina
at Chapel Hill (McCall, 1970)

Early in May 1970, a secretary at *Playboy* magazine discovered a recent memo by publisher Hugh Hefner in which he addressed a controversy among *Playboy*'s editorial staff, several of whom were women, over an article the magazine had commissioned on women's liberation. Not yet published, the article focused on the extremism of groups such as Redstockings and W.I.T.C.H. It "warned that the revolution's 'battleground will be the business, home, and bed of every man in the country,'" and it was perceived by some editors as insufficiently balanced and objective because it was overfocused on the "radical fringe" of women's liberation (Pitzulo, 2011, p. 142). In Hefner's memo, he affirmed that he was "interested in the highly irrational, emotional, kookie trend that feminism has taken in the last couple of years" (quoted in Pitzulo, 2011, p. 142). The *Playboy* secretary leaked the memo to women's liberation groups in Chicago, and excerpts from it eventually appeared in a Chicago newspaper as well as in *Time* magazine. They included Hefner's claim that "these chicks are our natural enemy" and "it is time to do battle with them. . . . What I want is a devastating piece that takes the militant feminists apart. [They are] unalterably opposed to the romantic boy-girl society that *Playboy* promotes. . . . Let's get to it and let's make it a real winner" ("Male and Female," 1970, p. 74).[1]

The sentiments Hefner expressed rang true for many feminists as representative of the attitude that they believed prevailed among the men who ran most media organizations. Marlene Sanders, whose documentary about women's liberation would appear on ABC a few weeks after Hefner's memo made the news, was no exception. One of only two female national correspondents for ABC and an early member of NOW, Sanders saw her report as an intervention into the dismissive news coverage the movement had received as a result of the attitudes of men like Hefner. In her memoir of her career, her rationale for the documentary was that "the emerging women's movement needed straightforward television coverage instead of ridicule," and she noted that early reporting on the movement "was done mainly by men" who treated women's liberation "with humor at best, and contempt at worst" (Sanders and Rock, 1988, p. 117). Recalling the 1969 granting of approval for the project by ABC's director of public affairs, Tom Wolf, Sanders called him "a man ahead of his time," implying that *most* men would not have been supportive (Sanders and Rock, 1988, p. 117).

Yet by the time the "Women's Liberation" documentary aired on May 25, 1970, as part of ABC's documentary series titled *NOW*, the recent explosion of attention to women's liberation in both print and broadcast venues meant that ABC was unlikely to be accused of giving extended time to an issue that no one cared about, a concern for a reporter who needed to be seen as objective and not as an advocate.[2] For example, when discussing her *LHJ* story, Sanders noted her relief that "the sit-in was also covered by the wire services and the major New York dailies. . . . If we had been the only major outlet with the story it would have been taken less seriously. Television news management at the time tended still to be print-oriented, believing that if print didn't have it, our exclusive might not be trustworthy" (Sanders and Rock, 1988, pp. 116–117).

Thus, for someone like Sanders, who sympathized with the movement and thought that it had been poorly represented in media reports, the opportunity presented by the documentary came with certain constraints. She clearly saw it as a chance to correct misimpressions about the movement and to improve its public image, but being known as a sympathizer by her colleagues in the news business heightened the need to project fairness and objectivity in the program. Susan Brownmiller, for example, recalled Sanders's attempts to recruit her to NOW during the days when Brownmiller worked as a newswriter at ABC. She noted that Sanders did so quietly, by simply dropping flyers on her desk, and she described the reporter as "muffled by the objectivity that newspeople are supposed to live by" (Brownmiller, 1999, p. 4).

In fact, when *TV Guide*'s May 23, 1970, issue described the "Women's Liberation" documentary in one of the Close-Up boxes used to highlight noteworthy programming, it included the following line: "Marlene Sanders (a working mother), produced, wrote, and narrated this report" (1970, p. A-35). At no point in the documentary did Sanders mention anything about her personal life, and the knowledge that she was a "working mother" had to have been derived from another source. The mention of this bit of personal information about Sanders in *TV Guide* suggests suspicion about her potentially self-interested point of view, especially given that the description went on to note that one of the topics discussed in the documentary was the need for day care centers. Certainly, some members of the movement saw Sanders as a comrade: Brownmiller (1999) termed her "a one-woman corrective in television" (1999, p. 140), and lesbian feminist Rita Mae Brown (1997) called Sanders "one of the best reporters in the business" who "actually understood the issues" (p. 237). Yet, almost twenty years after the fact, Sanders still couched her motivations in terms of standard reportorial concerns—for example, doing the story right and doing it first: "while the women's movement was making news in bits and pieces, it warranted in-depth attention. The one thing a television documentary could do was to put the parts together and see what it meant" (Sanders and Rock, 1988, p. 117).

The program Sanders would produce was not only the longest unified narrative about women's liberation to be broadcast in 1970, it also stands as 1970's preeminent example of self-consciously sympathetic reporting on women's liberation by a journalist who sought to package the movement in a fashion that would make its claims seem reasonable. To do so, Sanders narrowed the movement's meaning considerably, edging lesbians, women of color, and the movement's most radical implications out of the camera's eye while putting the ERA front and center. "Women's Liberation" brought the movement squarely into a liberal frame that relied heavily on a race-sex analogy, illustrating the profound inadequacies of the comparison as well as the limits of liberalism itself for encompassing feminism's complexity in 1970.

Sanders's own ultimate assessment of the documentary was that it "served as a primer, exploring the goals of the bra-less campus radicals as well as the more socially acceptable feminist theoreticians" (Sanders and Rock, 1988, p. 117). Yet it did far more than introduce its audience to the various goals of the movement; rather, it attempted to reshape the public identity of women's liberation so that it might be taken as seriously as those movements for social justice that had preceded it. Three crucial rhetorical strategies contributed toward this end, the first of which was its highly conventional documentary form. "Women's Liberation" eschewed any innovative aesthetic techniques; closely resembled, both verbally and visually, a traditional, if lengthy, news story; and hewed closely to the codes of realism and objectivity that distinguish expository documentary. Second, Sanders's framing discourse, most evident in her introductory and concluding remarks as well as in her frequent use of voice-over narration, did a great deal of interpretive work for the viewer and signaled her embrace of the rhetorical license offered by the documentary form. She used that license to construct a powerful, and powerfully reductive, analogy between feminism and black civil rights.

Finally, although Sanders claimed to offer a primer, a *first* attempt to explain what the movement meant, viewing the documentary as a *response* to the wave of media attention that preceded it is far more illuminating. An implicit refutation strategy permeates "Women's Liberation," and reading it as a refutative text elucidates the key role that imagined white male spectators played in its rhetorical design as well as highlights the centrality of a white, heterosexual, evolutionary liberalism to the documentary's overall logic. Uniting all of these strategies was the attempt to "fix" feminism, in multiple senses of the word. Sanders not only attempted to repair the image of women's liberation, she also endeavored to stabilize its meaning, to establish a unitary *telos* for it, and to give it a narrative coherence that had thus far been lacking in media representations.

The Rhetoric of Form

Film and television theorists have long argued that documentary serves as a vehicle for social commentary, making it inherently rhetorical and political. In the 1930s, John Grierson argued that documentary's "creative treatment of actuality" must have a social purpose (quoted in Plantinga, 1997, p. 27), a position echoed by William Bluem in his *Documentary in American Television* (1965). Bill Nichols (1991) has claimed that argument is central to documentary, and Carl Plantinga (1997) has written of documentary's "assertive" stance, arguing that it is fundamentally rhetorical (p. 17). Such characteristics can be articulated in a number of ways, and documentarians have developed a wide variety of approaches to their subject matter, ranging from traditionally journalistic form to uses of direct cinema and cinema verité techniques to self-conscious employment of dramatic narrative (Curtin, 1993; Hammond, 1981).

The form of "Women's Liberation," however, was quite conventional and journalistic, reflecting documentary's expository mode, the dominant trend in television documentaries at the end of the 1960s (Nichols, 1991). Expository documentary is the most epistemologically naïve—and the most common—mode of the genre; it privileges realism and "emphasizes the impression of objectivity" (Nichols, 1991, p. 35). In this sense, objectivity is a rhetorical stance, a particular mode of reasoning and presentation, rather than a "representation-free point of view" (Plantinga, 1997, p. 30). Achieving absolute correspondence with a preexisting reality is epistemologically impossible; on the other hand, journalistic discourse uses codes or strategies that foster the appearance of objectivity, and such tactics were easily visible in "Women's Liberation."

The documentary was structured topically; there were seven segments, and the movement from one to another was signaled by Sanders's verbal transitions, which used a "voice of God" style of narration to offer commonsensical descrip-tion of what the viewer saw or was about to see. The segments described the major concerns of the movement: those she specifically linked to radical groups (socialization and the sexual objectification of women); those she specifically linked to reformist groups (employment opportunity, pay equity, and the ERA); and those that she claimed united all feminists (abortion rights). Within most of the segments, images of events and activities were juxtaposed with brief in-terviews with participants and observers that functioned to assess or evaluate what the viewer saw. In a couple of cases, Sanders used one of the most com-mon objectivity codes: the presentation of commentary by two persons with differing points of view on an issue.

Sanders's was the only voice to directly address the camera or the viewer, and she retained epistemic privilege throughout. Although her interviews in-cluded those easily categorized as experts, such as former NOW president Betty Friedan or Senator Birch Bayh, as well as those who were either participants in women's liberation activities or merely observers of it, all of these interviewees spoke to Sanders, not to the camera itself. Typical of expository documentary, this approach weaves such voices "into a textual logic that subsumes and or-chestrates them" and in which they "provide evidence or substantiation for what the commentary addresses" (Nichols, 1991, p. 37).

The structure of the segments in the documentary followed a pattern in which Sanders introduced an issue and provided a brief orientation to it (matching her introductory words with a standard establishing shot of a locale), followed by a few minutes of unnarrated camera work that supported her contention and created the impression that she was simply presenting "events, or situations [that] actually occur or exist in the actual world as portrayed" (Plantinga, 1997, p. 18). When she interviewed participants or observers, these interviews were filmed in conventional style with the speakers positioned as talking heads in medium shots. The documentary as a whole was governed by "word logic," within which arguments are propositional and linear, major contentions are expressed by the reporter in direct address to the audience, and images offer visual support for verbal arguments (Bluem, 1965, p. 123).

Because such strategies were typical for news specials, news magazines, and short-form documentaries by the end of the 1960s, adhering so closely to them functioned strategically to accomplish one of Sanders's stated goals: to give women's liberation the treatment that any other hard news story deserved and to avoid the irony and ridicule that she believed had characterized earlier coverage. Sanders's approach reflected NOW's media pragmatism, which viewed "media, especially the national, elite news media, as a powerful movement resource" that could be used to give the public "an 'honest' picture of the movement" (Barker-Plummer, 1995, p. 312). The utter conventionality of the documentary's structure was part of its overall refutative design: It implicitly asserted that women's liberation was a legitimate story that could and should be made credible and compelling within dominant representational practices. As Nichols (1991) observes, "attaching a particular text to a traditional mode of representation and to the discursive authority of that tradition may well strengthen its claims, lending to these claims the weight of previously established legitimacy" (p. 34). This formal grounding was crucial to the documentary's central framing strategy: its analogy between the claims of women's liberation and those of black civil rights.

The Sex-Race Analogy

Framed by Sanders's narration, "Women's Liberation" performed extensive rhetorical work under the guise of making commonsensical "claims about the 'real'" (Plantinga, 1997, p. 38). Sanders exploited every opportunity for direct address of the viewer, "moving the text forward in service of its persuasive needs" (Nichols, 1991, p. 34–35). She spoke directly to the camera in the stand-ups that opened and closed the half hour; she provided voice-over narration introducing each discrete segment of the program (establishing relevance and comparing or contrasting to what had gone before); and she introduced and credentialed her interviewees. Her discourse performed the conventional function of framing: "to define particular aspects of reality in ways that support specific social interests within the field of public discourse" and to shape "the symbolic platform on which members of society think and talk about public issues" (Tucker, 1998, p. 143).

Two framing strategies dominated the narrative Sanders developed, and both were signaled in her opening commentary: first, her emphasis on the geographical, ideological, and political diversity of the women's liberation movement, and second, her attempt to situate the movement within the general climate of protest well known to television audiences by 1970. The latter strategy grew more dominant and more specific as the documentary proceeded. These were normalizing frames; they attempted to make women's liberation less frightening by demonstrating that its adherents were not limited to a radical fringe, and, more importantly, they positioned the women's movement as a natural outgrowth of the questioning of social and political inequality connected to black civil rights struggles.

Both the opening and the closing shots of the documentary focused on Sanders sitting on a stone bench in front of a fountain in what appeared to be a campus setting (likely University of North Carolina [UNC] or Duke, locations where she had filmed parts of the documentary the previous month). Using the by now familiar device of linking the first and second waves of feminism, she addressed the camera as follows:

> Fifty years ago, women got the vote. It was a bitter battle, but an easy goal to explain. Today, the things women want are more complex. Those involved in what has come to be known as the women's liberation movement do not necessarily agree on all of the objectives. But there is a serious questioning of the role of woman in our society. And the rhetoric of the civil rights movement has been contagious. The word "equality" is powerful.

Sanders accomplished a great deal of rhetorical work in a few seconds here. She connected women's liberation to the first wave of feminism while explicitly noting that the second wave had a greater rhetorical burden: Its issues were more diverse and feminists did not agree on all of them. This argument required a significant amount of historical erasure, as the first wave took on many more issues than simply gaining the franchise and it had its share of conflicts. But that erasure worked toward a rhetorical purpose: warning the viewer that women's liberation was harder to understand, and that what followed would reflect that. Her other connecting move, toward the civil rights movement, bolstered the credibility of women's liberation by giving it a place alongside other contemporary movements combating discrimination.

These two themes, the diversity of the movement and its connections to what was usually called "the black movement" or "black power" in the documentary, consistently recurred in Sanders's commentary and in the evidence she marshaled to support it. For example, she introduced the first segment, focusing on sex-role conditioning, as follows: "In big cities as well as on hundreds of college campuses, groups of women have joined the movement. Their numbers are increasing." Sander's words were accompanied by an establishing shot of the UNC campus that narrowed to focus on a poster advertising a women's liberation rally. A focus on UNC was strategic in itself—a southern campus, far from a major city, the active presence of women's liberation there demonstrated the geographical reach of the movement as well as featured an ostensibly organic feminism unconnected to the urban radicalism prominent in earlier network coverage.

The unnarrated film's focus then shifted to the advertised rally, where UNC feminists acted out a scenario dramatizing gender socialization. In the scene, an adolescent girl repudiated her doll and attempted to play with her brother's truck, asking why she could not wear pants, only to be reprimanded by her mother and informed that "little boys wear pants. Little girls wear dresses and keep their skirts down." Another sketch that followed depicted a young woman at a job interview. Though she listed her graduate degrees and academic honors, her interviewer asked only if she could type and make coffee. Such "guerilla theater," which first gained notice at the Miss America Pageant protest in 1968, was a common CR device of radical feminists that also made for good television. Sanders chose to include two scenes that were supportive of the liberal feminist goals that would ultimately dominate the documentary: both showed women frustrated by refusals to give them opportunities that their male counterparts enjoyed.

When Sanders interviewed a male spectator after the performance, he supported the connection of women's liberation to other movements: "I think it was a good show. I think it points out, maybe in a comical fashion, the real issues

Figure 8. ABC publicity photo for Sanders's documentary. The caption for the photo read: "Members of 'Women's Liberation No. 27' in North Carolina explain the symbolic chains that bind women for ABC News Correspondent Marlene Sanders." © American Broadcasting Companies, Inc.

behind this movement. And the issues are very real—they correlate somewhat to the black revolution and the youth revolution." Importantly, a man made this supportive connection between feminism and other movements. For purposes of objectivity, this affirming reaction was followed by a brief interview with another male spectator, more skeptical of claims for discrimination, who claimed, "if a woman really wants to be free, she may be." In standard expository style, this initial segment established context with visuals and narration, offered footage of an event, and closed with differing reactions to that event.

The opening segment not only worked to establish Sanders's objectivity, it also furthered the connection to civil rights. Lest the point be lost, when she moved to a segment on abortion activism in New York, Sanders again situated women's activism within the familiar practices of social protest. As the viewer saw large numbers of women marching down a city street, holding signs, and chanting "Free abortion on demand, sisterhood is powerful," she said: "Marches, sit-ins, confrontations. All are part of protest in America today."

After Sanders established abortion rights as a unifying goal for both the reformist and radical wings of the movement, viewers saw footage of a woman speaking to an abortion rally. Her words to the crowd reiterated the feminism–civil rights analogy:

> "We've learned an awful lot from the black movement and what it's done in the last ten years. We know that we've got to use every forum. Okay, so we've been trying in the legislature and we've been failing. But even *they've* heard us now. They just can't ignore the fact that we're all here. And we're trying the courts, and damn it, y'know, we're in the streets!

This segment fed Sanders's pragmatic goals in two key ways. First, in a classic example of the visual supporting verbal claims, the camera work showed the sheer numbers and diversity of women behind this issue—data for her claim that abortion rights were a "unifying goal" for the movement's diverse groups. It also included several shots of women carrying babies—a subtle argument that abortion supporters were not necessarily antifamily or antichild. Second, in a rhetorical move that functioned to justify feminist protest tactics, viewers heard the young woman at the abortion rally argue that, like blacks, when women's attempts to use conventional channels for social change were unsuccessful, they would take to the streets to dramatize their demands.

This strategy of analogizing women and blacks reached its peak in the final segment of the documentary, which focused on the ERA. As was the case in Aline Saarinen's NBC story, locating this issue last in the program's narrative underscored Sanders's implicit contention that the amendment was the logical policy solution to the problems laid out earlier. Tellingly, this segment came on the heels of the program's focus on feminist activism concerning employment and equal pay issues. That penultimate segment showcased the formation of the Professional Women's Caucus, and Sanders introduced it as follows: "Professional women are taking the battle off the streets, away from the campuses, and into the Congress and the courts. Members of the academic, professional, and business world met recently in New York to form a Professional Women's Caucus. The basic reason? Only 1 percent of all working women in the United States earn ten thousand dollars a year or more." She followed this introduction with additional evidence of inequality in wages, and viewers then saw footage of a lawyer offering yet more statistical proof of discrimination to a rapt audience of watching women.

Thus, before Sanders even mentioned the ERA, she had taken care to establish the grounds for its necessity, using the least controversial rationale: workplace inequality. Visual effects were crucial to the rhetorical impact of this move: the camera's pan in this segment showed a group of primarily middle-class, middle-aged, professionally coiffed and clothed white women, the standard visual codes for reformist feminists. The contrast to the groups of students and protesters seen earlier was hard to miss, and this image signaled the completed transition in the documentary's evolutionary narrative. That transition—from radicalism to liberalism, from youth to maturity, and from socialization to legislation—simply had to be solidified in the documentary's final segment.

Preceding a segment on the ERA with information on pay discrimination was a strategic move, an attempt to present the amendment as a solution to a concrete and easily comprehended social ill. Yet, the ERA would not have done more to ameliorate employment and pay inequity than had already been legislated by the Equal Pay Act of 1963 or by Title VII of the Civil Rights Act, which prohibited job discrimination on the basis of sex (although legal battles over the interpretation and enforcement of these measures was ongoing in 1970). In her account of the ERA's defeat, Jane Mansbridge (1986) bluntly noted that the amendment "would have had almost no effect on the gap between women's and men's wages" (p. 36). This reality did not stop ERA advocates from emphasizing pay equity, and "equal pay for equal work" would become a primary rationale for the ERA in the discourse of its supporters in the 1970s.

In the documentary's final segment on the ERA, the civil rights analogy was given additional weight by a white male U.S. senator. In a standard interview set-up (the interviewee behind a desk, the reporter facing him with her back to the camera in a medium shot) that appeared to take place in his office in Washington, D.C, Sanders interviewed Indiana Senator Birch Bayh, the chairman of the hearings on the Equal Rights Amendment that had begun earlier in May:

> SANDERS: Most people assume that women already have full equality under the law. The 1964 Civil Rights Act banned discrimination on the basis of sex, but discrimination does not end by decree alone. Forty-seven years ago, an Equal Rights Amendment to the Constitution was proposed but never passed. Senator Birch Bayh was chairman of the most recent hearings on the Constitutional Amendment and he told me what it would accomplish.
>
> BAYH: It would do the same thing for women as was done for Negroes after the Civil War when we amended the constitution and said that no one should have their rights abridged because of race, color, or creed. We would just merely say "or sex."

Bayh went on to occupy a larger speaking role in the documentary than anyone except for Sanders herself. He spoke for virtually the entirety of the ERA segment, during which he gave examples of several state laws that discriminated against women and that would be eradicated by the ERA.

At the end of the interview, in the last discourse in the documentary before Sander's closing comments, Bayh reiterated the liberal goals of the ERA (and, by implication, of feminism itself) and closed with the rhetoric of choice and equal opportunity:

> I think many people can and have wrongly interpreted the women's liberation movement or whatever you want to call it. None of us who are concerned about this discrimination feel that it's our responsibility to tell a woman what she should do—whether she should work or go to school or raise a family. This is none of our responsibility in government. But I think it is our responsibility in government to give all of our citizens, whether they are male or female, black, white, yellow or brown, the opportunity to utilize their total talents as they want to use them to the ultimate of their abilities.

In the climactic segment of the documentary, then, the analogy to civil rights occurred twice. First came Bayh's reference to the Reconstruction Amendments (a comparison that hardly boded well for the efficacy of the ERA given the problematic enforcement history of those amendments, not to mention the fact that they were designed to guarantee rights to black *men* but not black *women*). Second, in his final sentence, Bayh again compared (white) women with those who faced discrimination based on skin color. Coming from a respected U.S. senator, who took it upon himself to counter misinterpretations of women's liberation, the expression of this ultimate rationale for the amendment's necessity was a powerful culmination of the documentary's refutative form.

The analogy to black civil rights—and to the tactics of the civil rights movement—that recurred in the "Women's Liberation" documentary was a legitimation strategy, one that had already appeared in various news media treatments of the movement. The NBC series on women's liberation had used the strategy in a truncated fashion, but it was far more developed in "Women's Liberation," an indication of Sanders's own political sympathies as well as of key shifts in the developing public memory of the civil rights movement. By 1970, the legitimacy offered by the sexism-racism analogy had spread beyond leftist circles. The successes of the civil rights movement; the discourses and the deaths of Martin Luther King Jr., Malcolm X, and Robert Kennedy; and the public embrace of moderate civil rights ideals by three presidents—one of them posthumously made a martyr to it—had given claims about racism powerful legitimacy with the public at large.[3] As Catherine Stimpson (1988) has observed,

> The civil rights movement scoured a rusty national conscience. Moral and political struggle against a genuine domestic evil became respectable again. . . . Confrontation politics became middle class again as the movement helped to resurrect the appealing American tradition of rebellion. The real domino theory deals with the delusions of contentment. Once these delusions are exposed for one group, they tend to be obvious for others. . . . Being treated like Blacks became proof of exploitation. (pp. 32–33)

And, just like the civil rights movement, women's liberation had its radical and its reformist elements and its youthful and its professional factions, who worked together on some issues and were at odds over others.

Most importantly, just as was the case with civil rights, it was the reformist, legalistic, and/or legislative solutions that ultimately were rhetorically presented by dominant media as the most sensible and viable; indeed, the rising visibility of the Black Panthers in 1970, and their depiction in white media as "violent, anti-social thugs," made the nonviolent civil rights movement seem an increasingly attractive model (Rhodes, 2007, p. 300). Sanders's utilization of the feminism–civil rights analogy was fully in line with the goals and media strategy of NOW, an organization that attempted to borrow "the rhetoric and moral authority of the Civil Rights movement" and that had put the ERA at the top of its list in the "Bill of Rights" written at its first national conference in 1967 (Barker-Plummer, 2002, p. 198; "NOW Bill of Rights," 1970).

That the "Women's Liberation" documentary concluded with a segment on the ERA, a segment built around an interview with a white male senator discussing the need for a constitutional amendment that would guarantee equality under the law, just as the Constitution had done for blacks, was powerful proof of Sanders's adherence to NOW's media pragmatism strategy and of her commitment to the liberal ideology of the expository documentary. She fulfilled the typical expectation of viewers that such texts will "take shape around the solution to a problem or puzzle" (Nichols, 1991, p. 38). Despite its tour through both liberal and radical feminist activity, the documentary built toward the demonstration of clearly identifiable, statistically verifiable gender discrimination—the kind that could be remedied by legislation designed to level the playing field.

Sanders's concluding remarks that followed the ERA segment made this even more apparent. In them, she implied that, when the radicalism of the movement was spent, it was the demands based in equality—those capable of being met within the system—that would endure:

> The women's liberation movement will not disappear after the singing, march-ing, and shouting have died down. Man himself may not be the enemy, but his practices are under attack, whether they are motivated by prejudice, profit, or habit. This is a search for equality of opportunity, not the wish to be just like men. It is the desire for more options, for choice, for a shattering of stereotypes. For women to choose more freely the kinds of lives that they want to live, and if we choose to work, to be paid in full. The status quo is being challenged by the women's liberation movement. Today, it's still a man's world—and just look at it. Move over, gentlemen—maybe you can use some help.

From her opening statement, which claimed that the second wave, in compari-son to the first, was "more complex" and harder to explain, Sanders had moved to a position in her conclusion, thirty minutes later, in which the second wave's complexity had been reduced and its meaning had stabilized around the liberal mantras of choice and equality of opportunity (for which the only concrete ex-ample was being "paid in full" for work).

This accomplishment required invoking a nostalgic, oversimplified vision of the civil rights movement, one in which that movement was only about equality under the law and in which it had been successfully concluded at this point in 1970 so that it could be used as a model for feminism. This perspective erased ongoing activism by groups such as the Black Panther Party and assumed that goals such as voting rights and the elimination of Jim Crow composed the entire agenda of the civil rights movement. Likewise, Sanders's framing relied on a narrow vision of women's liberation in which the work of the first wave merely had to be completed by passing the ERA, which, she noted, was first introduced in 1923 (interestingly, the documentary's subtitle, spoken by an announcer after the *NOW* opening credits but not seen on screen, was "The Unfinished Revolu-tion of American Women.")

In this version of feminism, there were no lesbians and no women of color, and many of the issues raised by radical factions—the issues that most afflicted the movement's image—would be recast in personal, rather than political terms, as I discuss shortly. If a crucial aspect of Sanders's media pragmatism was to legitimize the goals of the movement by analogizing them to a romantic memory of civil rights, then an equally important task was to convince those who feared feminist radicalism that they had, as Senator Bayh put it, "wrongly interpreted the women's liberation movement."

Men and the Movement

Sander's last sentence in her closing, "Move over, gentlemen," was offered somewhat humorously, cushioned by her smile and the subtle joke that preceded it. Yet this comment also explicitly marked a presumed male audience for the documentary, and it was not the only aspect of the program that indicated Sanders's concern with men's reaction to the movement. Men were the presumed audience for most news discourse, as the skepticism and spectacle that characterized some previous print and broadcast treatment of the movement reflected. Sanders, in contrast, took feminists very seriously: She interviewed them and marshaled visual and verbal evidence to support their claims. At the same time, however, she took the presumed male spectator for the documentary quite seriously as well, particularly in terms of implicitly recognizing the gender anxiety provoked by feminism's claims.

The documentary presumed an audience deeply concerned about the movement's implications for men, and Sanders worked hard at refuting the widespread belief that feminists hated men or that the movement was necessarily bad for men. This emphasis was very much within the bounds of media pragmatism that NOW advocated—unlike radical feminist groups, NOW welcomed male members, hence the careful wording of its name as the National Organization *for* Women, rather than the National Organization *of* Women. Given NOW's orientation toward legislative and legal reform, and given the gender composition of courts and legislative bodies at both state and national levels, reducing hostility from men was only sensible. In addition, NOW (and Sanders, too) wanted the support of moderate women, and the organization eschewed linking feminism to extremism of any sort, recognizing that many of the women it wanted as members were unwilling to be perceived as man-haters.

The refutative strategy began early in the documentary and was introduced, as always, by Sanders herself: "Some men view the women's liberation movement with scorn or amusement. The rhetoric is sometimes strident and men often feel threatened by it. But these members of a group at the University of North Carolina and nearby Duke are married, and several have children. They're militant, but Linda Fisher told me she thinks there's something in the movement for men." This opening contained an example of an effective, if logically flawed, rhetorical strategy: feminists cannot really hate men, because many of them are married and have children (within this logic, one would have to accept that there are no married misogynists).

Adhering to the documentary's expository structure, Fisher's commentary that followed supported Sanders's expressed claim about the movement's benefits for men:

> The very first thing is that men will no longer have to be solely responsible for the financial health of their family; they don't have to get ulcers and other things because they're the only wage earners. If a woman follows her desires throughout life and if that desire happens to be to work, to have a career, or simply to work at a job that she enjoys, then any given man that she is married to does not have to feel the sole responsibility for taking care of her then, and later on, if say the marriage breaks up, as under the law now he's responsible. The other thing things that he has to gain have to do with emotional needs. A lot of men have said "I wish I could cry," but they're long past learning how because they've spent so long believing that it's inappropriate.

Although Sanders called her militant, Fisher's arguments represented conventional liberal feminist reasoning: Men would be liberated from their own restrictive gender roles that required financial responsibility and emotional inaccessibility. A radical feminist analysis would point out that this outcome represented more than relief from responsibility; it would also mean the relinquishment of *power*. The absence of such analysis underscored the inherently liberal tone of the documentary, one that posited that men simply needed to be enlightened about the rewards they would reap from women's liberation.

A more radical analysis of the relations between men and women was voiced in a later segment, one that Sanders introduced as an exploration of conflict within the movement. As the camera panned over the shelves of a bookstore, focusing on the variety of titles addressing different aspects of women's liberation, Sanders noted, "There are many ideological battles being waged among the various factions. A vast outpouring of literature on 'the woman question' has appeared since 1963, when Betty Friedan's *The Feminine Mystique* signaled the revival of the feminist movement." In what followed, four interviewees purportedly answered the question "Who is the enemy?" that Sanders posited as central to the movement. Yet only Betty Friedan appeared to find it important enough to address it directly, as she seized the opportunity to counter the perception that feminists saw *men* as the enemy.

What follows is a near complete transcript of the remainder of the segment, edited only for repetition and to omit paralanguage. The camera work in each interview was virtually the same—each speaker focused her remarks at Sanders while facing the camera, and each was framed in a medium shot. After Sanders's introductory words, there was no verbal transitional discourse separating the interviews, although Sanders inserted a short identifying statement for each woman after she began to speak:

SANDERS: More radical voices have been raised since then [1963]. The question of "Who is the enemy?" gets varied responses, like this one from a member of The Feminists.

MEMBER OF THE FEMINISTS: The purpose of women's liberation . . . is to liberate women. I mean, we see rape as a[n] integral part of a terrorist activity to keep women down. (*Insert from Sanders: "What about marriage?"*). Well, marriage, as I've said, is unpaid labor . . . it's a free household slave for each man.

PAT SCULLEY: Well, we can't take that position because so many of us are married . . . (*voice-over from Sanders: "Pat Sculley, student"*). We don't see many viable options to marriage in this society, and we also think that marriage meets some important human needs for intimacy . . . and prevents loneliness and things like that. And there aren't any viable alternatives. Even if we criticize marriage, it's got to be in a constructive way in terms of thinking of new institutions this society needs and new values people have to have relating to marriage.

MARY ALICE WATERS: Society would have to take major collective responsibility for the care and the raising of children . . . (*voice-over from Sanders: "Mary Alice Waters, editor of* The Militant). There would have to be a provision made for twenty-four hour daycare/childcare centers controlled by the people who use them, to make sure that women are able to leave the home, that they aren't tied to their children twenty-four hours a day. The oppression of women is so tied in to class society, its roots are so deep . . . that it will take a major social revolution for women to be truly liberated.

BETTY FRIEDAN: Strangely enough, I don't think man is the enemy. I think man is a fellow victim (*voice-over from Sanders: "Betty Friedan, author"*). Man is a fellow victim with women in the world of half equality we're in now. He's as much oppressed by the burdens and the guilts and the hostilities that are bred by the current sexual definitions and the lack of equal responsibilities and equal opportunities and challenges that each man and women has to suffer alone in his or her own family, bedroom or kitchen, but yet must be solved by whole social and political change. Man's not . . . the enemy.

Despite Sander's relative silence, the structure and editing of the segment accomplished a great deal; as it progressed, radicalism was refuted and liberalism looked ever more reasonable. A brief interview with a member of one of the most radical New York feminist groups, The Feminists, stood in for radical feminism as a whole, and its representative articulated an analysis clearly based in issues of power, although she was given almost no time to explain it (this moment in the documentary is strikingly similar to David Culhane's use of The Feminists in his CBS story). And she was immediately refuted by a married feminist, who focused on the pragmatic problems of doing away with marriage. Sanders then gave voice to another feminist who offered an analysis of familial roles that was somewhat more systemic, given her references to class and to history; in fact, this was the documentary's unacknowledged featuring of socialist-feminist analysis (Waters was a member of the Young Socialist Alliance, and *The Militant* was a socialist publication). However, much of the bite was taken out of it when it was followed by Betty Friedan, who ended the segment by providing the answer to the question "Who is the enemy?" Crucially, Friedan was quite clear that men were not to blame.

Taken as a whole, this segment implied that the likeliest candidate for blame was "tradition" or "ignorance," the conventional enemies of liberal progress. In an ingenious move on Sanders's part, Friedan's discourse merged the radical rhetoric of social transformation with the same liberal claims about the benefits for men that had appeared earlier in the documentary. The ultimate liberal feminist, Friedan somehow managed to make the argument that feminism required the elimination of patriarchy while still maintaining that men would be better off. This worked especially well because the availability of child care—the concrete issue raised by Mary Alice Waters when she spoke of social revolution—had long been an issue for Friedan and the liberal wing of the movement.

Child care was, in fact, one of the safer issues that a feminist could be depicted as advocating. It was an issue that united radicals and liberals and would be one of the three demands (along with abortion and equal pay) that were agreed on by the various feminist groups involved in the August 1970 Women's Strike for Equality. Moreover, advocating publicly funded child care—unlike analogizing rape to terrorism or characterizing married women as slaves, as the member of The Feminists had done—was not as direct an attack on men's character or their privilege, and it reinforced the traditional belief that children were women's responsibility. That is, if women wanted more freedom, they had better figure out who was going to mind the children.[4]

Sanders's concern to alleviate men's anxiety about what feminism meant to them was part and parcel of the media pragmatism strategy, although I do not mean to discount the ways that this strategy worked for women as well, many of whom were—and are—concerned that to identify as feminist requires hating men. This strategy was striking in two respects: First, such a focus on making feminism palatable to men was absent from earlier mainstream coverage of the movement, in which it was generally assumed that men *were* the enemy; indeed, men's role, except as oppressors, was not a major focus for feminist discourse as a whole during the early second wave.[5] Sanders's considerable time and attention to the issue should be seen as part of her goal to correct the poor media image of the movement. Her focus on marriage in the documentary appears explicitly designed to counter the excesses of David Culhane's earlier series on the movement. Culhane had asserted that all radical feminists shared the stance that "the institution of marriage must go," yet Sanders's treatment of marriage featured feminists, both liberals and self-identified militants, who thought it was worth saving.

Second, the documentary's focus on the movement's benefits for men clarifies one of the unique rhetorical burdens of women's liberation, an additional way in which the analogy to civil rights was problematic. Trying to claim that relations between blacks and whites were not based in power would have been ludicrous, and listing the pragmatic benefits that black liberation would accrue for whites was hardly a priority for civil rights advocates. Certainly, some, like Martin Luther King Jr., avoided naming whites as the enemy and appealed to a moral and religious rationale for civil rights, but even King hardly tried to deny that it was white people who were behind discrimination and brutality against blacks and that many whites resisted the loss of power—of white supremacy— that civil rights represented.

Conversely, what white people *gained* from civil rights—and this was implicit in much of the discourse produced by rhetors like King as well—was the opportunity to demonstrate their moral courage and the satisfaction of distinguishing themselves from racists. The history of white involvement in civil rights activism indicates that that reward was quite meaningful to many. It was meaningful to broadcasters as well. In her analysis of the intersections of the agendas of the Southern Christian Leadership Conference and of network news in the 1950s and 1960s, Torres (2003) argues that television news' attention to civil rights activities, particularly those relying on the "moral authority of Christian nonviolence," was a route to the "political and cultural *gravitas*" the medium craved (p. 15).

But sexism, unlike racism, has never achieved the status of a moral issue in American culture. Promising men the satisfaction that would come from renouncing sexism—from separating themselves from their fellow patriarchs— was not enough, and thus the rewards Sanders's interviewees described were pragmatic rather than moral, and they positioned men as ignorant or out-of-date rather than actively oppressive. And, certainly, many feminists—like the ones interviewed by Sanders—believed that their sexual and emotional relationships with men could only be preserved by avoiding enmity. Given that many women continued to participate in and to defend sexist relationships, practices, and institutions, declaring men the enemy was hardly a good strategy for swelling the ranks of the movement. Finally, and particularly interesting given Sanders's downplaying of analyses of power, another way to read this conciliatory strategy is as simple recognition of a power imbalance. Feminists were outmanned and outgunned, so to speak, and they could hardly afford to alienate men more than they already had, especially given that Sanders saw legislation that had to be passed by overwhelmingly male legislators as the best path for the movement. As she explicitly remarked, "man must be an ally if there is to be meaningful change," a contention underscored by the fact that the documentary's most voluble advocate for the ERA was, in fact, a man.

Sanders's efforts to assuage male anxiety about the movement's implications were equally apparent when the documentary turned to karate, an especially troubling issue for feminism's public image. The representation of feminists' advocacy of martial arts was, by this time, a mainstream media staple, as it functioned to condense militancy and man-hating into one image—women learning how to beat up men. Articles on feminism in *Life* (Davidson, 1969), in *Time* ("The New Feminists," 1969), in *Atlantic Monthly* (Gerrity, 1970), and in *Newsweek* (Dudar, 1970) in the year previous to the broadcast of the documentary had all focused, to some degree, on the role of martial arts within the second wave. Many radical feminists did advocate the learning of self-defense as a response to male violence against women, but for media that hardly acknowledged the systematic nature of that violence and that found the notion of physically aggressive women both absurd and repugnant, the political analysis was almost always displaced by spectacle. David Culhane's discourse in the CBS series on feminism was the exemplar of this approach, both visually and verbally. As he presented it, women were learning judo so that they could physically assault the men who oppressed them; such skills were an outlet for women's rage, and men had better beware.

In contrast, Sanders's segment on karate transformed a radical feminist analysis of power into a less threatening issue of women's self-esteem. No women or feminists had spoken about their attraction to martial arts in the CBS report, and Culhane's interpretation of their motivations went unchallenged. But Sanders not only offered a sympathetic introduction to the issue (in which, importantly, she put it under the rubric of "self-defense"), she also allowed a young feminist to articulate a thoughtful rationale. Perhaps most importantly, the visuals in Sanders's segment did not emphasize a mano a mano "battle of the sexes" as Culhane's had. Instead, the camera panned across a college gym full of women in comfortable street clothes (rather than martial arts garb), kicking softly, trying out judo holds on each other, smiling and laughing, as Sanders narrated:

> On the campus of Duke University, women are learning to discard something they have long felt inappropriate for them—their role as victims, weak and vulnerable. One of the offshoots of the women's liberation movement has been the growth of self-defense classes. Students and local residents hired an expert to teach them how to overcome their physical limitations. The classes have an ideological basis, according to student Mary Thad Ridge.

The screen shifted to a medium shot of Ridge, who offered the following justification for self-defense:

> Well, I think that if women are going to want to really take the position that belongs to them, then one of the most important things is mobility. It means to be able to go where you want to go, when you want to go, without the protection of a man. And I think that this means that women should be able to walk the streets at night with the same facility that men are able to. Not only does this mean self-defense . . . but I think one of the most important things is a woman's confidence.

The "ideological basis" for martial arts that Ridge offered (despite the references to "being able to walk the streets," which always implies the specter of the male attacker) was about mobility, about equality of access to public space, and, most importantly, about confidence. Here, the building of confidence replaced the practice of physical aggression, and karate and judo became something women were doing *for* themselves rather than weapons they wanted to use *against* men.

Remaining unspoken in all of the televised treatments of martial arts was the radical feminist analysis of power, within which women's development of physical skills was a direct response to men's violence against them.[6] Sanders's skillful segment completely reconfigured the threat that images of karate and judo posed to men and to the image of the movement. Images of attractive female college students, tentatively learning to "overcome their physical limitations," replaced those of angry militant feminists wrestling with men, and the rationale for self-defense was relocated from the battle between the sexes to women's struggle for self-esteem—in short, from the political to the personal. Indeed, men were *not* the enemy.

Fixing Feminism

Sanders's good intentions were quite evident in "Women's Liberation," and she largely accomplished the goals for the program that she articulated in her memoir: She gave a sense of the breadth of the movement, of its ideological diversity, and of some of its major issues, all in a serious and respectful tone. The documentary has been lauded in at least three accounts of the second wave; for example, in *The World Split Open,* Ruth Rosen (2000) calls the program sympathetic and "lively" and claims that it provided "in depth coverage of women's desires, needs, and issues" (p. 299; see also Brownmiller, 1999; Cohen, 1988). Rosen (2000) also reports that "viewers wrote appreciative letters to Sanders, asking how they could join the 'cause'" (p. 300).

Yet Sanders's treatment of the movement—even with its sympathetic framing and its efforts to refute negative stereotypes—was mostly an echo of the dominant themes of earlier network reports. The topics that received the most attention—women's socialization as wives and mothers, abortion, equality of opportunity and pay—were already the topics most likely to get favorable coverage, as they had in the CBS and NBC series. Moreover, the documentary further developed the equality narrative that had emerged in Sanders's earlier story on the *Ladies Home Journal* sit-in, in which she emphasized equal opportunity issues and downplayed the protestors' critique of sexist magazine content. Sanders was attempting to move the movement toward the center, presenting its membership (at least that part of it to which she paid the most attention) as white, middle-class, and married. This was an audience strategy designed to make women's liberation more amenable for identification by the kind of women she believed the movement needed to attract and, equally if not more important, to downplay its radicalism for male opinion leaders whose support would be necessary to pass the ERA. The emphasis on clearly quantifiable types of discrimination—and on remedies like the ERA—functioned similarly.

Yet, unlike some past coverage, the documentary did not demonize those radical voices that it included. Nor did it largely eliminate and/or assimilate them, as the NBC series had so deftly done. Rather, it simply muted them, allowing them to be outweighed by voices urging reform rather than revolution and analyses that talked about equality and choice rather than power and violence. Particularly clear in the closing and in the segment on self-defense, this primer on women's liberation told the viewer that feminism was about women—and their self-improvement—not about patriarchy and its dismantling. Sanders's ultimate message was that the system could and should absorb the changes that feminists sought. The documentary operated within a variation of liberalism that "believed fairness was primarily accomplished by overcoming prejudicial thinking," a theme familiar from dominant understandings of the civil rights movement (Bradley, 1998, p. 168).

Sanders did not *mis*represent the movement in the "Women's Liberation" documentary: As is always the case with mediated representations, the rhetoric was in the choices of what was included and what was omitted and in how the former was framed. The documentary relied on the ideology of liberal pluralism and its implicit claim that "competing voices contribute equally to fashioning public policy on difficult social issues. What gets repressed is the incontrovertible fact that some voices are given legitimacy through representation and others are not, some get airtime and others get stifled" (D'Acci, 1999, pp. 135–136). "Women's Liberation" attempted to provide legitimacy for the movement, to "fix" feminism by analogizing it to civil rights, by emphasizing its benefits for men, and by highlighting its possibilities for individual opportunity and self-improvement, presenting these goals within an implicit "call to a generosity of spirit, as if the inclusion of what had been previously left out was the correction of an oversight" (Bradley, 1998, p. 168). Rhetorically, it functioned as intended: In Sanders's vision, the movement was easier to understand, less threatening, and, most importantly, it was simply another forward move in an evolutionary historical narrative of progressive social change.

In the process, "Women's Liberation" furthered the already normalized whiteness, classism, and heterosexism of the movement and ignored its ongoing and earnest conflicts over those issues. The absence of the concerns of women of color in a narrative that revolved around a race-sex analogy not only indicates the irony of the comparison, it also demonstrates just how powerful the "all the women are white, all the blacks are men" assumption was in public consciousness (Hull, Scott, and Smith, 1982). The only blacks in Sanders's story were the romanticized (black male) civil rights activists who had asked for and received the kind of equality that (white) feminists deserved as well. "Women's Liberation" served as a classic example of the "depressing habit white people have of first defining the black experience and then of making it their own" (Stimpson, 1988, p. 34). Likewise, the only lesbians in Sanders's story were those in the imaginations of her audience, and they were countered by all the straight married women on the screen. Poor women were invisible as well: When "Women's Liberation" featured discourse on wage and job inequality, the focus was specific to professional women. The white, middle-class women who dominated the documentary might have been making lots of noise, but they ultimately bore no special grudge against men and would be satisfied with the passage of the ERA.

In fact, the role of men in the "Women's Liberation" documentary was both rhetorically astute and politically problematic. The assumption that men were the audience for national network news often resulted in reports on feminism that were characterized by thinly veiled amusement, derision, and/or demonstrable gender anxiety. Yet, Sanders took the focus on men in a new direction, as her report on the movement seemed designed to reassure them that they had less to fear than they might have imagined. The price of such peacemaking was high for radical feminists, however.

Man-hating was not just a media-created chimera; many radicals saw it as a necessary part of the movement's politics. That is, if women could not allow themselves to hate their oppressors (or, at the very least, to name and blame them), they risked turning their anger at their situation toward themselves and other women (Kearon, 1973). As Hogeland (1998) has put it, "because hatred is a logical and psychological human reaction to oppression, claiming the legitimacy of man-hating becomes a political strategy to resist internalized misogyny" (p. 82). Equally as important, if feminism had no enemy, it lost force as a politics and risked "the slippage from the political to the psychological" that ends in a vision of women's liberation as a self-improvement enterprise (Hogeland, 1998, p. 101). Sanders's documentary facilitated rather than forestalled such an outcome, although she simply contributed to a process that was already underway in other venues such as women's magazines.

"Women's Liberation" absorbed a complex, diverse, and often revolutionary set of political ideas into a vocabulary of equal rights, choice, and self-improvement, and it eventually focused on those aspects of feminism that were pursued through the legislatures and the courts, thus upholding the "legitimacy of the economic-political system as a whole" (Gitlin, 1980, p. 273). The decision to make the documentary was a decision to package the movement, and Sander's vision, though far more benign than some that had come before and many that would come after, was still partial and ideological, requiring a distinction between *negative* coverage (which "Women's Liberation" certainly was not) and coverage that drastically *limited* the movement's meanings and implications. Yet, the ideological work that the documentary performed was barely visible, because the current of liberal individualism that ran through all of the perspectives through which its narrative was filtered—expository documentary, news pragmatism, and an evolutionary theory of social change derived from a romantic memory of civil rights—was so thoroughly naturalized that it passed for objectivity.

The rise in media attention to the second wave and the eventual ascendance of liberal, equal opportunity feminism as the only kind of feminism that dominant media would recognize were mutually reinforcing processes. As even the promovement and well-intentioned "Women's Liberation" documentary demonstrated, those threatening aspects of radical feminism that had to be culled out before women's liberation could become a truly mass movement were precisely the elements that did not translate well to journalistic norms: systemic critique of patriarchy (and men's role in it), an awareness of the intersections of race, class, gender, and sexuality, and, finally, recognition of the difference between the liberal, pluralist concept of "choice" and the radical notion of freedom.

Sanders would have the opportunity to report on the ERA again a couple months later when it passed the House of Representatives in early August. The national broadcast stories on the ERA were fairly perfunctory and would be far overshadowed by the attention the networks lavished on the Women's Strike for Equality that occurred a few weeks later. The stories on the strike were the first network hard news treatments of women's liberation since the *Ladies' Home Journal* protest, and, unlike Sanders's story from March, they would exemplify all of the problems of event-centered reporting on the movement.

CHAPTER 5

Making a Spectacle of the Movement

The August 26, 1970, Women's Strike for Equality

> Betty Friedan was 20 minutes late for her first scheduled appearance
> in connection with the Women's Strike for Equality yesterday because
> of a last-minute emergency appointment with her hairdresser. . . .
> "I don't want people to think Women's Lib girls don't care about how
> they look," she said . . ."We should try to be as pretty as we can.
> It's good for our self-image and it's good politics."
>
> —"Leading Feminist Puts Hairdo before Strike,"
> in the *New York Times* (1970, p. 30)

On August 10, 1970, the U.S. House of Representatives passed the ERA by a wide margin, and each of the three network evening newscasts dutifully reported the event. The stories were strikingly similar. Each included, for instance, a quotation from a supporter—Representative Martha Griffiths from Michigan—and from an adversary—Representative Emanuel ("Manny") Celler of New York. Griffiths was a logical choice to speak for the amendment; she had pushed hard to include the prohibition of sex discrimination under Title VII of the Civil Rights Act of 1964, and she had led the discharge petition drive that finally freed the ERA from the control of the House Judiciary Committee (which Celler chaired) and brought it to the floor of the House for debate (Davis, 1991). Her statement in NBC's story, that the effect of the amendment would be the repeal of discriminatory state laws, was a neat summation of the position that had been taken by feminist advocates of the amendment.

Like Griffiths, Celler was a Democrat with a history of antidiscrimination advocacy. In office since 1922, he had opposed immigration quotas that made it difficult for Jews fleeing the Holocaust to emigrate to the United States, had been an early opponent of Senator Joseph McCarthy, and had been deeply involved in the passage of the Civil Rights Act of 1964 (Carroll, 1981). Yet he not only opposed the ERA, he also had spoken against the inclusion of sex discrimination under Title VII. Even so, Celler's opposition to the ERA was not articulated as simple sexism. His central concerns, as he expressed them to reporters, were that the amendment was too abstract, that its implications were vague, and that its potential effects should be further studied. Like the leaders of major labor organizations, he claimed that the ERA would harm women by making protective labor legislation unconstitutional (an issue about to become moot because of ongoing EEOC actions to enforce Title VII), and he called it "a historic step backward" in ABC's story. But times were changing, and Celler was on the wrong side of history. In 1972, at age eighty-four and still chair of one of the most powerful committees in Congress, he would lose the Democratic primary to thirty-three-year-old Elizabeth Holtzman. Holtzman would go on to win the seat, and she would later lead the fight in Congress to extend the ERA's ratification deadline to 1982.

ABC's report on the House passage of the ERA on August 10 was followed by Marlene Sanders's story about a group of women's liberationists who demonstrated at the Statue of Liberty to coincide with the House vote. As always, Sanders was judicious, describing the several dozen demonstrators who marched with signs on Liberty Island, chanting "Freedom now!" as both "peaceful" and "ladylike." The only interviewee in the story analogized discrimination against women to discrimination based on race, echoing Sanders's rhetorical tactic from her May documentary. Of the four network news stories and one commentary between August 9 and 11 that treated the House passage of the ERA, Sanders's was the only one that included the twenty-four–word text of the amendment itself, which Sanders read aloud: "Equality of rights under the law shall not be denied or abridged by the United States or by any state on account of sex."

Perhaps most striking, in hindsight, is that each of the network stories communicated the conviction that the ERA would be easily passed by the Senate (the vote in the House was 346 to 15) and ratified by the states forty-seven years after it was first introduced to Congress.[1] Coexisting with this general recognition of the momentum of the women's movement was the sentiment that women/feminists had let that momentum go to their heads and did not quite know what they were doing. All three networks noted in their stories that women might have to be drafted and to pay alimony (issues that had emerged in House debate), and the NBC story quoted Manny Celler saying, "the women themselves do not agree on what equality means." NBC's reporter closed the story noting wryly that the amendment might end up "giving women more liberation than they bargained for." In Frank Reynolds's commentary for ABC, he approvingly repeated Celler's statement that "there is more difference between a male and a female than between a horse chestnut and a chestnut horse," and observed that a major impediment to women serving in combat was that they could simply "never be ready on time."

This dynamic in the early August ERA stories, in which recognition of the movement's momentum was coupled with patronizing observations about feminists' failure to think through the implications of their demands, is helpful for understanding the quantity and quality of network news coverage of the biggest women's liberation story of 1970 that occurred later that same month: the Women's Strike for Equality. Held on August 26, the fiftieth anniversary of the day the Nineteenth Amendment guaranteeing women the right to vote became law, the strike was the largest demonstration yet conceived and executed by second-wave feminists. On "Strike Day," as it came to be known, thousands of women marched up Fifth Avenue in New York City to dramatize feminist concerns. Smaller groups of women marched in other U.S. cities, including Washington, D.C., Chicago, Los Angeles, Boston, Detroit, Milwaukee, Syracuse, San Francisco, Baltimore, and Miami; all told, women mounted strike-related events in forty-two states (Rosen, 2000). In a show of international solidarity, a small band of French women marched in Paris, women demonstrated in Quebec and turned out in Norway, and Dutch women marched on the U.S. Embassy in Amsterdam (Davis, 1991; Giardina, 2010).

If the success of media activism is measured by the amount of news coverage generated, the Strike for Equality hit the mother lode. It was the first

Figure 9. An aerial view of Strike for Equality marchers stretching across Fifth Avenue in New York City. © JP Laffont/Sygma/CORBIS.

major feminist event to receive front-page, above-the-fold, coverage in major national newspapers, including the *New York Times,* the *Los Angeles Times,* the *Washington Post,* and the *Chicago Tribune,* as well as extensive, on-the-scene coverage from all three national television news networks. Strike Day was the brainchild of Betty Friedan, who had proposed it in a lengthy speech at the Chicago NOW convention in March 1970 as she was leaving the organization's presidency after four embattled years. In her memoir, Friedan (2000) claimed that a central part of her motivation for proposing the action was to create "a serious action to get the focus off sexual politics" and back to equal opportunity issues (p. 231). From Friedan's (2000) perspective, the "trivializing media attention" that was threatening to derail the public's understanding of the movement included "stories about the extremists who continued to make literal analogies of the women's movement with class warfare or race warfare. Down with men. Down with marriage. Down with motherhood. Down with anything women have ever done to attract men. . . . [T]he anti-man manifestos which the media loved to write about were not real, did not express the feelings or the situations of most women" (pp. 231, 232). From the beginning, the strike was conceived as media activism, but not simply in terms of getting media attention for what Friedan saw as feminism's "real" issues, long a concern for NOW—a corollary goal was to take the focus *away* from those issues that imperiled the movement's image.

Not all NOW members shared Friedan's enthusiasm for the idea of urging women to walk out on their jobs on August 26, her original plan for the action. In her speech to the convention, and later on a Chicago radio station, Friedan (1985) described the strike as "a resistance, both passive and active, of all women in America against the concrete conditions of their oppression." She proposed that "women who are doing menial chores in the offices cover their typewriters and lose their notebooks, the telephone operators unplug their switchboards, the waitresses stop waiting, cleaning women stop cleaning, and everyone who is doing a job for which a man would be paid more—stop—every woman pegged forever as assistant, doing jobs for which men get the credit—stop" (p. 144). Friedan (2000) later wrote that Aileen Hernández, NOW's new president, resisted the idea because she thought it was a "wild scheme" that was likely to "flop" (p. 233). Jo Freeman's (1975) account concurs that the idea was greeted with skepticism: It "got instant attention from the press and instant groans from NOW members who despaired of how ridiculous they would look when the majority of American women failed to strike" (p. 84).

NOW leaders later decided to scale back expectations for the strike by redefining it as a march that would begin around 5 P.M., thereby not requiring that women literally leave their jobs. NOW members worked feverishly to make it a success, setting up organizing committees in cities around the country, raising money selling buttons and posters, and passing out thousands of leaflets. The organization secured an array of sponsors to lend visibility to the strike, including Gloria Steinem, Congressmember Shirley Chisholm and soon-to-be-elected Congressional candidate Bella Abzug, as well as former Congressmember Jeanette Rankin, feminist author Kate Millett, civil rights activist and American Civil Liberties Union attorney Eleanor Holmes Norton, and Flo Kennedy (Cohen, 1988).

NOW board member (and later president) Jacqui Ceballos managed to hold together a coalition of women's groups that would be represented at the strike in New York, among them the Young Women's Christian Association, NYRF, Redstockings, Radicalesbians, the National Coalition of American Nuns, the National Welfare Rights Organization, W.I.T.C.H., Women's Strike for Peace, the Socialist Workers Party/Young Socialist Alliance, the Third World Women's Alliance, and Columbia Women's Liberation (Bradley, 2003; Cohen, 1988). By Strike Day, Governor Rockefeller had declared August 26 a holiday in New York; President Nixon had issued a proclamation commemorating the anniversary of woman suffrage; and the mayor of New York had proclaimed August 26 Equality for Women Day (Cohen, 1988; Charlton, 1970). Although police officials estimated the turnout in New York at ten thousand, while feminists claimed it was between thirty-five thousand and fifty thousand, there was little doubt that the march had been a success for the women involved in it (Davis, 1991). Friedan (2000) later called it "a great day" and a "high point" of her political life (p. 241).

The Strike for Equality was the largest media activism event mounted by feminists in 1970, and NOW did everything possible to make it amenable to positive media coverage. Its success, in terms of national and international participation and the volume of news coverage, demonstrated the long distance the movement had traveled by August 1970. Even so, the strikingly consistent qualities of the three networks' reporting on Strike Day took the problems of event-centered and conflict-focused reporting that had plagued previous treatments of feminist protest to a whole new level. The movement's growth and its profound challenge to the social order were becoming apparent, and the palpable gender anxiety in the networks' coverage of the strike manifested recognition of that context by depicting an event forwarding liberal goals as a radical assault on traditional social mores. The respectable liberals, depicted as moderate and reasonable in previous reporting (in contrast to the radical fringe with their crazy ideas and disruptive behavior), were now the ones *in the streets,* leading the charge, making noise, and mouthing off, and thousands of women had joined them. To see this as a danger to traditional gender roles (and their attendant masculine prerogatives) was not paranoia; rather, it was recognition of reality. The networks scrambled to contain the implications of Strike Day and brought to bear everything in their arsenals, from visual spectacle, to the disavowals of "ordinary women," to patronizing editorial commentaries by male reporters.

In the end, the effects of the strike were quite contradictory. The events of August 26, 1970, conclusively demonstrated the mass appeal of women's liberation and precipitated further movement growth, thus helping to pave the way for many of liberal feminism's legislative and judicial victories in the early 1970s. At the same time, television coverage of the action presented an interpretation of feminism as, at its base, an attack on the various binaries that undergirded traditional gender ideology—private versus public, masculine versus feminine, the personal versus the political—and served as a harbinger of the antifeminist arguments that would eventually derail the ERA and help to usher in a post-feminist era.

Framing the Strike

As an event conceived and largely directed by NOW, the design of Strike Day reflected the organization's media pragmatism. The action had the qualities that attract extensive media attention: It was a public, observable event (with the possibility for producing compelling images); it was deviant (such huge demonstrations by women were unusual); it had the potential for conflict (between feminists and antifeminists); it could be personified (hence the recruitment of highly visible women as sponsors); and it could be linked to issues already on the media agenda (such as abortion law repeal, Title VII enforcement, the ERA, and other topics treated in the wave of media attention in 1970). The strike was designed to dramatize three major issues that NOW had extensively emphasized to reporters and that Friedan (1985) repeated again in her speech on August 26 in New York: "real equality of opportunity in education and employment, a whole network of . . . twenty-four hour child care centers, and the right, the inalienable human right, to control our own bodies, to medical help in abortion" (p. 153).

This brief list of demands had taken months to hammer out, as the coalition between the older, liberal branch of the movement, and the younger, radical branch, was precarious. The radicals, for instance, wanted the phrase to be "free abortion on demand" rather than Friedan's more cautious right to "medical help in abortion." In fact, the phrase "free abortion on demand" made it into both print and broadcast accounts of the strike, probably because of its presence on signs held by radicals. The most surprising sacrifice NOW made to placate radical feminists, however, was the decision to forego official use of the strike to create pressure toward Senate passage of the ERA. Even with that concession, the final three demands were likely to be generally understood as representing the interests of the liberal wing of women's liberation; more importantly, they were demands that had been treated as uncontroversial in earlier network coverage of the movement.

Bradley (2003) describes print treatment of the strike as "mixed," with a tendency to combine "fairly straightforward news coverage with jocular sidebars" (p. 116), and a review of the coverage in the *New York Times* supports her assessment. The *Times*'s reports did an accurate job of describing the activities of the day in New York and in other cities, highlighted the strike's three primary demands, and noted the various personalities and groups involved. However, along with coverage of strike events, the paper carried additional stories that undermined representation of the event as serious political activism. The epigraph to this chapter is one example. Another story, headlined as "For Most Women, Strike Day Was Just a Topic of Conversation," included disavowals of women's liberation from housewives, one of whom said "we're busy squeezing tomatoes, like we do everyday," from working women, one of whom commented that she was "against the whole equality thing" because she was "afraid of being drafted," and from a company spokesman who presumably was speaking for his female employees when he claimed that "the movement is regarded with some ridicule here" because women employees were uninterested in issues such as abortion or day care (Lichtenstein, 1970b, p. 30).

Despite problems of emphasis or interpretation, the *Times* took the strike story seriously enough to devote a front-page, above-the-fold photo and story to it, as well as to continue that story on an inside page that included several related items. Among them were a brief column on feminist efforts to lobby the Senate for the passage of the ERA, a report on the agreement reached between women employees and management at *Newsweek* following the EEOC complaint lodged in March, and the text of President Nixon's proclamation commemorating the anniversary of the Nineteenth Amendment. Generally, the *Times* situated the event in the context of various aspects of reformist activism, although its coverage also included a profile of Kate Millett, a featured speaker at the strike who was receiving a significant amount of media attention that August because of the publication of her book, *Sexual Politics*. The latter prompted the *Times* to term her the "principal theoretician of the women's liberation movement" (Prial, 1970, p. 30).

In contrast, although each of the networks noted the strike's three major demands, their stories did a much less complete job of reviewing the major events of the day or the speakers at the rallies. Friedan was the only member of women's liberation with a speaking role; she was briefly shown addressing a crowd in two reports, and an even briefer shot of an unidentified Steinem holding a microphone appeared in another. Otherwise, the speakers at the rally in New York's Bryant Park—which also included Bella Abzug, Kate Millett, and Eleanor Holmes Norton—were unmentioned in the network reports broadcast on Strike Day. The reports also contained no interviews with participants in the strike, as, for instance, the *Times* did. Even so, the television coverage was extensive. It featured reports on strike activities in other cities, interviews with antifeminists (all of whom, save Senator Jennings Randolph, were women), and editorials from commentators for each network (all of whom were men).

There were some differences, in both tone and substance, between the networks. For example, ABC's coverage was by far the most egregiously sexist. Its lead story on August 26 began with anchor Howard K. Smith quoting Vice President Spiro Agnew's observation that "three things have been difficult to tame: the oceans, fools, and women," and that while the oceans largely had been tamed, "fools and women will take a little longer." At the close of the report, Smith quoted West Virginia Senator Jennings Randolph, who had called feminists a "small band of braless bubbleheads" (the senator's identical comment would appear in all three networks' coverage). Finally, Smith's editorial commentary on August 25 had as a central focus his fear that women's liberation would mean that women would cease wearing miniskirts, a garment that he called "the biggest advance in urban beautification since Central Park."

Smith's comment, relying as it did on an assumption of women's function as objects of visual pleasure for men, presumed a male spectator, and this supposition reverberated in various ways throughout the stories, which exploited the event's visual potential as only television could. The strike coverage relied on cultural associations of women with visual pleasure in three respects: through its positioning of the strike as sheer spectacle; through its verbal and visual framing of the strike as entertainment rather than reasoned protest; and through its emphasis on the issue of femininity under attack, a focus within which femininity was largely represented by women's bodies.

As a whole, the television coverage of the Strike for Equality betrayed a conspicuous sense of gender anxiety; that is, a fear that feminism's assault on patriarchal privilege was, at its heart, an attempt to eradicate gender difference, represented in news stories as those feminine attributes that made women pleasing visual objects for men. In some fascinating ways, this coverage betrayed a realization that femininity was unstable, contingent, and performative, rather than a natural attribute (Butler, 1990). The strike's three major demands—abortion, child care, and equality in pay and employment—were about public policy and not sexual politics (at least not explicitly), but television news' featuring of the latter indicated just how easily any change in women's status was understood as a threat to cherished gender roles.

A STRIKING SPECTACLE

For television news, in addition to its fulfillment of the basic categories of newsworthiness, Strike Day had a central, irresistible, feature: It presented the opportunity for some great pictures. Television's tendency to "let pictures tell the story" was immediately apparent in the opening footage in the three network stories. Following an introduction by their respective news anchors, each of the reports began with film of women marching. Very little information was given to frame the initial footage. Instead, the spectator saw the spectacle of crowds of women, sometimes angry women, shouting, singing, and carrying signs in front of watching onlookers in various cities (most reportage focused on New York, Boston, Washington, D.C., Chicago, and Los Angeles).

Although NBC's John Chancellor recited the strike's major demands in his introduction to the story (while also including Jennings Randolph's "braless bubbleheads" remark), NBC's coverage relied the most on visual spectacle, something the other two reports did to lesser degrees. On NBC, three and a half minutes of unnarrated footage were shown during the four-and-a-half-minute report. The story began rather ominously, with a somber drumbeat and a shot of marchers in Boston in which a police officer could be seen on the edge of the frame, serving as a reminder of the danger such crowds of women inherently represented. It moved on to close-ups of some protest signs and of women carrying various symbolic objects, such as a huge typewriter and a female mannequin made of papier-mâché.

The report then cut to a scene in Lafayette Park in Washington, D.C., and showed a black woman singing "O, Freedom," a popular Student Non-Violent Coordinating Committee song familiar to those who remembered Joan Baez's stirring performance of it at the 1963 March on Washington. This was the only specific focus on a woman of color during any of the coverage on any of the networks, exemplifying news workers' habit of connecting women of color to issues of race rather than gender. Moreover, it was framed as entertainment, reflecting a tendency in television reports on civil rights to include "gratuitous example[s] of African-American performance" within an "ostensibly political narrative" (Torres, 2003, p. 46). The camera spent several seconds panning the crowd in the park, depicting the listeners' relaxed posture as they enjoyed the music and ate ice cream. The only hints that this was, in fact, a political protest and not simply an afternoon concert were the camera's close-ups, during the singing, on pro-ERA signs. This moment in NBC's coverage brings to mind critiques charging that television reports on the 1963 March on Washington depicted it as "a big picnic, a hootenanny combined with the spirit of a revival prayer meeting" (Bradley, 2003, p. 120). Douglas (1994) makes a similar point in reference to this specific scene from strike coverage, noting the implicit race-sex analogy when she writes that the "juxtaposition of the song's lyrics [e.g., 'Before I'd be a slave, I'll be buried in my grave'] and the images of extremely comfortable [white] women enjoying a leisurely picnic put the lie to claims that women were 'oppressed' in any way like other groups had been" (p. 182).

The CBS and ABC reports were similar to NBC's, although they included more narration to accompany their images. After brief introductions, viewers saw footage of marching, singing women; there were no interviews and no attempt to elaborate on the strike's aims or its meaning. Walter Cronkite's introduction to CBS's story on the strike was noteworthy, however. Observing that the Nineteenth Amendment was passed fifty years earlier, Cronkite then said, "On this anniversary, a militant minority of women's liberationists were on the street across the country to demand equal employment for women, care centers for mothers, child abortions for anyone who wants them, and general equality between men and women."[2] Designating the protestors as a "militant minority" characterized them as deviant, from women in general and among feminists as a whole, although there was no context and no evidence provided to substantiate their militancy. As in earlier coverage of feminist protest, any crowd of women was assumed to be an army on the march.

Moreover, the militant minority Cronkite referred to included current and former members of Congress, editors from *Ladies' Home Journal* and *McCall's,* and *Cosmopolitan* editor Helen Gurley Brown, hardly radical feminists. For Cronkite, simply marching in public was apparently enough to make you a militant feminist, illustrating how transgressive such behavior was perceived to be. Yet the CBS report's featuring of mayoral approval, when it showed brief footage of Betty Friedan accepting a proclamation from the mayor (also included in ABC's report) would seem to cast doubt on Cronkite's militant minority claim. Generally, CBS's narration served the purpose of supporting Cronkite's initial interpretation of the feminists' radicalism. As the screen showed the march down Fifth Avenue in New York, for example, the male CBS reporter noted that "most of the day the tone of the protest stayed moderate and orderly. The radical feminists in the movement attempted no confrontation." Akin to the famously loaded question, "when did you stop beating your wife?" the unstated presumption of these comments was that the absence of confrontation was somehow remarkable.

NBC, to its credit, was the only network that included information in its story fleshing out any of the strike's main demands. A portion of its coverage showed film from a Chicago rally in which a woman addressed a large crowd about the need for legalized abortion. She spoke of the dangers of back alley abortions and woman's inherent right to control her own body as the camera scanned the crowd, focusing on the faces of various women. Out of all of the coverage on the three networks, this was the only moment in which a participant was featured making anything approaching a reasoned political argument. Importantly, however, the attitude of the camera work in this instance was very similar to that in the segment focusing on the woman singing: It was not as much about information as it was about the display, or spectacle, of the throng of women gathered around the speaker; as the camera panned the crowd, the speaking woman was seen only briefly.

Television critic John Fiske (1987) has argued that spectacle is not about meaning; rather, it emphasizes "the pleasure of looking. It exaggerates the visible, magnifies and foregrounds the surface appearance, and refuses meaning or depth" (p. 243). The lack of narration in NBC's report was an implicit message that what was interesting about the strike was not what it meant to the participants, or what it might mean about the position of women in American society. Rather, it was interesting simply for the spectacle of large numbers of women, gathered in public, taking themselves very seriously. This was a rarity and simply seeing it was enough. To act as a feminist, to step outside the bounds of conventional womanhood and take to the streets, was to become a spectacle, something to be looked at rather than engaged with; in short, the participants in strike events were bearers rather than makers of meaning (Mulvey, 1975/1999). Such spectacle, as Fiske (1987) observes, "works only on the physical senses, the body of the spectator, not in the construction of a subject," and "its emphasis on excessive materiality foregrounds the body, not as a signifier of something else, but in its *presence*" (p. 243, emphasis in original).

Although the feminists who created the strike were attempting to exert control over the image of the movement—by making it visible, by demonstrating widespread support for it, and by dramatizing its demands—television's framing of the action within dominant cultural representational norms undermined those purposes. Suzanne Kappeler (1986) argues that "representations, compositions that determine our perspective and how we look at things, are a crucial strategy in the supreme subject's endeavor to maintain his position of power and privilege and the social, political, and economic organization that supports it" (p. 165). Offering a vision of the striking women as spectacle drew on longstanding representational conventions, dominant in visual genres from fine art to pornography, in which women's bodies were displayed for consumption. Within a representational logic dependent on the objectification of women, "the surveyor of women is the male gender" (Kappeler, 1986, p. 50), a presumption made increasingly clear as the television news reports described reactions to the strike.

ENTERTAINING THE MALE SPECTATOR

Theorists of visual pleasure have long and persuasively argued that images of women's bodies presume their enjoyment by a male spectator. As Mulvey (1975/1999) explains, "in a world ordered by sexual imbalance, pleasure in looking has been split between active/male and passive/female. The determining male gaze projects its fantasy onto the female figure.... In their traditional exhibitionist role women are simultaneously looked at and displayed ... so that they can be said to connote *to-be-looked-at-ness*" (pp. 62–63, emphasis in original).[3]

Mulvey's perspective is helpful for elucidating the function of the camera work in the Strike Day reports, which constructed a male spectator *within* the news stories themselves as well as presumed a preexisting male television spectator. In both cases, the male viewer was cast as amused and entertained by the spectacle. In one portion of its coverage, NBC's camera shots of onlookers focused on men wearing benevolent smiles as women marched by. The film then quickly cut to another angle, behind the men, and shot over their shoulders at the passing women. At this moment, the camera projected a male gaze literally as well as figuratively. The ABC report on activities in New York was verbally explicit about the gender of the spectators and their attitude toward the proceedings when a reporter noted that a demonstration outside the Stock Exchange caused a "bemused sort of traffic congestion" and that "amusement rather than outrage prevailed among the overwhelmingly male crowd."

The reporter's characterization of audience reaction as amused was an indicator of the motif of ABC's coverage of the march. As in NBC's report, there was an emphasis on women as spectacle that functioned as entertainment. ABC reporter Virginia Sherwood's opening narration of the network's strike coverage introduced "a guerrilla theater that painted a portrait of the so-called 'captive woman' sold to the country as the slick ideal by Madison Avenue." At this point, feminists had their first speaking roles in ABC's report as a group of three women took turns delivering the following analysis of American advertising's "perfect female" to a watching crowd in Washington, D.C.:

> What are the qualifications, you're wondering? Well you all see all of those television commercials. You've got to be, first of all, thin, rich, blond, of course, with a thirty-eight inch bust with a nice uplift, hips firm and fully packed, young, juicy, and wrinkle-free: a finished product of the cosmetic industry, specially packaged and ready to become Miss Super Slick of 1970!

No narration or analysis followed this performance, and the ABC footage cut quickly to the scene outside the New York Stock Exchange.

However, when the coverage moved to Chicago, the report focused again on feminist protest against beauty images, as a young woman offered the following analysis to a crowd gathered around Picasso's *Head of a Woman* sculpture in front of the city's Civic Center:

> Who in our society decides what is beautiful and for whose benefit is a woman beautiful? Who has the right to decide what is the proper shape of your body with confining undergarments? There's something wrong when an attractive girl can make more money as a Playboy Bunny or a covergirl than as anything else.

As in the NBC report, ABC's camera focused on the speaking woman only briefly, concentrating instead on close-ups of various women in the crowd, as if gauging their beauty, and then offered brief shots of murals and paintings of women's faces.

On the one hand, this camerawork could be interpreted as an attempt to take the issue seriously: what is beauty? On the other hand, it could as easily be seen as simply another excuse to focus on women's visual appeal at the exclusion of their thoughts or their discourse. In 1972, John Berger offered his now-famous commentary on woman's role as the object of surveillance: "How she appears to others, and ultimately how she appears to men, is of crucial importance for what is normally thought of as the success of her life. . . . Men look at women. Women watch themselves being looked at." They are "an object of vision: a sight" (pp. 46–47). This logic was precisely what many feminists were resisting, but the rhetoric of the camera in reports on the Strike for Equality bolstered it with its implied male gaze. ABC's focus on the watching crowds in all of its coverage was a sign of its framing of the events as entertainment, both for the assembled crowds and for the assumed male spectator, and the network's selection of events furthered this interpretation by emphasizing the issue of women's visual appeal (and feminists' critique of it). The final segment in ABC's report, in which a reporter interviewed an antifeminist in Los Angeles, continued the theme.

Importantly, in all three network stories, the only interviews with women were for the purpose of demonstrating *opposition* to the strike or to the movement as a whole. ABC's interviewee was introduced as Jaquie Davison, a housewife with seven children and "proud of it." When asked why she was against women's liberation, Davison replied, "I like being a girl. It's fun. We are free. The liberation movement wants to eliminate the words masculinity and femininity. Gregory Peck says that life without femininity would be like life in a desert. Well, to me, life without masculinity would be like life in a desert." Davison's remarks were a succinct articulation of the perspective that the strikers' "real" goal was to attack gender roles, a prominent theme in the coverage as a whole.

Visual elements were particularly important to the impact of this segment. Jaquie Davison powerfully resembled Jayne Mansfield or Marilyn Monroe. She was a young woman (thirty-two at the time) with teased, bleached, blond hair and large breasts, wearing ample make-up. She represented the apotheosis of sexualized American femininity, indicating that the feminine beauty ideal under attack by feminists earlier in ABC's story was under attack only from those who could not achieve it, a familiar theme from earlier reports on the movement. What ABC's report did not tell its viewers was that Davison's opposition was hardly a spontaneous defense of femininity by a typical housewife. Davison was, in fact, an activist, organizational leader, and the founder of Happiness of Womanhood, a group she had begun in her home state of Arizona a few months earlier specifically to fight against the passage of the ERA, which, in her words, "would legislate out the differences between male and female, thus changing our entire way of life" (Davison, 1972, p. 51). For the previous two years, Davison had been leading Fascinating Womanhood seminars, based on Helen Andelin's (1963) book of the same name, which, ostensibly based in biblical principles, "emphasized women's duty to embody moral purity and submit to their husbands" (Wood, 2010, p. 91).

By the time Davison appeared in ABC's story on the strike, she had been the subject of national print media profiles and was a frequent guest on radio and television talk shows. She traveled to Los Angeles several days before the

Figure 10. Jaquie Davison in the early 1970s. From Davison's 1972 book, *I Am a Housewife*, courtesy of Mary Brooks.

strike to make media contacts, and she called a well-attended press conference on August 20 to publicize Happiness of Womanhood's countermarch on
Strike Day (Davison, 1972). One result was a front-page story in the *Los Angeles
Times* that described Davison as "a blonde mother of 7 who looks as if she just
stepped out of a magazine centerfold" (Shuit, 1970, p. A1). In short, Davison
was as politically interested and as motivated by media attention as were the
feminists she was opposing, but such context was absent from her ABC appearance, where she was presented as simply one example of the "ordinary women"
who opposed the movement.

The other networks carried similar antifeminist segments. NBC's attempt
to introduce conflict into its coverage of the day's events consisted of a brief
interview with a young couple at the marriage license bureau in New York City.
Asked about the strike by an unseen female reporter, the woman in the couple
commented that the feminists were "giving up their femininity." Her prospec-
tive husband disagreed, underscoring the primacy of women, rather than men,
as opponents of feminism. When asked next if his wife would be equal in their
marriage, his reply was "No, I don't think she wants to be equal," thus putting
the onus of antifeminism on her once again. This segment also marked the
only use of a woman reporter in NBC's coverage of the strike. She was not only
unseen, but her function was to elicit opposition to feminism.

As the *Times* had, CBS's August 26 story positioned housewives as foes of
feminism and featured brief interviews with three women defending their traditional roles as they went about their lives far from the strike (all three appeared to
be interviewed in parking lots as they entered or left stores). Sound bites such as
"I'm a very happy housewife and a very happy mother" implied that these women
perceived themselves to be the target of feminist attacks. Another contributed
the following tortured analysis: "I think it's ridiculous. I think it's stupid. I don't
think women should just stay at home all the time, but I don't think they belong
out, either." These examples from the CBS report were especially illustrative of
the ways that such disavowals worked against feminists' credibility. That is,
while "women with complaints were shown only in highly charged, dramatic,
public demonstrations," the "women without complaints were in more tran-
quil, everyday settings" (Douglas, 1994, p. 183). In short, feminist deviance was
underscored by its contrast with visions of satisfied "real" women who were
dismissive of feminist claims as they went about their private lives. As if to drive
the point home, this was the point at which CBS showcased Senator Jennings
Randolph's "braless bubbleheads" commentary, which included the claim that
feminism's "strident" voices did not "speak for women."

The most unscrupulous moment in CBS's construction of antifeminism occurred in the final segment of its report, which used former woman suffragist

Alice Paul to criticize contemporary feminism. Paul, the original author of the ERA in 1923, was asked by CBS reporter Marya McLaughlin for her opinion of "the tactics of the women today, like the bra-burners?" thus presenting another example of the use of a female reporter to prompt opposition to the movement. Paul's reply was that she did not think that bra burning had "anything whatsoever to do with this woman movement," which was about equality "throughout our whole legal system and in our constitution." First, there was no bra burning at the strike (or anywhere else for that matter). Second, had McLaughlin asked Paul her opinion about the actual events of the day, she likely would have given a different answer. She was, after all, the planner and organizer of the largest suffrage demonstration and march ever mounted in this country on March 3, 1913, the day before Woodrow Wilson's inauguration (Moore, 1997). Not only that, but several former suffragists were among the marchers in New York on Strike Day. Paul was no stranger to the use of public protest to create visibility and pressure, but few viewers would know this. In the context of the CBS story, Paul seemed to be dismissing the relevance of the strike.

Even more ironic, in retrospect, are the parallels between press reactions to early-twentieth-century suffrage parades and to the 1970 strike, an indication that the perceived threat that crowds of women in public posed to traditional gender ideals had not greatly diminished in the intervening half century. In her analysis of press response to the suffrage parades, Jennifer Borda (2002) quotes a *New York Times* reporter from 1912 who might just as well have been describing the 1970 strike when he wrote that "for the most part, the onlookers seemed to be there to see spectacle, to cheer or to laugh as they would at a circus parade and without any thought as to the political significance of the event for which the women had toiled so hard and to which they dedicated such earnest effort" (p. 45). Like the strike, suffrage parades were designed as an intervention into negative public images of feminists. Also like the strike, they ran squarely into the ridicule, scorn, and outrage precipitated by their participants' blatant violation of the "boundaries of masculine and feminine, public and private, and domestic and political" (Borda, 2002, p. 42). For Alice Paul, watching the networks' coverage of the strike might have produced a profound sense of déjà vu.

FEMINISTS, FEMININITY, AND GENDER ANXIETY

Given that the CBS segment featuring Alice Paul's dismissal of bra-burners came on the heels of Senator Jennings Randolph's "braless bubbleheads" comment, bras actually came up twice in the final moments of the CBS report on the strike, making the potent image of bra-burning one of CBS's viewers' last associations with Strike Day. Indeed, by this point, not quite two years after the 1968 Miss America Pageant protest, bra burning had already solidified as a synecdoche for second-wave feminism. Its appeal lay in its ability to represent a number of key issues at once: feminists' attack on conventional womanhood, the spectacle of women protesting, and, most importantly, the bra's function as a signifier of femininity.

Broadcast news' treatment of the Strike for Equality was quite consistent, across networks, in its interpretation of the protest as an attack on cultural notions of femininity. Despite the fact that the strike's three demands were rooted in public policy issues, and despite the fact that no feminist was ever asked for any analysis of the issue of femininity, the network reports raised the topic repeatedly. This emphasis on issues of femininity in the news coverage seemed to work inferentially, as though viewers were expected to know what was meant by the term. There were some clues. ABC, for instance, interpreted the issue as one rooted in women's appearance with its focus on two strike events that questioned beauty standards as well as through its visual display of Jaquie Davison's hyperfemininity. Howard K. Smith's commentary on ABC, while approving of the action's three major demands, interpreted the problem as a "demand for sameness" that was "abhorrent." He continued:

> When American women adopted the miniskirt, displaying much more woman, it was the biggest advance in urban beautification since Central Park was created in Manhattan. Imagine a street scene of men in miniskirts. All those knobby knees and stringy legs would be downright aesthetic pollution. To me, women's liberation has that in common with the midi that is now threatening us—it is a kind of de-feminization.

For Smith, then, feminism meant defeminization, which meant a loss of women's visual appeal for men, which meant, somehow, that men would begin wearing skirts? The logic was twisted, but not impossible to dissect.

Within patriarchal logic, nothing is "more ridiculous than a woman who imitates a male activity and is therefore no longer a woman. This can apply . . . to the way a woman looks, the job she does . . . and so on *ad infinitum*. Sex differentiation must be widely upheld by whatever means are available, for men can be men only if women are unambiguously women" (Cameron, 1985, p. 155–156). Recognition of the interactive relationship of masculinity and femininity elucidates a great deal about the gender anxiety manifest in coverage of the strike. For instance, a portion of CBS's report featured a group of feminists in Los Angeles being confronted by a man holding a sign reading Vive la Différence (the sign was created by Jaquie Davison's group, although the CBS report did not mention them). The feminists' response was to chant at him: "Go do the dishes." This segment was a rather clear illustration of precisely what the male spectator was presumed to fear: If feminism triumphed, he might end up doing the dishes (perhaps while wearing a miniskirt).

Eric Sevareid's commentary at the conclusion of the CBS report revisited the issue. As a whole, Sevareid's discourse was somewhat contradictory (although consistent in the importance it placed on men's reactions to the strike). He began by noting that men dominated by their wives were "startled" to hear of women's oppression and relieved to know that a Gallup poll showed that two-thirds of women "don't think they're oppressed either." Yet he then noted the wisdom of the strike's "three practical aims with which a great many men also agree." His final comments, however, reiterated the theme from the early August ERA stories that feminists were meddling in issues they did not fully understand:

> when the liberation spokeswomen enter the realm of the human psyche and insist on a radical transformation of feeling between the sexes, at that point most men, and a great many women, feel baffled and reluctant to follow. The usual formulation of the militant women is, 'think of us as persons, not as women.' The instruction manual for this has not yet been written. It is hard enough to separate nationality from personality and impossible to separate one's personality from one's sex.

Like Smith, Sevareid gave perfunctory approval to the public policy aims of the strike before expressing caution about feminism's larger and less desirable implications: the potential elimination of gender difference. His effort to distinguish the "practical" from the "militant" aims of the movement was a succinct expression of van Zoonen's (1992) argument that "the press can only understand body politics, gender relations, sexual violence, etc., as part of a social psychological domain, not politics" (p. 470).

NBC commentator Frank McGee was more judicious; he offered approval of work-related issues while largely steering clear of sexual politics: "Surely a reasonable person would agree that if a woman can do a job she should have it, that if she has it she should receive the same pay as a man doing the same work, and most of us would agree that many bright and some brilliant women have lived wasted lives serving less competent males who happen to be their husbands." Indeed, McGee seemed to strike the most tolerant note among the three commentators when he concluded his remarks with the following: "For those who want careers, fine. For those who want careers and marriages, fine. For those who want marriages only, fine. Fine. Thank you and good evening." Yet McGee's tone carried a note of exasperation, as though the protests of feminists were much ado about nothing and could be easily addressed if women would simply make up their minds.

Just as the commentators did not question the reasonableness of the strike's major demands, the antifeminist interviewees did not either. Nor, in fact, did the network reports as a whole. That inequality existed was not at issue in this coverage. No one, it seemed, doubted that there was a lack of parity in men's and women's pay and jobs, or that feminists might have a point about abortion and day care. The issue, then, was not whether equality existed, but whether it was *desirable* and what it might mean. The commentators seemed willing to grant the desirability of equality as the strike's demands defined it, but they also seemed dedicated to the notion that such equality could and should be achieved without affecting traditional gender roles and relationships. The Strike Day coverage foregrounded the anxiety produced by the prospect that feminism could upset traditional notions of masculinity and femininity to the extent that women might eschew their traditional function as the aesthetic objects of men's desires, thus undermining the "eroticizing of sexual inequality" that resulted from it (Bem, 1993, p. 164). As the antifeminist discourse implicitly recognized, this possibility had far-reaching consequences, for patriarchy depends on "the construction of males and females whose gendered personalities mirror the different and unequal roles assigned to them in the social structure" (Bem, 1993, p. 152).

As a whole, the television news coverage of the Strike for Equality displayed a fascinating tension between power and anxiety. If "the ability to scrutinize is premised on power," the camera in these reports was simply an extension of the male gaze as feminist film theorists understand it (Walters, 1995, p. 66). This factor, combined with the condescension of much of the reporters' narration and of the network commentators, seemed to bear out Jo Freeman's (1975) claim that "the press treats women's liberation much as society treats women—as entertainment not to be taken seriously" (p. 112). A key aspect of women's function as entertainment is *looking at them*: "the objectification of women is a result of the subjectification of man. He is pure subject in relation to an object, which means that he is not engaging in communication with that objectified person who, by definition, cannot take the role of a subject" (Kappeler, 1986, p. 50).

To have engaged the feminists, that is, to have actually interviewed them or probed their claims, would have been to transform them into subjects, a move that these reports carefully avoided. Thus, despite the lengthy attention to the strike, the actual form of the coverage worked in direct opposition to the point that the feminists were trying to make. The women who participated in the event felt empowered by its "coordinated release of anger and joy" (Brownmiller, 1999, p. 148), but networks' representation of the strike employed a variety of strategies to take that power away and give it instead to the male spectator. John Berger (1972) is useful again here, as he notes that "women are depicted in a quite different way from men . . . because the 'ideal' spectator is always assumed to be male and the image of woman is designed to flatter him" (p. 64).

However, this coverage did more than simply reiterate news organizations' refusal to take women's liberation seriously. There was fear and anxiety beneath the dismissals and sexist humor; objectifying the feminists as entertaining spectacle kept them at a safe distance and functioned as a shield against the unsettling potential of gender disorder the protest signified. Masculine power exists in a synergistic relationship with feminine submission, and defeminizing women has the corollary effect of demasculinizing men, thus the emphasis on maintaining difference and avoiding, in Howard K. Smith's term, "sameness." Despite Eric Sevareid's corollary comment that it was "impossible to separate one's personality from one's sex," this coverage betrayed a realization that gender identity was, at base, performative, and that "being male or female is something to work at, to accomplish, and to be sure not to lose, rather than something one *is* biologically" (Bem 1993, p. 148, emphasis in original). The interviews with female antifeminists were not just instantiations of the tried and true media strategy of pitting women against women. The antifeminists also functioned as surrogates for the presumed male spectator, simultaneously articulating and assuaging his anxiety by affirming that there were still women who understood the masculine-feminine balance and who were dedicated to preserving it. The strike coverage implicitly supported the position that characterizes news generally: It asserted that, in the end, the world was still relatively stable and the status quo was preferable to the prospect of radical change. The (gender) system works.

Ultimately, the strategies in the networks' coverage of the Strike for Equality were *not* that original, *not* somehow peculiar to coverage of feminism. Rather, they were simply an adaptation of conventions for representing "woman" that had long existed in other media and that were profoundly hostile to feminist ideals. When women function as spectacle, when they are valued more for entertainment than for ideas, when their essence is reduced to their appearance, they are not subjects. The demand for women to function as subjects, to speak and act in their own interests, was at the heart of second-wave feminism, and yet that basic demand was precisely what this coverage worked so hard to subvert.

Conclusion

The Strike for Equality was the second wave's peak moment in 1970. The six months between CBS's dismissive feature stories in March (broadcast barely a week before Friedan proposed the strike) and Strike Day saw the movement transition from the margin to the mainstream in the nation's collective consciousness, a shift reflected in the tone of the early August reports on the ERA's easy passage through the House. Earlier network reports on women's liberation had presented it as a sort of emergent phenomenon, one that warranted explanation and for which the implications were still developing. Some of those implications, as in the CBS series treatment of radicals, were presented as ludicrous and/or alarming, while others were depicted as reasonable, as ideas whose time had come, especially clear in the NBC series and in ABC's documentary. Yet none of these previous portraits of the movement did what the national television coverage of the Strike for Equality would do: present incontrovertible visual evidence that women's liberation was a national phenomenon that could no longer be understood as only a concern for what Cronkite had termed "a militant minority." A week later, *Life* magazine made the event its cover story under the line "Women Arise: The Revolution That Will Affect Everybody" ("On the March," 1970). Measuring success in terms of media coverage and turnout, the planners of Strike Day saw it as a victory on both counts, and the effect was felt in all corners of the movement.

The contradictions in reactions to Strike Day—a triumph for the movement that was presented as a spectacle for the national television audience—can partially be chalked up to the transgressive elements of the event itself as they were understood within prevailing gender norms. The groups of professionally dressed middle-class women holding orderly meetings that had represented the liberals in earlier network reports had become thousands of women marching in the streets, and the latter were automatically categorized as militant, typifying news workers' tendency to characterize feminist activism on the basis of behavior rather than goals or ideology. Crowds of angry women were automatically unfeminine and dangerous, and what strike planners saw as a demonstration of the movement's strength and unity became, on national television screens, a demonstration of its deviance, fueling the gender anxiety that characterized the reports.

In contrast to the divergences in earlier network narratives that reflected the rhetorical freedom of feature reporting, the strong similarities in the networks' narratives about the events of August 26 displayed the influence of routine news practices for representing protest as well as for representing feminism. For example, NOW's leaders had claimed it would be a nationwide event, and thus each network offered coverage from more than one city. Pictures took precedence over analysis or explanation, and, while supporters of the action far outnumbered counterprotestors, the search for balance meant that the latter were given ample airtime. Fulfilling media affection for conflict, interviews with "ordinary women" created the implication that feminism's foes were traditional women, rather than patriarchy or sexism, as though the purpose of the strike had been to condemn housewives. If such women had been asked their opinion about the strike's actual demands, one wonders if their response might have been different (on the other hand, as I discuss in chapter 6, this "women versus women" tactic would be used quite successfully in media reports on the ERA battle that was soon to begin).

Other predictable elements were present as well. "Militant" and "strident" made their ritualistic appearances as descriptors of feminists, and, also a ritual by this point, Betty Friedan embodied feminist leadership at an event that had been openly supported and attended by a wide range of well-known women and men who were never seen in the television coverage. Despite the fact that Strike Day was perhaps the most racially diverse event yet mounted by the second wave (and certainly the most diverse one to get extensive media attention), women of color went unmentioned in the coverage, which positioned the action as relevant only to (a certain kind of) white women with its solicited reactions from white housewives. Yet members of the Third World Women's Alliance were part of the march; the featured speakers included at least two black women, Dorothy Height, president of the National Council of Negro Women, and Eleanor Holmes Norton, and many still photos of Strike Day clearly show women of color among the participants. Moreover, neither of the two women reporters who were visibly involved in the networks' reports—Marya McLaughlin, CBS's only woman correspondent, and Virginia Sherwood, one of two women

Figure 11. Some of the diversity that went unnoticed by the networks among the marchers at the Women's Strike for Equality in New York. This photo appeared in *Life* magazine's September 4, 1970, cover story on Strike Day. John Olson/Time & Life Pictures/Getty Images.

at ABC—disrupted the problematic tone of the coverage. Sherwood used the term "strident" when describing Betty Friedan in her preview story on the day before the strike, and McLaughlin reported the inexcusable segment on Alice Paul. In contrast to NBC's concerted effort to use women reporters in its earlier stories on the movement, all of its visible reporters on the strike were men (it was, after all, hard news).

The triumph of event-centered reporting was most evident in the reports' refusal to engage with the major demands of the strike, about which there was little information provided and around which the coverage constructed no controversy. The focus on public policy and public discrimination that had protected liberals from dismissive network coverage earlier in 1970 ceased to be effective in the same way in the Strike Day reports, and NOW's media pragmatism could not thwart media inclination to turn their political goals into a referendum on private behavior. The strike presented clear evidence that feminism's claims had touched a nerve in American women, and that things might never be the same. According to the networks, the event's most dangerous implication was not that women might get equal pay, or child care, or abortion rights; rather, it was that *women might stop acting like women,* not just that day, but every day, in every way. And then hell truly would break loose. This was precisely the goal of radical feminists' pursuit of a sex-role revolution, but it was decidedly not what Betty Friedan, who spent the morning of the strike having her hair done, had in mind.

In the end, like the Miss America Pageant protest two years earlier, the Strike for Equality did not require supportive media attention to achieve its goals, and its positive impact on the movement's visibility, regardless of the tone of the reports and commentaries, was undeniable. In the months following, NOW's membership increased by 50 percent; the publicity of the strike "made it the most obvious place to go" (Freeman, 1975, p. 86). The growth in individual chapters was sometimes as much as 70 percent, and this influx was made up of working women who were younger than NOW's traditional membership but also had a different profile than the younger members of radical groups did in that they had less education and no previous movement experience. NOW's growth also included housewives who were "concerned with the emptiness in their own lives and worried lest the same fate befall their daughters," and such women joined NOW simply because it was easy to find and because it seemed "more respectable" than other groups (Freeman, 1975, pp. 85, 86).

Indeed, respectability was a key issue. Even as network reports presented a peaceful march as a radical assault, the images from Strike Day made the scale of the event, and thus its popular appeal for women, undeniable. The mainstreaming of the movement made so clear by Strike Day and by the easy House passage of the ERA created the outlines of a public identity for women's liberation that was far more respectable than it had been even six months earlier, not to mention two years earlier when the Miss America Pageant protest first thrust the movement into the spotlight. Sympathetic network reporting in April and May that presented the ERA as a logical solution to issues raised by women's liberation laid the groundwork for the movement's coalescence, in the public eye, around what seemed to be an easily understood public policy measure guaranteeing legal equality. Strike coverage added to this impression; despite radicals' insistence that the action not be used to promote the ERA, they could not keep reporters from making the connection. For example, ABC reporter Virginia Sherwood included a segment on feminist efforts toward Senate passage of the ERA in her preview story on August 25, and she began her description of the day's events the following night with "there were protest songs, speeches, and a push for passage of the Equal Rights Amendment."

The impact of Strike Day was the culmination of a period of transition that women's liberation had been undergoing throughout 1970. Positive network reporting on liberal issues like workplace equality and the ERA, coupled with NOW's increasing organizational and political muscle and the tumult in the radical movement over feminist identity (most prominently lesbianism) and political priorities set the stage for the ascendance of liberal feminism as the only feminism that mass media would recognize. As I discuss in the next chapter, the negative network reporting on Strike Day failed to derail feminism's evolution, in the eyes of mass media and the public, from an insurgent social movement to a political force that increasingly would be linked to electoral politics and public policy issues in the years that followed. News worker's proficiency with issues that could be framed through the routine processes of courts, legislatures, and campaigns produced more respectful coverage, giving liberal feminism, for a time, the political credibility that had long eluded radicals. Another crucial factor was the emergence of Gloria Steinem, who met movement and media needs for an attractive and articulate representative.

Yet progress produces resistance, and the network coverage of the strike was an early omen of backlash against feminism. The gender anxiety so evident in reports and commentaries on Strike Day would not disappear; rather, it would find new forms of expression as the organized antifeminism that went unrecognized as such in the network reports on the strike found firm footing and a powerful platform in the rebirth of political conservatism after 1970.

CHAPTER 6

After 1970

Second-Wave Feminism, Mediated Popular Memory, and Gloria Steinem

Thank God for Gloria Steinem.

—Widely reported remark by the mother of the first U.S. woman
astronaut, Sally Ride, as Ride lifted off into space aboard
the initial flight of the Space Shuttle Challenger in 1983

When 1970 began, national television news was just turning its attention to women's liberation, playing catch-up with the story that elite print media had been intermittently covering for close to two years. The multiplicity of reports the networks subsequently produced made the movement into a nationally visible phenomenon in a way that was only possible through television. The narratives they offered about the constituencies, the convictions, and the consequences of women's liberation were distinguished by their initial variety as well as by their underlying stability that became more apparent as the year proceeded.

Early stories, such as much of the network attention to the birth control hearings disruption and David Culhane's CBS series, categorized radical feminist activity within what Michael Schudson (1995) has called the "zone of deviance," a location that puts "issues, topics, or groups beyond the reach of normal reportorial obligations of balance and fairness" (p. 13; see also Hallin, 1986). Because radical ideology and behavior were outside the realm of social consensus, particularly where women were concerned, they could be "ridiculed, marginalized, or trivialized" without concern that professionalism was being breached (Schudson, 1995, p. 13). Feminist activities merited coverage because they were aberrant and could make for compelling television, but that did not mean that the coverage need be respectful, particularly given that the target audience for that coverage was presumed to be white men with little interest in the movement's grievances.

Yet Culhane's stories in March were the most dismissive and sensationalizing treatment among the three networks' portraits of the movement in the first half of 1970. Although the CBS reports provide plenty of fodder for the oft-made claim that television news trivialized many facets of women's liberation, they are not representative of the national television news coverage of feminism that year except in one important respect: Like other reports that year, they treated demands for employment opportunity and child care as reasonable issues raised by liberal feminists. Importantly, however, part of that effect was achieved through the contrast created by Culhane's less respectful treatment of issues raised by radicals; in effect, his reports created a "division between legitimate emancipatory concerns and deviant feminism" that was quite pronounced but was not characteristic of network coverage as a whole (van Zoonen, 1992, p. 470).

In fact, the most inventive rhetorical strategies deployed in the network reporting from 1970 were geared toward making the movement more credible, not less. For instance, what the CBS series exacerbated—feminism's lack of legitimacy as a political movement—Marlene Sanders tried to fix in her documentary, downplaying the transgressive elements of feminist unrest by tying it to a larger countercultural climate and stressing the similarities of liberal feminist claims to the demands of the nonviolent civil rights movement. Her contextualization of feminism in ways that made its arguments and its adherents appear rational and thoughtful required considerable rhetorical effort in terms of structure, framing, and editing. NBC's reporters took another tack, framing sexism as a social problem rather than a feminist claim. Liz Trotta's story on sexism and socialization, for example, offered a version of radical feminist analysis of women's internalization of sex roles yet omitted feminist voices, instead using the testimony of ordinary citizens. One of the most unusual aspects of NBC's reporting—its featuring of women of color—was achieved through a visual variation on the "ordinary women" strategy within which women of color simply became part of the visual backdrop of anonymous working women used to illustrate sex discrimination in the workplace.

These more sympathetic and substantive treatments of the movement required far more creativity and subtlety than simply exploiting radical feminists' violation of social consensus and conventional gender expectations. Instead, each carefully reframed the movement and its issues in ways that took advantage of the legitimacy offered by form—expository documentary and the social problem story—as well as emphasized feminism's liberal and reformist goals in ways that did not rely on the demonization of radicals. A related conclusion suggested by my readings of these texts is that feminist claims were made most persuasive when they did not come from members of women's liberation, whose testimony was rarely taken as representing the opinion of the average (white, middle-class, heterosexual) woman. The real genius of the NBC series was that the majority of its stories did not feature feminists at all; instead, they focused on the impact of sexism in the lives of women ostensibly unaffiliated with women's liberation who qualified as rhetorically appealing feminist subjects because of their traditional roles as mothers. The most sympathetic portion of David Culhane's CBS series—the human-interest segment on child care—also relied on this strategy. Although Marlene Sanders's documentary featured ample discourse from self-identified feminists, the most extensive speaking role in her report was held by a male U.S. senator who made the case for the ERA, a strategy that had kinship with Aline Saarinen's use of an elderly first-wave feminist, Alice Paul, to do the same in her NBC story.

In all cases, these rhetorical choices reflected reporters' sensitivity to their imagined audiences. Culhane's stories relied on the masculine sensibilities that guide news practices, and his targeted audience of male viewers was presumed to share the ironic, even derisive, perspective that characterized his reporting on radical feminism. Sanders also targeted a male audience, but, rather than playing to their prejudices, her purpose was to disabuse them of perceptions of feminist excess (particularly man-hating) and to pull the movement's meaning back within social consensus around the desirability of equality. The NBC series' assimilation of radical feminism within the liberal goals of women's liberation can be understood as serving a similar purpose, making Catherine Mackin's targeting of a female audience in her reports on the EEOC and abortion all the more remarkable.

Indeed, that the reporting on women's liberation in 1970 primarily addressed an implied male audience is a crucial context for making sense of the choices that guided both sympathetic reporting and its opposite. The upshot of those choices was to push the meaning of the movement toward easily understood and largely uncontroversial (at least at the time) public policy goals that fit within dominant understandings of what counted as politics in a masculine public sphere. Each of the feature stories on women's liberation embraced this tactic to some degree through the approving treatment given employment rights (and the related need for child care), the ERA, and abortion. The attempt to bring feminism within social consensus around the desirability of fairness and equality that such public policy measures symbolized, while rhetorically powerful, limited the import of women's liberation in far-reaching ways that had a variety of consequences for the movement.

At the most basic level, these liberal goals upheld the division between public and private that radical feminists were dedicated to dismantling. Such reformist remediation did not address their wide-ranging critique of gendered power dynamics in all arenas of women's lives, it entirely sidestepped issues central to the movement in 1970, namely lesbian feminism, and it contributed to a vision of the movement as the province of white women. In particular, the recurring deployment of the sex-race analogy as a legitimation device for what were almost entirely depicted as white women's complaints worked to make black women largely invisible as a constituency for feminism. This dominant characteristic of reporting on women's liberation served only to further distance women of color from the movement, a problem that continues to this day despite a history of feminist coalitional work across race and class lines. Tellingly, when the National Black Feminist Organization formed in 1973, representing the first such large-scale endeavor to organize black women, the opening line of its statement of purpose launched a critique of "the distorted male-dominated media image of the Women's Liberation Movement," which "has been characterized as the exclusive property of so-called white middle-class women" (Davis, 1988, p. 46).

Thus, even sympathetic reporting on women's liberation contributed to a vision of the movement that excised crucial aspects of feminist politics and hastened the sidelining of radical feminism that was largely accomplished by the end of 1970. But that outcome was multicausal, rooted in the movement itself as well as its representation. Network features on women's liberation certainly contributed to a distillation of the movement, in the eyes of the public, to one that centered on a few public policy issues—workplace discrimination, the ERA, and abortion—but that result also was the product of the well-organized interest groups affiliated with the liberal movement that exerted tremendous pressure to keep such issues on not only the media agenda but the agenda of government agencies, the courts, legislatures, and Congress (efforts that fed each other, given journalists' affection for the routine processes of such bodies).

Radical groups' quest for a cultural revolution was hampered by the volatility of the radical movement itself and by its quest for political purity rather than political (or mediated) efficacy. Eschewing the conventional political capital pursued by groups like NOW, radicals "often chose for themselves another form of capital—counter-cultural capital—which gained them power within the movement [both women's liberation and the larger left] rather than outside" (Barker-Plummer, 1995, p. 320). As the aftermath of the *LHJ* sit-in demonstrated, even when feminist protest effected (some of) what radicals wished for, that result was measured by its failure to live up to an idealized vision of what might have been.

Moreover, CR, radical feminism's greatest strength and central asset for building the movement and its ideas, simply could not be translated to television. CR was the source for many of the radical movement's brilliant insights about the politics of gender; it politicized countless women and led to the radical zap actions that enabled feminism's initial emergence as a national news story. But the CR process that worked so well to enable women's understanding of the sexism that permeated their lives and took root in their subjectivities was not only ill-suited to televisual representation, it also was a phenomenon that had to be experienced rather than witnessed or described. Absent that experience, the claims made by radicals about the perniciousness of the Miss America Pageant, or Playboy Bunnies, were easy to dismiss as exaggerated, mean-spirited, and personally motivated. Radical feminism attacked "the psycho-social reality of the culture," and news practices guided by adherence to social consensus were unlikely to carry its message well (Campbell, 1973, p. 81). When radical feminists articulated the insights of CR—a deeply analytical process—in television news sound bites, even the movement's most gifted thinkers, such as Shulamith Firestone, sounded (and looked) irrational rather than intellectual.

In an important contrast with feature reporting, distinctions between the representation of radical and liberal feminism largely disappeared when network news coverage focused on public protest. The stories produced in the wake of feminists' public media activism, beginning with 1968's Miss America Pageant protest and culminating in the reporting on Strike Day, tended to be event-centered, exploiting the deviant behavior of women who publicly rebelled against conventional gender norms that they always be "friendly, accommodating, compliant, docile, and obsequious" while providing little insight into their motivations for doing so (Douglas, 1994, p. 188). In contrast to the creativity of the NBC series or the ABC documentary, most reports on feminist protest followed the established playbooks of routine news practices as well as norms for representing women; they presented culturally deviant behavior with little context for making sense of it and relied on conventionalized representations of women's bodies as spectacle. Even on Strike Day, while the reasonableness of the public policy issues upon which NOW staked the action went unchallenged, the "radical" implications of the rebellious behavior of the thousands of women in the streets became the story for the networks. NBC's reporting on the birth control hearings and Marlene Sanders's story on the *Ladies' Home Journal* sit-in stand as noteworthy interventions into this pattern.

The relative emphases on behavior versus ideas and events versus issues, and the ways they played out in news coverage, proved to be key indicators of the valence of reporting on women's liberation. At the same time, the substance of that coverage was not a reliable predictor of the *impact* of feminists' attempts to use media to achieve their goals. The outcomes of the interaction of feminist media activism and news practices in 1970 present a kind of paradox that is only intelligible through context-sensitive analysis. When evaluated exclusively through the kind of national coverage that resulted, actions such as the Miss America Pageant protest, the birth control hearings, and the Strike for Equality (and the *LHJ* sit-in as well, in terms of print treatment) did little to build legitimacy for feminist claims; rather, they built a case for feminist extremism. On the other hand, the visibility that national reporting produced was a boon for the movement in other ways—it galvanized existing members, attracted new ones, and contributed to significant achievements, such as warning labels on the pill, changes in women's magazines, and the building of momentum for the ERA. Indeed, the massive growth in the movement after the Strike for Equality indicates that women, despite the assumptions of most reporters, were among the national television audience watching women's liberation, and thousands of them saw past the condescending coverage to grasp the movement's promise of a different future for themselves and their daughters.

After 1970

The pivotal events of 1970 would set the stage for a period of liberal feminist triumph over the next several years, as feminists made good use of the movement's momentum. As Gail Collins (2009) puts it, "The world had turned, and the conviction that what women needed most was protection had given way to a call for an equal playing field" as "the nation's consciousness was quickly, and sometimes painfully, evolving" (pp. 206–207). That evolving consciousness would be fostered by the creation of new feminist institutions, such as the National Women's Political Caucus (NWPC, founded in 1971 by Gloria Steinem, Betty Friedan, Fannie Lou Hamer, Shirley Chisholm, Myrlie Evers, and Bella Abzug), and *Ms.* magazine, which put out its first issue in 1972. As I will discuss shortly, Gloria Steinem's centrality to these developments—and to media attention to feminism—was another crucial post-1970 outcome.

Liberal feminism's ascendance after 1970 was facilitated by the disintegration of radical groups that were splintered by ideological conflicts and by the rise of a separatist, often lesbian, cultural feminism that was invisible to mass media. Some radicals turned to NOW as the most viable and stable alternative for doing movement work, and the organization would become the chief beneficiary of radical feminism's decline; its member total was around 3,000 in 1970, but would swell to more than 50,000 by 1974 (Davis, 1991; Echols, 1989).

Liberal feminists enjoyed a hospitable political climate in the early 1970s, when "the U.S. Congress seemed hell-bent on figuring out what women wanted and giving it to them," and the courts cooperated by issuing a series of favorable rulings (Evans, 2003, pp. 62). Because of liberal feminist activism, legislation such as Title IX, the Equal Opportunity Act, the Women's Educational Equity Act, and the Equal Credit Opportunity Act all passed early in the decade. By 1972, both houses of Congress had passed the ERA, and the amendment would be ratified by thirty states by the end of 1973, the same year that the Supreme Court issued the *Roe v. Wade* decision.

The confidence about ERA ratification so evident in 1970's stories about the House passage would turn out to be short-lived. Within a few years, opponents of the amendment, led by women such as STOP ERA's Phyllis Schlafly, would launch a powerful countermovement, and even the granting of a four-year extension to the 1979 ratification deadline would not make a difference. Yet the ERA's difficulties also were a product of the larger political and cultural context; by the mid-1970s, economic stagnation, post-Watergate cynicism, and post-Vietnam disillusionment had created fertile ground for backlash against feminist goals (Evans, 2003). That context would be exploited by antifeminists like Schlafly, who argued, in ways strikingly similar to some of the network coverage and commentary around the Strike for Equality, that the ERA would force the elimination of gender distinctions in all arenas of public and private life, making it illegal, for instance, for men to support their wives and outlawing other protections that traditional women treasured (Mansbridge, 1986; Solomon, 1979). The conflict created by conservative opposition kept the ERA in the news, as did routine coverage of ratification efforts in various states and the campaign to extend the ratification deadline. Abortion also maintained its newsworthiness because of conservative backlash and ongoing efforts to limit the implications of *Roe v. Wade* through the courts and state legislatures.

Yet maintaining a distinction between feminism itself and its representation in mass media is crucial. For example, radical feminism's disappearance from national television coverage of feminism does not tell the tale of its legacy for women's liberation. Radicals' CR-based analyses of the systemic power imbalance between men and women would become the foundation of later reforms pursued at local, state, and national levels (and supported by NOW and various social welfare agencies) around issues such as rape, domestic violence, and sexual harassment (Bronstein, 2011; Cuklanz, 1995). Issues once deemed personal and private eventually became the focus of public policy and public institutions, and it was radical feminist thinking and activism that initiated that shift. Even so, they were framed as "women's issues" and were usually relegated to the soft news category, where they appeared most often in the women's pages (renamed as Life or Style sections) of national and local newspapers, as well as in women's magazines, including *Ms.* (Bradley, 2003). Although radicals did not see the total revolution they sought come to fruition, their efforts contributed to various kinds of social transformation through the growth of feminist institutions across the nation (e.g., battered women's shelters, sexual assault centers, women's health centers, women's bookstores, and women's studies programs) and through shifts in public discourse around issues that they first brought to public attention.

Rape is a useful example. Although it was a persistent topic in early consciousness-raising groups (see Connell and Wilson, 1974), the 1970 network reports mentioned rape only once, and in passing, in a comment in the ABC documentary. In January 1971, NYRF organized the first speak-out on rape, followed by a conference in April, and thus began the feminist antirape movement (Matthews, 1994). That same year, the first important works of feminist theory about rape appeared, when Susan Griffin (1971) published (the widely reprinted) "Rape: The All-American Crime," in the leftist outlet *Ramparts* and Pam Kearon and Barbara Mehrhof (1973) of The Feminists, published "Rape: An Act of Terror" in the feminist collection *Notes from the Third Year*. In 1975, Susan Brownmiller would publish her groundbreaking book, *Against Our Will: Men, Women, and Rape*, that would help push rape onto the national news agenda (Bronstein, 2011). Media attention and rape law reform efforts intensified throughout the late 1970s, although, particularly in national broadcast news, such attention came in the form of crime reporting and stories on high-profile legal cases rather than as reports on feminist activism (Cuklanz, 1995).

Another post-1970 outcome was that coverage of organized, institution-based feminist activities became somewhat routinized, at least for several years. For example, the networks ran stories on the founding of the NWPC in July 1971, as well as on the anniversary of Strike Day that August and on the founding of *Ms.* in 1972. In 1973, they covered the first convention of the NWPC as well as NOW's annual meeting. When the National Women's Conference, an outgrowth of the United Nations' designation of 1975 as International Women's Year and the first and only women's conference funded by the federal government, was held in Houston in November 1977, it was the subject of multiple network stories (Evans, 2003). In fact, it received substantial hard news coverage from national and international outlets, and "the fact that 60 percent of the people requesting press passes were women attested to how responsive the media had become on the subject of their own personnel policies and their image" (Tobias, 1997, p. 110).

3 first
Ladies

On the one hand, that a conference dominated by feminists was attended by three first ladies (Betty Ford, Rosalynn Carter, and Lady Bird Johnson), who opened the proceedings, could be seen as a triumph for feminism's acceptance and/or as a sign of feminism's co-optation by the establishment (assessments that are by no means mutually exclusive). On the other hand, that the conference managed to create a twenty-six plank "Plan of Action" encompassing issues as diverse as equal credit for women, national health insurance, abortion, child care, lesbian rights, violence against women, and the ERA (a prominent demand to come out of the conference involved extension of the ratification deadline), was a sign that feminism's agenda was still broad, as was its constituency. In fact, 35 percent of the delegates were nonwhite, and there were more than a hundred women there who identified as lesbian (Evans, 2003; Tobias, 1997).

But the conference also was a sign of the growing strength of the conservative antifeminist forces that would enable the defeat of the ERA and aid in the election of President Ronald Reagan in 1980. A group of more than 10,000 conservative antifeminist women, led by Phyllis Schlafly, set up their own gathering across town to protest what they saw as a radical antifamily conference wrongly subsidized by the federal government. Their keynote speaker, Representative Robert Dornan of California, called the National Women's Conference delegates "sick, anti-God, pro-lesbian, and anti-patriotic" (Evans, 2003, p. 142). In ad-

Figure 12. Phyllis Schlafly surrounded by reporters and supporters at an anti-ERA rally in 1977. © Bettman/CORBIS.

Figure 13. Representative Barbara Jordan (D-Texas) delivers the keynote at the 1977 National Women's Conference. Front row, left to right: Representative Bella Abzug (D-New York), First Lady Rosalynn Carter, former First Lady Betty Ford, former First Lady Lady Bird Johnson. © 2013 Associated Press/ *Houston Chronicle*, Sam C. Pierson Jr.

NOW Largest Womens organizat.

dition, a number of the delegates at the National Women's Conference were also conservative, anti-ERA women, representing states that had not ratified the amendment, such as Mississippi and Utah (Evans, 2003). Their opposition to various resolutions—particularly those concerning lesbian rights and abortion—would result in sometimes rancorous debate, and network stories predictably focused on the conflict and underplayed unity around other issues.

Perhaps most importantly, the Houston conference was the beginning of a "rhetorical commingling" by antifeminist forces that implied that support for the ERA was support for abortion rights (despite the fact that the former would have no effect on the latter), thus bringing the formidable power of religious antiabortion forces (the National Conference of Catholic Bishops, Mormons, and Protestant fundamentalists) into the anti-ERA camp (Bradley, 2003, p. 268). The adoption of a lesbian rights plank by the conference provided further ammunition for the ERA opposition, which used the danger of homosexual contagion as a potent rhetorical resource. Interviewed ten years later, Phyllis Schlafly claimed that the "display of feminist solidarity with lesbians that day in Houston clinched her victory" over the ERA (Tobias, 1997, p. 156; see also Tate, 2005).

Like the Women's Strike for Equality, the National Women's Conference was viewed as a triumph by those who had planned and participated in it. It was not only proof of feminist power and solidarity, it had the official imprimatur of the U.S. government. The conference's Plan of Action was delivered to President Jimmy Carter, who sent legislative recommendations to Congress based upon it. They died there, as the rise of the Republican Right was already underway. At the 1980 Republican National Convention at which Ronald Reagan became the Republican nominee for president, the GOP would remove support for the ERA from its platform (a reversal of a forty-year tradition), and Reagan would become the first U.S. president actively opposed to the amendment (Evans, 2003).

By this time, pro-ERA forces had mounted a July 1978 March for Equality in Washington, D.C., in support of the ratification extension and had fought efforts to rescind ERA ratification in a dozen states. Participants in the March for Equality, around a hundred thousand, far outstripped the Women's Strike for Equality but received far less network coverage (Davis, 1991). The antifeminist seeds sown at the National Women's Conference had come to fruition, and feminism was struggling to maintain its footing in a new political environment, a problem made more acute when the June 30, 1982, deadline passed and the ERA was three states short of the thirty-eight required for ratification. In *Why We Lost the ERA*, Jane Mansbridge (1986) argues that the ERA, even if passed, would have had few short-term, direct effects on women's legal equality, which made great strides during the 1970s anyway as Supreme Court interpretations of the Fourteenth Amendment made unconstitutional many of the discriminatory laws that the ERA had been designed to address. However, she also maintains that the amendment's indirect effects on the attitudes of legislators and judges might have been substantial.

By placing the ERA at the conclusion of my narrative about the evolution of feminism and its presence in network news after 1970, I do not mean to participate in a version of feminist history that pinpoints the defeat of the amendment as the end of the second wave (although there are reasons to believe that mass media saw it this way). Instead, following Mansbridge, I mean to highlight the amendment's tremendous rhetorical and symbolic power as an issue that kept feminism in the media spotlight in the latter half of the 1970s. At the same time, that attention enabled the perpetuation and amplification of problematic media strategies already attached to women's liberation (most prominently the "women versus women" dynamic and/or "feminists hate housewives" charge) as well as precipitated the generation of new ones, such as the claim that feminists were, as a whole, antifamily/antimotherhood and prolesbian (as though the two were the same thing and as though there were no lesbian mothers). The antifamily charge, in particular, shows how quickly the worm can turn, given that child care was not only a central concern for feminists, but it had been approvingly featured as a reasonable feminist issue in network coverage of the movement in 1970.

In many ways, the narrowing of national television coverage of the movement to a focus on the ERA was the logical extension of network coverage in 1970 that had endorsed the amendment as the obvious cure for women's ills. Moreover, by the early 1970s, NOW, the nation's largest feminist organization, had thrown all of its energies behind ratification. This choice came at a cost. For one thing, the amendment's failure would be viewed by many as the failure of feminism itself, an interpretation promoted by mass media. In addition, a focus on the ERA, and the emphases of that focus, did little to displace public perceptions of feminism as a movement of white, middle-class women. By the time women of color were founding their own feminist groups, such as the National Black Feminist Organization, television news' interest in women's liberation as a social movement, rather than as a special interest group fighting for specific political issues, had waned.[1] Media casting of the ERA struggle as a battle between careerist feminists and traditional women (i.e., privileged white homemakers) defending their families left little room for the concerns of women of color who did not fit either of these narrow images. Although lesbians had finally entered media discussion of feminism, they did so as a scare tactic deployed by the opposition, not as a group with unique and legitimate concerns.[2]

In the end, the ERA's abstraction was a simultaneous strength and weakness. It was a powerful symbol of support for women's equality, and public equality had long been treated as a fairly uncontroversial goal in news treatment of women's liberation, embodying, as it did, the virtues of liberalism and reformism while also functioning as the moderate alternative to the radical calls for revolution in all areas of public and private life. Yet the ERA also was vague enough that mass media were able to use their default mode for representing feminism and thus to frame discussion of the issue within the limited concerns of white, middle-class womanhood. At worst, the lack of specificity in the amendment made it into a kind of empty vessel into which all kinds of gendered fears and anxieties could be poured. Conservative voices poured them eagerly and skillfully, and mass media dutifully reported the accusations that the ERA would wreck homes and families, make abortion easier, and serve as the vehicle for lesbian liberation.

At a time when the country as a whole was turning to the right, and when backlash against the perceived excesses of the 1960s counterculture was building, the ERA was tainted by its association with women's liberation, the movement that had brought it out of decades of legislative limbo. This quintessential liberal feminist policy goal, long scorned by radical feminists, became *the* symbol of radical feminism for many Americans, an ironic outcome that was partially made possible because radical feminists themselves had vanished from newspaper pages and television screens.

Thus, after mass media were instrumental in making the ERA the central goal of the movement, the failure of the amendment's ratification provided an impetus for television news to "post" feminism; that is, to treat it as a phenomenon that had largely receded into the past, for good or ill. The term "postfeminism" began to enter the media lexicon around this time, and one of its first appearances was in a 1982 cover story in the *NYT Magazine,* titled "Voices from the Postfeminist Generation" (Bolotin, 1982). The article detailed young women's rejection of feminism as "the province of angry, bitter women too dedicated to pointing out the problems of being female," demonstrating the power of certain mass-mediated interpretations of the movement (Dow, 1996, p. 89). A wave of media stories and mass market books would follow, cohering around the assumptions that the second wave had "accomplished all that it set out to" and that it had "outlived its usefulness," while also arguing that what feminism hath wrought had come at a great cost to postfeminism's preferred subject—white, middle-class, largely married women—whose lives were more complicated and less happy (Vavrus, 2002, p. 184). In response, feminists argued that that the problems contemporary women faced were the result of too little feminism, not too much, and that the blame lay with governments' and society's failure to adequately respond to the changes in women's lives, including the lives of those women who, unlike postfeminism's ideal subject, were not "well situated socially or materially" (Vavrus, 2002, p. 184; see also Dow, 1996; Faludi, 1991).

Little more than a decade after the triumph that was the Women's Strike for Equality, a decade in which feminist activism had involved thousands of women and had produced transformative legal, social, and political change, the organized movement was on the defensive. Much of feminism's work in the 1980s, largely absent from television screens, would be focused on forestalling the erosion of the gains of the 1970s, gains from which women had barely begun to benefit.

The Rise of Gloria Steinem

One constant in feminism's triumphal years in the 1970s, as well as in the more challenging years that followed, was the near ubiquitous presence of Gloria Steinem, the movement's longest-lasting media icon. Contrary to much popular memory, Steinem was not a visible presence in 1970s wave of network news coverage. She had begun to write and to speak about the movement as a

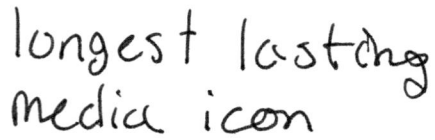

longest lasting
media icon

journalist by 1969, but she was not a member of any of the feminist groups on which that coverage focused (or any feminist group, period), and she had yet to be recognized as a movement leader by national media.

By 1972, however, Steinem had become the face of feminism for mass media and the public, a position that she arguably still holds. On March 18, 2012, the front page of the *New York Times* Style section carried an article titled "A Woman Like No Other" that began by observing that "for more than 40 years, Gloria Steinem has been the near-singular voice of the women's movement," and went on to explore why no worthy successor to Steinem had emerged (Hepola, 2012, p. ST1). The *Times*'s math is a bit generous, given that "more than 40 years" ago places Steinem at the movement's helm *prior* to 1970. In 1970, the *Times* used the appellation "high priestess" of women's liberation to refer to both Kate Millett and Betty Friedan in different articles in the space of four months, but only briefly mentioned Steinem in the paper's coverage of the Women's Strike for Equality, the first organized movement action in which she participated (Klemesrud, 1970, p. 47; Prial, 1970, p. 30).

Steinem's centrality to feminism—and its media presence—in the 1970s and beyond is unquestionable, but I am most concerned with the ways that mediated popular memory has shaped that centrality, and in turn, has shaped memories of the movement itself. In the final portion of this chapter, I take up the portrait of Steinem, second-wave feminism, and mass media's relation to both offered by a 2011 documentary, HBO's *Gloria: In Her Own Words*, which echoes the *New York Times'* assumption that modern feminism would not exist without her. *Gloria* is an intriguing exercise in public memory construction because of the tale it tells about the second wave and Steinem's place in it as well as the one it does not. Certainly, it simplifies a complex story, which is to be expected in a narrative framed as biography. More compelling to me are the paradoxical ways in which the documentary implicitly functions as a story about mass media and women's liberation while, in various implicit and explicit ways, eliding the centrality of mass media to Steinem's life in the movement as well as to its account of that life. Thus, I approach it as an illuminating postscript to my assessment of the problems and possibilities of early mediated narratives of the second wave, suggesting that its most powerful lesson is that the contradictions that characterized feminism's image politics in 1970 persist in the present.

Gloria Steinem, Mass Media, and the Movement

The second wave did not make Gloria Steinem a celebrity, although it did make her a *feminist* celebrity. By the late 1960s, Steinem already enjoyed considerable fame as a glamorous and socially active journalist in New York, where she was as well known for her connections—both professional and romantic—to powerful men as for her writing. She had been toiling as a freelance journalist for almost a decade at that point, and, as she would later lament, much of her published writing was on fashion, lifestyle, celebrities, and other frothy cultural topics. Yet she quickly gained notice and was soon not just the writer of celebrity profiles but the subject of them as well. Her 1963 publication in *Show* of "A Bunny's Tale," her now-famous exposé of the Playboy Club, was instrumental in this development.

The story could not help but draw attention to the fact that Steinem was a journalist attractive enough to qualify for an undercover role as a Bunny, and it was illustrated with photos of her wearing a Bunny costume. The press took notice. In 1964, a feature in *Glamour* described her signature style, a lengthy 1965 *Newsday* story was titled "The World's Most Beautiful Byline," and articles in *Ladies' Home Journal* in 1966 and the *Washington Post* in 1967 were headed, respectively, as "Easy on the Eye" and "Writer's Life Can Be Glorious and Beautiful." During this same period, she was involved with a number of well-known men such as Kennedy intimate Ted Sorenson and director Mike Nichols (Stern, 1997).

In 1968, Steinem became a contributing editor at the newly created *New York* magazine, and an April 1969 column she wrote for *New York,* "After Black Power, Women's Liberation" (Steinem, 1969), was her initial launching pad into movement politics, and, by her own account, precipitated her feminist awakening (Steinem, 1983). Researching the piece, she attended Redstockings's February 1969 disruption of the New York State Assembly's hearings on abortion law reform as well as the abortion speakout that the group held a month later in New York's West Village.[3] Steinem's column on the movement generated speaking invitations, and she and a series of speaking partners, all black women (Dorothy Pittman Hughes, Flo Kennedy, and Margaret Sloan), began to travel around the country lecturing on feminism on college campuses and in other venues.[4] The speaking tour brought her additional publicity that began to link her with women's liberation in the eyes of the public and mass media.

Even so, by 1970, when viewers watched women's liberation explode onto television screens, Steinem had some fame as a journalist who talked about women's liberation but was not yet perceived as a movement player. In addition to her absence from network stories treating women's liberation that year, her role in print stories about the movement, although on the rise, was fairly small. She was quoted in the *Washington Post*'s coverage of the Senate hearings on the ERA in May (Lardner, 1970); she was interviewed—and her photo was included—in a *NYT Magazine* article about Betty Friedan in November (Wilkes, 1970); and she was mentioned—and pictured—again less than a month later in the *Times* story about

Figure 14. Photo accompanying an Associated Press feature story about Steinem published in April 1970. The caption read, in part: "Gloria Steinem, writer-activist-antiwar-gorgeous bachelor girl has managed to make the whole world accessible to her." © 2013 Associated Press.

the press conference that she helped to organize at which feminists vocalized their support for Kate Millett after her outing by *Time* (Klemesrud, 1970). On the other hand, her reputation as a celebrity journalist in New York received yet another boost that summer when she penned an article about her recently redecorated apartment for the July issue of *House and Garden* (Steinem, 1970b).

Steinem was operating in a liminal space with regard to her relationship to the movement throughout most of 1970. Although she was speaking about feminism with increasing frequency, she was not seen as a feminist leader by national media, which was likely related to her lack of membership, let alone leadership, in any existing feminist group. Steinem's appearance at the ERA hearings is an instructive example of the ways that her media visibility, rather than her movement connections, facilitated her rise as a feminist figurehead. Brenda Feigen, a NOW vice president who had once worked for Senator Birch Bayh, was asked by Bayh to coordinate the hearings' pro-ERA testimony. She recalled having seen Steinem on *The David Susskind Show* in 1969, after Steinem's column about the movement had appeared in *New York,* and she called and asked her to testify (Heilbrun, 1996).

At the time, Steinem primarily identified as a journalist; in the *Times* article on Millett, for instance, she was described as such in a paragraph that included movement group affiliations for the other women present. Although she published (remarkably similar) pieces about the movement in the *Washington Post* and in *Time* in 1970, she was identified as a journalist and contributing editor of *New York* magazine in each of them (Steinem, 1970a, 1970c). Within the liberal movement in New York, however, the power of her public profile, including her fundraising abilities in her powerful and wealthy social circle, were seen as enough of an asset by the summer of 1970 that she was asked to join the coordinating committee for the Women's Strike for Equality.

Figure 15. The Kate is Great press conference called on December 17, 1970, to show support for Kate Millett. Despite the many representatives of various feminist groups in attendance, this photo that accompanied the *New York Times* and Associated Press stories centered on Steinem. © 2013 Associated Press.

By 1971, Steinem would complete the transition from journalist to feminist activist when she cofounded the NWPC, which occasioned her first speaking appearance on national network news (although she had already appeared on a variety of local and national talk shows), and the Women's Action Alliance. The NWPC was targeted at raising the visibility of women and women's issues in national electoral politics, while the Women's Action Alliance was designed to foster local grassroots projects combating social and economic discrimination. By this point, Steinem also was involved in the planning and production of the preview of *Ms.* that appeared in a December issue of *New York* magazine and that would set the stage for the debut of *Ms.* as a stand-alone publication in the spring of 1972.

Her national media presence in relation to the movement expanded dramatically during this period as well. In August 1971, she appeared on the cover of *Newsweek* below the coverline "The New Woman." The story inside was subtitled "A Liberated Woman Despite Beauty, Chic, and Success," thus calling attention to her deviation from perceived feminist norms, an element essential to her irresistibility for news workers (Boeth, 1971, p. 51). In the *Times*'s coverage of the first anniversary of the Women's Strike for Equality that summer, the paper carried an article by Steinem (1971), adapted from her recent speech at the Harvard Law Review banquet.

By January 1972, in the *McCall's* issue accompanying her selection as the magazine's Woman of the Year, she was termed the movement's "most persuasive evangelist" (Mercer, 1972, p. 68), and praised for her ability "to bridge the gap between the early militants, whose vehemence frightened away the people they most wanted to reach, and the thoughtful dedicated women who understand that women's status *must* change. She is, in short, a transitional figure, proof that change is not so frightening after all" ("Woman of the Year," 1972, p. 67, emphasis

in original). That same month, Steinem was the focus of an extensive interview in *Redbook,* headlined on the cover as "Gloria Steinem: Blunt Answers to Questions about Love, Marriage and Angry Women" (Smith, 1972).

At the time, some attributed Steinem's rapid ascent in terms of visibility and influence as much to her celebrity, pleasing appearance, and connections to powerful men (e.g., Clay Felker, editor of *New York*, who facilitated the founding of *Ms.*) as to her hard work as an organizer and advocate (e.g., Levitt, 1971; "Lib Rip-off?" 1972). Contemporary accounts credit commercial mass media with her rise to prominence; happy to find a feminist they could sell, journalists saw Steinem as the "compromise" they had been looking for, "a feminist who looks like a fashion model" (Douglas, 1994, p. 230; see also Bradley, 2003). Steinem's media-friendliness functioned at several levels: She was not only physically attractive and rhetorically skilled, making her an ideal spokesperson for media purposes, but she was also well-networked in the media world and smart about how it worked, making her expert at fashioning her own image and well-equipped to spearhead a mass-market feminist magazine.

Not surprisingly, she was viewed as an opportunistic arriviste by some radical feminists, for whom she signified the selling-out of the movement. Not only did she lack authentic movement credentials, having never been a member of a feminist organization that she did not help to create, but she made a career out of co-opting radical ideas and packaging them for the mainstream. For example,

Redstocking Ellen Willis (1992), who would briefly work for *Ms.*, counted Steinem among liberals who "supported feminist reforms . . . but basically ignored the existence of power relations" as they sought to transform feminism into a strategy of "individual and collective self-improvement" (p. 137). Moreover, Steinem's penchant for publicity flew in the face of radicals' antielitism, a problem she was largely able to sidestep by creating a power base outside of existing movement groups. Carole Hanisch (1978a) would subsequently acknowledge that the radical movement's "no leadership line" had stymied its efforts to reach out to women and had cleared the path for media-friendly liberals like Steinem "who have access to the press and money" (p. 163).

Steinem had always been interested in bringing attention to the problems of traditional heterosexual relationships, a perennial topic for radical feminist CR and writing since the movement's beginnings. Yet when she discussed the problematic roles that men and women needed to "unlearn," her rhetoric was liberal and pedagogical, claiming that such changes would benefit men and women alike, and she omitted the complex analyses of power dynamics that characterized radical feminist theorizing (Steinem, 1971, p. 37; see also Steinem 1970a, 1970c). Steinem's ultimate rhetorical tactic was her attempt to transcend ideology altogether and to turn feminism's claims into a kind of common sense (always an ideology in itself) that sidestepped the theoretical disagreements—between liberals and radicals and among radicals themselves—that had characterized the early second wave and with which she had no experience and little interest in her quest to make the movement meaningful to the masses. By framing her feminism as a humane quest for fairness and equality—whether in private male-female relationships or in the public sphere through the ERA and reproductive rights—she followed the movement's public trajectory and helped to shape it as well.

Steinem's amalgam of attenuated radical and liberal ideas also characterized *Ms.* magazine under her leadership. Ellen Willis's (1978) critique of *Ms.*, issued when she left its ranks in 1975, usefully describes Steinem's politics as enacted through the magazine: "the party line was an obsession with electoral politics, self-help, a presentation of sisterhood as sentimental papering-over of divisions," and "an emphasis on attacking sexual roles rather than male power" (p. 171). Yet the failure of *Ms.* to serve as forum for radical feminist writing and theory was about more than Steinem's reformist vision. By the mid-1970s, the growth of women's studies programs and feminist academic publishing meant that the innovative theorizing, largely grounded in CR, that had fueled the development of the early feminist underground press was moving into the academy, where it was increasingly separate from grassroots feminist activism (Messer-

Davidow, 2002). By the early 1980s, feminist scholarship would increasingly be "claimed as a form of activist intervention" in itself (Dever, 2004, p. 149).

Indeed, Steinem's emergence as a central figure in the second wave—both in the eyes of mass media and among feminists themselves—was partially produced by the dramatic changes the movement was undergoing after 1970. *McCall's* description of Steinem as a "transitional figure" was an apt one; she both benefited from and facilitated liberal feminism's movement into the mainstream (and radical feminism's concomitant decline) that had begun in earnest with the House passage of the ERA and the Women's Strike for Equality. By bringing her already considerable visibility and networking skills to movement work, she broadened feminism's appeal with the public at large and with key constituencies, such as the Democratic Party, which gave her a speaking slot at the 1972 Democratic National Convention.

Steinem's commitments to public policy issues meant that she was generally well-regarded among liberal feminists, many of whom were her allies in her organizing work. However, she was famously the target of Betty Friedan's rancor—Friedan accused her in 1972 of "ripping off the movement for profit" ("Lib Rip-off," 1972, p. D2)—a phenomenon that was often chalked up to the NOW founder's jealousy that she was losing the media spotlight to someone younger and prettier who lacked her many years in the trenches (e.g., Ephron, 1972). Yet Friedan saw her differences with Steinem as political and strategic as well. To her, the famously antimarriage Steinem was insufficiently attentive to the need to translate the movement's ideas into terms that would attract the support of middle-class married women. Friedan's general dismay at what she saw as feminists' dismissal of the importance of marriage and children to most women would manifest in her 1981 book, *The Second Stage,* in which she charged that feminists should reorient their efforts toward ensuring that women could enjoy full lives that included husbands and children. Different reactions to Steinem indicate the malleability of what counted as "liberal" versus "radical" feminism as the 1970s proceeded, when ERA opponents labeled the amendment and its advocates as radical while longtime radical feminists viewed the measure as pointless reformism. Those radical feminists still committed to the revolutionary goals of the early movement saw Steinem as a liberal careerist, while Friedan saw her as not moderate enough.

Despite Friedan's discomfort with Steinem's general disdain for marriage, the latter's vivid heterosexual appeal was a crucial ingredient in the mainstreaming of the movement, as the cover stories in *Newsweek* and *McCall's* demonstrated. By 1974, she would make the cover of *People* with the coverline "fighting sexism with new tactics" ("Gloria Steinem," 1974). In each of these cover stories, the photos were remarkably similar: close-up headshots that emphasized her leonine mane of hair and striking face. Steinem's adherence to conventional beauty standards was a signal that she "accepted the rules of society" thus making her "a safe choice for media celebrity" (Bradley, 2003, p. 151). Her always visible womanliness was a crucial antidote to the gender anxiety provoked by earlier feminist protest, and she did indeed project a public identity for feminism that was "not so frightening after all" ("Woman of the Year," 1972, p. 67).

Steinem's equanimity, her measured, often pithy, discourse, and her camera-friendly visage made her an ideal popularizer for a movement that had, until she entered it, lacked a principal and persuasive personality to carry its ideas. Friedan was seen as abrasive and overbearing even by her own feminist colleagues (partially accounting for her exit from NOW leadership in 1970), Kate Millett's brief moment as a media-appointed movement leader that year ended with the revelation that she was bisexual, and Ti-Grace Atkinson was too radical to function as more than good copy for feminist extremism. Steinem, on the other hand, became an institution-builder as well as a media personality, and thus was always perceived as representing a constituency. Yet, unlike Shirley Chisholm and Bella Abzug, who also were committed to movement ideals and were quite visible in the 1970s, she was not constrained by elective office. In short, her success at becoming the face and voice of the movement was about the confluence of that moment in the movement's development, her existing media image and connections, *and* her movement work, central to which was her willingness to travel and speak almost anywhere her presence was requested to represent feminism, and, not incidentally, the interests of *Ms.* magazine.

Steinem *was* a media-created feminist heroine in important ways, but she was not *only* that, and much of the dismissive treatment she received reflected the same kind of sexism that resulted in the erasure of feminists' political credentials in early reports on women's liberation. Reactions to Steinem's role in the movement in the 1970s tend to assign her either too much agency, charging that she single-handedly deradicalized feminism by packaging it in a mass-market publication (thus oversimplifying a transition to liberal feminist dominance and to feminism's commodification that was multicausal), or too little, claiming that mass media simply anointed her as the movement's primary leader because of her attractiveness (thus ignoring her considerable hard work).

Regardless, Steinem became the movement's first real celebrity, and her function as such both broadened its popular appeal and narrowed its political potential. She met a hunger in mass media, existent since 1968, for a marketable individual who could represent and speak for what the movement meant. That that meaning was largely interpreted through her own personal characteristics—white, beautiful, single, childless, and careerist—was an outcome impossible to avoid, given mass media emphasis on liberal individualism. Despite her work with feminist organizations that involved women of different races, classes, sexual identities, and life situations—and promoted the interests of the same—she herself became the enduring message.

Mass media promotion of Steinem as a feminist icon would do little to counter existing interpretations of the movement as relevant only to a slender slice of American women, impressions that gained power from feminism's increasing commodification in the 1970s. Steinem became one of the symbols of a developing lifestyle feminism that was driven by identity rather than ideology, was sold in *Ms.* and other women's magazines, and was bolstered by various popular culture forms—music, advertising, television programming, and film—that packaged feminist themes for mass consumption. Songs such as Helen Reddy's "I Am Woman, Hear Me Roar" (1972), sitcoms like *The Mary Tyler Moore Show* (1970–1977), and movies such as *An Unmarried Woman* (1978) enabled the creation of a new stock feminist character and preferred feminist subject—the independent working (white) woman who made her way without a man—that Steinem typified (Douglas, 1994; Dow, 1996, Lehman, 2011).

News reports on the movement drew from and contributed to this wider media context, fitting Steinem into a narrative that cast the feminist-antifeminist conflicts of the 1970s as a kind of catfight among women; for example, a 1977 ABC special was titled "ERA: The Battle between the Women" (Douglas, 1994). Steinem herself was wary of this dynamic and refused to debate opponents like Phyllis Schlafly, believing that to do so simply validated the canard that women could not get along (Heilbrun, 1996). But her participation was not necessary for the women versus women narrative, long a staple of media reports on feminism, to find new footing. On one side was Steinem, the unmarried and childfree careerist who championed the lesbian cause along with the ERA and abortion rights, and on the other was Phyllis Schlafly, the married mother of six who charged that feminists like Steinem wanted to destroy the traditional family and the protections it afforded women.

Chroniclers of Steinem's role in the movement consistently remark on the effort she expended to control her public image—an endeavor to which she is still clearly committed in the *Gloria* documentary—but she could not control all of the uses to which her image was put (Bradley, 2003, Stern, 1997). She became the omnipresent face of the movement quite quickly, and, just as it was possible to discuss the state of women's liberation in 1970 without mentioning Gloria Steinem, it became impossible to discuss the state of feminism *after* 1971 without mentioning Gloria Steinem.

Gloria's Feminist History

One of the consequences of Steinem's status as the personification of the second wave is a shortening and flattening of the movement's history. The second wave's early and earnest conflicts over ideology and tactics, race, class, and sexuality, as well as its relationship to the countercultural ferment of the 1960s, are eclipsed in the story of Steinem's equally earnest personal crusade, begun in the 1970s, to champion all that was good for women and to oppose all that was bad for them. In 1974, *People* magazine claimed that Steinem had been "the feminist movement's most visible spokesperson" for five years, thus, much like the 2012 *Times* story, inserting her into second wave history in 1969, when she had no relationship to the organized movement ("Gloria Steinem," p. 8). Despite its ample use of network footage from 1970, *Gloria* similarly implies that second-wave feminism *really* began when Steinem entered it.

Interviewed in the *New York Times* around the time of the program's first broadcast, HBO producer Sheila Nevins revealed that her purpose for the project was straightforward. Aghast that most of the young men and women on her staff had not heard of Steinem, she called it "an inspirational film about St. Gloria. We made it for the kids on the floor who didn't know who she was" (Jensen, 2011, p. AR16). The article also contained disclaimers from Steinem about her discomfort at being singled out and her insistence that "the fight for equal rights for women 'has been a collective effort'" (Jensen, 2011, p. AR16).

This backstory sheds some light on dominant strategies in the documentary, including its universalization of Steinem's experiences that positions her as an everywoman representing collective womanhood of her generation, an interpretation of her glamorous past that presents it as more of a problem than an asset, and, true to the "St. Gloria" designation, a portrayal of her as a selfless vessel for the movement's interests and the betterment of womankind. My purpose here is not to set the record straight with regard to Steinem's "true" history in the second wave, but, rather, to explore the ways in which the narrative offered by *Gloria* simultaneously reveals and obscures the critical intersections of Steinem's career and the movement's development, and mass media's relationship to both.

Gloria: In Her Own Words is an appropriate title, given that Steinem's is the documentary's only sense-making voice. It contains no ongoing narration and no contemporary interview footage save that involving Steinem herself, who sat down for a lengthy interview conducted by Nevins and director Peter Kunhardt (who are never seen and never heard) in her New York apartment. Transitions between segments are signaled by epigraphs, on a black screen or superimposed over a photograph, taken from Steinem's own discourse. For example, the segment on Betty Friedan's relationship with Steinem is preceded by an epigraph that reads, "People have the false impression that Betty Friedan and I were close." With the exception of the excerpts from the interview with Steinem that are woven throughout the documentary (pieces of which are also used as narration for images), the rest of the narrative is made up entirely of photographs and video footage, most of it from news reports on the movement and previous interviews with Steinem.

The bulk of *Gloria* is spent on Steinem's early life, feminist awakening, and movement work in the 1970s, what Steinem, in the documentary, calls a "heady and exciting and naïve" period "because we thought these injustices are so great, surely if we just explain them to people, they will want to fix them." Forty-three of the documentary's sixty-one minutes focus on events before 1982, the year of the ERA ratification failure. As it begins, a montage of video clips precedes the appearance of the program's title; they include images from the Miss America Pageant protest (taken from one of David Culhane's 1970 CBS stories), from the Strike for Equality (taken from the August 26, 1970, CBS report), from the founding of the NWPC (also from CBS coverage), and from the 2004 March for Women's Lives, a feminist action for reproductive freedom heralded as the largest march on Washington ever held in the United States. A couple of talking head shots of Steinem from the 1970s are interspersed, including one in which she utters one of her memorable aphorisms, "What we are talking about is a revolution, not a reform," followed by a clip in which she articulates a familiar theme about the need to "humanize" the roles of men and women.

The montage also includes footage of antifeminists such as Phyllis Schlafly, who comments, "Of course the women's libbers are sincere. The homosexuals are sincere. But they want to change the supreme law of our land." Toward the end of this opening sequence, Barbara Walters's voice calls Steinem "the most visible symbol of the women's movement," after which viewers see images of suffragists as Steinem's voice quotes Susan B. Anthony, the most visible symbol of the *first* wave, on the importance of making young women "ungrateful" so that they will continue the work of the movement. After the title appears on the screen, the program's first image is of Steinem in her apartment in 2011, defining a feminist as someone "who believes in the full social, economic and political equality of women and men" and "also acts on it."

In these first few moments, *Gloria* establishes Steinem's longtime centrality to feminism, illustrates resistance to the movement, and demonstrates the ongoing nature of feminist activism, even going so far as to make a connection to the first wave. By the time Steinem defines feminism as a belief in gender equality—importantly, she precedes the definition by saying that hers is the same as that which can be found in the dictionary, thus establishing it as noncontroversial and commonsensical—the stage has been set for a telling of her story. Her early experiences with sexism—the difficulty of renting an apartment as a single woman in New York, her inability to obtain assignments for the serious political journalism she wanted to write, and her sexual harassment by an editor—are recounted in *Gloria*'s initial segments. Each is universalized as a symptom of the sexism that afflicted all women at the time, reflecting a long-standing tendency of Steinem's, when asked to comment on her experiences, of putting them "in service to a larger point" (Bradley, 2003, p. 162). In an account of Steinem's experience of writing "A Bunny's Tale," she recalls that she regretted the article for years, because it exacerbated her problem of being taken seriously as a journalist, but that she would later realize its feminist import.

Although *The Feminine Mystique* (which appeared in 1963, the same year as "A Bunny's Tale") is never mentioned in this review of Steinem's early career, the segment includes several visuals of 1950s era magazine and television ads depicting white homemakers touting the satisfaction of a clean house, thus making a subtle link to Friedan's critique of housewifery and implying both that Steinem sought to escape such a fate and that her early career was limited by the traditional expectations that Friedan's book deconstructed. Betty Friedan herself, in a 1971 *Newsweek* interview, would insightfully describe Steinem as someone who "rebelled against the feminine mystique without an ideology" (quoted in Stern, 1997, p. 226). In fact, later in the documentary, when Steinem recounts her difficult adolescence as a caretaker for her mentally ill mother, she attributes Ruth Steinem's nervous breakdown to her "inability to be the perfect wife and mother and to have a pioneering career at the same time." Such an interpretation of her mother's illness can be understood as an extreme manifestation of what Friedan (1963), in *The Feminine Mystique,* famously called "the problem that has no name" (p. 57). An epigraph that appears at this point reads, "A lot of my generation are living out the unlived lives of their mothers."

When *Gloria* moves on to Steinem's feminist awakening at the March 1969 Redstockings abortion speakout, the segment opens with footage of women protestors in the streets carrying abortion law repeal signs. As images of the 1970 birth control hearings (misidentified in a caption as abortion hearings) appear on the screen, Steinem describes the abortion protest and the speakout as the "big click" that "transformed me and I began to seek out everything I could find on what was then the burgeoning women's movement." Steinem had had an abortion in her early twenties, and, as she says in *Gloria*, "I never told anyone." As she describes it, she was radicalized by the realization that she was not alone, that the criminalization of abortion was a problem for all women, and that "I wasn't crazy, the system was crazy."

Even so, she did not join any movement groups or participate in any organized feminist actions until the Women's Strike for Equality, roughly a year and a half later. Steinem comments, "When the women's movement started, I was the in-between person. I was neither the mother nor the daughter, I was in-between and perhaps that was helpful." Of course, as her discussion of her mother later reveals, in personal terms at least, she *was* the daughter avoiding her mother's fate. I suspect that she is attempting here to articulate her lack of identification with either the older women of NOW or the younger radicals, and she makes a useful point. In 1969, she was thirty-five, several years older than radicals such as Shulamith Firestone and Robin Morgan and more than a decade younger than Betty Friedan. Another, and related, potential meaning for this remark is that her feminist politics were neither wholly liberal nor completely radical; rather, they were a user-friendly combination of both that she adapted to her goals of combating women's oppression in both private and public contexts. Steinem is never specific about how her in-between position was helpful or to whom, although one can draw the inference that it was helpful in allowing her to chart her own path in the movement, given that she launched her speaking tour soon after the *New York* column was published.

A series of news clips that follow, however, imply her presence in the early movement events depicted in them. For example, a clip of the February 1969 protest at the Berghoff in Chicago is followed by a clip of Steinem saying, "Bars and restaurants are to us what lunch counters were to the black movement," although I know of no evidence that she participated in one of NOW's public accommodations protests. A brief excerpt from one of Walter Cronkite's introductions to the CBS series of movement stories follows, followed by a portion of Norma Quarles's NBC story on sexism in the workplace, after which an epigraph appears that reads, "I began to understand that my experience was an almost universal female experience." In a sense, this epigraph aptly summarizes Steinem's framing of her life thus far; that is, she retrospectively employs a "personal is political" frame to interpret her individual experiences as a reflection of the universal position of women: All women are Bunnies; women aren't taken seriously in the workplace; women are refused control of their bodies; sexual harassment is "just life" to working women, etc.

The documentary's discussion of her glamorous life during the same period is similarly depersonalized. In her commentary, Steinem disavows any agency in or benefit from her early visibility. For example, when discussing reactions to her media profile as a journalist in the 1960s, she both downplays its importance and uses it as evidence of sexism, making an abstract observation about all women: "The idea that I had a glamorous life came in part at least from the idea that if you were a pretty girl, whatever that meant, that you must be getting assignments for that reason or, if you were ever photographed at a party, that was your whole persona, you couldn't also be serious." At another point, she remarks, "I worked really hard and the result was attributed to looks." The only moment in the documentary when Steinem acknowledges that her glamorous persona might have been useful is when she comments that her image might have been helpful in dispelling stereotypes of feminists as "super serious, and anti-sexual and anti-humorous," which is "one way to stop the movement."

Steinem never acknowledges her own participation in the construction of her persona during this period, but *Gloria*'s visuals offer a somewhat contradictory message. The documentary's images of the various articles about her as well as its use of ample interview footage of her from the time—in which, for example, she discusses her much-remarked upon appearance and her romantic life, and in which one clip shows her applying make-up and dressing in her apartment—indicate that her involvement in the creation of her own celebrity was far from unwitting.

Although the universalization strategy is quite pronounced in *Gloria*'s early segments, it recurs at later points in the documentary, where it coincides with the depiction of Steinem's selflessness as a feminist leader. The segments of the documentary that focus on her early feminist work—the Women's Strike for Equality, her speaking tour, the founding of the NWPC, the creation of *Ms.*, and feminist activism at the 1972 Democratic National Convention—offer several examples of both strategies. For instance, Steinem remarks that she began to travel and to speak about the movement because she was unable to publish about it, a claim that furthers *Gloria*'s portrayal of her as an altruistically motivated convert to the cause but which is also difficult to believe, given the barrage of stories about women's liberation, most of them by women journalists, during this period.

By and large, the segments on her rising visibility and influence cast her as a woman battling the odds. For example, a clip of ABC anchor Harry Reasoner predicting that *Ms.* would fail because everything that needed to be said was contained in the first issue illustrates Steinem's triumph over expectations. Similarly, the controversy over a 1971 article in *Esquire,* titled "She: The Awesome Power of Gloria Steinem" (Levitt, 1971), that depicted her as an ambitious, publicity-seeking gadfly who had, as Steinem describes it in the documentary, "glommed on to movements insincerely" depicts her struggle against such belittling treatment. The epigraph for this segment reads, "A woman who aspires to something is called a bitch."

In this segment, Steinem interprets the issue as media treatment of the movement—rather than herself—saying that women's liberation was treated with ridicule in the early stages, but when "it started to really change the mainstream of the culture, it became a threat." A clip from the 1971 press conference at which Steinem's supporters gathered to defend her against the *Esquire* piece shows her commenting that the "issue is the whole way in which non-establishment people are treated in the press," a typically universalizing response that seems somewhat disingenuous given that part of the point of the *Esquire* critique was that Steinem was, if anything, *too* well-connected within the establishment to be sincere in her activism against it. Earlier in the documentary, discussion of Betty Friedan's resistance to Steinem's meteoric rise elicited a remarkably similar depersonalizing interpretation from Steinem: "*Anybody* who threatened her ownership of the movement came in for this. The movement was hers, she was the mother of the movement" (my emphasis).

The documentary's featuring of the *Esquire* episode segues into the founding of *Ms.* magazine, as though one had led to the other (although the preview issue of *Ms.* was well underway before the *Esquire* article appeared), when Steinem is heard saying, "I realized that that there was really nothing for women to read that was controlled by women and this caused me along with a number of other women to start *Ms.* magazine." The transition to the segment on *Ms.* features an epigraph reading, "I learned to use anger constructively," offering the implication that her personal experience with media sexism was meaningful insofar as it motivated her to advance the interests of *all* women by founding a feminist magazine. Discussing the early struggles of *Ms.*, Steinem again expresses her experience in terms of the movement's uphill battle rather than her own ambition: "The idea of a feminist magazine seemed scary to people. It was chaotic and scary, we were afraid we would not succeed and it would embarrass the movement."

The hagiographic tone of the documentary is briefly disrupted during segments focusing on Steinem's admiration for her friends in feminist struggle in the 1970s, Flo Kennedy and Bella Abzug, offering the only moments in *Gloria* when Steinem herself is not the focus and when a woman of color is more than briefly visually featured. For those familiar with Steinem's renowned public unflappability, Kennedy and Abzug, who both had reputations for abrasiveness and confrontational tactics, can be understood as the id to her superego. For example, the epigraph for a segment on the 1972 Democratic National Convention is "There's such huge punishment in the culture for an angry woman." Yet, in the segment itself, which shows footage from feminists' confrontation with a CBS news crew on the convention floor, Steinem is nowhere seen. Instead, the focus is on Kennedy, whose behavior as she shouts at and curses the CBS crew would likely have been labeled militant and/or strident had it appeared in a movement story in 1970. Steinem's interview commentary that accompanies this clip—"sometimes the only way you can call attention to the problem is to freak out people" and "you have to break the form, you have to stop playing the game, in order to change the content"—is not, in fact, a reference to her own behavior, which was famously unruffled, nonconfrontational, and essential to the generally positive media treatment she received.

As the portions of *Gloria* focusing on Steinem's movement activism conclude, viewers see brief footage of her advocacy for abortion rights and the ERA, as well as of her speaking at the 1977 National Women's Conference, about which she comments "the lesbian issue was serious," because lesbian discrimination "was not agreed upon as a feminist issue until 1977." This marks the only moment at which the "lesbian issue" is mentioned in the program, and the claim that it was not agreed upon as a feminist concern up to that point erases its importance in the early movement, which, not part of Steinem's experience, is simply invisible. The final quarter of *Gloria* focuses on her career as an author, her star-studded fiftieth birthday party in 1984, a discussion of her breast cancer scare, her depression in the late 1980s after years of unremitting movement work, the death of her close friend Bella Abzug, and Steinem's marriage, shortly followed by widowhood, at the age of sixty-six. It concludes with Steinem's recognition of the importance of ongoing feminist work among young women. She characteristically dismisses her own relevance to the current movement, noting, "the thing is not that they [young women] know who I am, but that they know who they are."

Conclusion: Reading *Gloria* as Mediated Popular Memory

One potential feminist reading of *Gloria* could highlight and celebrate Steinem's expression, at every turn in the program's narrative, of variations on the feminist truism that "the personal is political." This recurring sense-making device of turning Steinem's personal story into a meditation on the status of women as a group constitutes the documentary's central yet unacknowledged debt to radical feminism. This is the preferred reading, I suspect, and, while it is not necessarily a wholly misleading or counterproductive one, it leaves a great deal unsaid about the ways in which Steinem's experiences and her role in the movement were also unique and beg to be understood through the pivotal role that mass media played in them.

Despite her many subsequent decades of work on behalf of feminism, demonstrating a dedication that I do not wish to minimize, Gloria Steinem's initial ascent as a feminist icon in the 1970s was undeniably facilitated by her easy fit within existing media logics as well as by her considerable ability to use those logics to her own and to feminism's benefit. Perhaps the most disingenuous tendency in the *Gloria* documentary is its positioning of Steinem as a victim of media attention (rather than as a manipulator and beneficiary of it) and as an underdog who battled the forces of resistance, despite her entrance to the movement at a moment when its momentum and her own were quite powerful.

From my own perspective, Steinem deserves more admiration for her continuing commitment to feminist work during the challenging postfeminist decades that followed, a time when conservative opposition became much more formidable and "is feminism dead?" and "how feminism failed" stories became a media perennial (Dow, 1996; Faludi, 1991). I suspect this later story receives little attention in *Gloria* because, although her role in it is heroic, the tale is a less riveting and uplifting one to tell. Indeed, as the years wore on, the backlash built, and postfeminist media logics took hold in an increasingly conservative political climate, Steinem retroactively earned, many times over, the status as a movement stalwart that mass media had too easily awarded her in the early 1970s.

Steinem deftly combined aspects of liberal and radical feminism in her positions in the 1970s, but her approach to mass media had the most in common with NOW's media pragmatism. Although, like radical feminists, she founded a feminist publication to provide an alternative to mainstream media, *Ms.*, unlike the early feminist underground press, operated within the bounds of market logic and consumer culture. That logic was not simply about the need to attract advertisers but the need to attract a wide range of readers as well, to create a "popular feminism" that reached beyond movement circles and made feminist thinking available and accessible to women everywhere (Farrell, 1998). Like the leaders of NOW, the editors of *Ms.* saw themselves as speaking "on behalf of a group called 'women'" as they attempted to represent the movement's interests and to influence public policy while converting women to the cause (Barker-Plummer, 1995, p. 312).

The story of Steinem and the movement told in *Gloria* repeats many of the dominant tendencies in early news treatments of women's liberation. Like *Gloria,* those early television reports had little interest in the movement's ideological, racial, or sexual diversity and its related internal conflicts and took for granted the reasonableness of liberal feminist demands for workplace equality and abortion rights. Early network reports on the movement actually gave more time to the second wave's radical roots than does the documentary, which uses footage of radical feminist actions only as unnarrated scene-setting devices. Faulting *Gloria* for the absence of attention to CR, radical feminist activism, and the complexities of early feminist theory and writing seems unfair; those aspects of the movement were not, in fact, part of Steinem's experience. Yet those aspects of the early movement created the conditions for her feminist career; radical feminist protest was the catalyst for national media attention to the movement in the first place, and the confrontational conduct of early protestors enabled the contrast effect that made Steinem's even-tempered approach so attractive.

Actions such as the Miss America Pageant protest, the birth control hearings protest, and the *Ladies' Home Journal* sit-in put the second wave on the news agenda and helped to create the climate that made a mass action such as the Women's Strike for Equality possible. As radical feminism receded from the media spotlight and feminism became a public policy issue covered in routinized ways, Steinem's familiarity, accessibility, and visibility became an asset to the movement and to mass media. In retrospect, that her initial participation in a public, organized movement action came on Strike Day is especially fitting. That day was the movement's moment of peak media visibility thus far, and it was also, not incidentally, when feminism's mainstream appeal became impossible to ignore. Both factors were critical to her success. To say so is not to posit that Steinem was only an opportunist; rather, it is to say that the "collective effort" (Jensen, 2011, p. AR16) to which she refers when describing the movement's success is not only about the women with whom she worked in the 1970s and beyond but is also about the years of activism that preceded her entry into the movement and that are almost completely unremarked on in *Gloria*.

The documentary, like 1970's movement reports, omits feminists' early and earnest struggles over race, class, and sexuality; more surprising and equally lamentable, it omits Steinem's considerable efforts in her own movement work to ameliorate those divisions. She insisted on the representation of women of color in the NWPC, in the Women's Action Alliance, in the pages of *Ms.*, and in just about every feminist effort in which she was involved, including her early speaking tour in which she always shared the stage with a black woman. Similarly, in contrast to Betty Friedan, she cultivated lesbians as a movement constituency, and one of her earliest public appearances on the movement's behalf was her presence at the so-called Kate is Great December 1970 press conference defending Kate Millett, throughout which she visibly held Millett's hand (Klemesrud, 1970; Stern, 1997, p. 219). Sensitive to the ways that the lesbian label was used to discredit feminists, Steinem showed her solidarity by deflecting inquiries about her sexuality, refusing to either confirm or deny that she was a lesbian when asked, famously replying to male reporters, "Are you my alternative?"

Yet, with the exception of the mention of lesbianism in connection with the 1977 National Women's Conference (a somewhat predictable move given that the lesbian issue became a focal point of national news reports on the event), *Gloria* gives almost no attention to racial and/or sexual diversity in the movement. The only other mention of such issues is in the segment on Betty Friedan, in which Steinem comments that Friedan "identified up" rather than down, thus Friedan resented her for bringing lesbians and poor women into the movement (this remark is accompanied by a photo of Steinem holding a black child and another of her at the Millett press conference). From the beginning, and across media genres, feminism has always been easiest to represent through its easily understood liberal reforms and their impact on the lives of middle-class, heterosexual, white women, and *Gloria* follows this longstanding precedent.

The limitations of biography as a vehicle for telling the story of the second wave are powerfully evident in *Gloria*, just as the attractions of biography for telling that story are equally as evident. In many ways, the documentary presents Gloria Steinem as the movement's foremost feminist entrepreneur, a portrayal well suited to neoliberal times. Certainly, her life, as *Gloria* tells it, has ingredients that make for a compelling story: a troubled and economically unstable childhood, early struggles to make her way in a man's world, and a moment of revelation that led her to dedicate her life to a cause larger than herself while fighting entrenched interests.

Such a heroic narrative inevitably undermines the collective nature of movement work, despite *Gloria*'s efforts to present Steinem as an everywoman, and it participates in media affection for representing feminism through individuals and as a matter of identity rather than politics or justice (while, ironically, denying the power of Steinem's personal identity in her rise as a movement heroine). Such a focus, present in the initial reports on the Miss America Pageant protest, in the wave of network coverage in 1970, and in the construction of Steinem's celebrity in the 1970s, manifested in attention to the heterosexual appeal, marital and procreative status, and general adherence (or lack of it) to traditional femininity that feminists embodied and enacted, pushing aside political experience and ideology as relevant elements for understanding and evaluating the movement's import and appeal.

Forty-plus years later, *Gloria* demonstrates the durability and the drawbacks of this enduring media strategy. Like the early television reports upon which it draws so heavily, it fails to illustrate the second wave's geographic reach and social impact, the diversity of its membership and constituency, and the rich variety of its political commitments and achievements. The second wave was always about more than those parts of it that appeared in and on the news (still the case for feminism), but mass media played a powerful role in its development, constructing its meaning and implications for Americans who watched the drama of women's liberation unfold on their television screens.

Much of this book has been about the many ways in which the interests of the early movement and the interests of mass media collided, but the story of

Gloria Steinem's climb to media stardom is one in which those interests coincided, at least for several years, broadening the reach of the movement while limiting its radical potential. Radical feminism receded into the past, available to be conjured up now and again through references to bra-burning that were disconnected from any knowledge of the actions and ideas of the intense and inventive young women who launched the second wave into public consciousness in 1968.

When I reached my teens in the mid-1970s, still an avid watcher of the Miss America Pageant, I put ERA stickers on my school notebooks and grew my hair out like Gloria's. I understood feminism as a trend and an identity long before I understood it as a politics. Such contradictions still afflict feminism's presence in American culture. From the beginning, second-wave feminism was simultaneously dismissed and dreaded, co-opted and commodified. That it accomplished as much as it did, and that it lives on in countless visible and invisible ways, is a testament to the many lives the movement touched, both through mass media and in spite of it.

Notes

Introduction

1. The most likely explanation for the networks' failure to cover the protest when it happened was its poor timing, in national television news terms. NBC, which broadcast the pageant on Saturday night September 7, would have been the most likely network to carry a story about the protest given its ample camera presence there. Its Saturday evening newscast, like that of CBS, aired at 6:30 P.M. ET, before the disruption inside the pageant itself (the most newsworthy aspect of the day's events because it led to police action) had occurred. NBC's only other weekend news offering was a fifteen minute news digest at 11 P.M. ET on Saturday and Sunday, which both CBS and ABC had as well (Brooks and Marsh, 1999). The first chance for an extended story on the pageant and/or the protest came on Monday, September 9, when the evening newscasts were dominated by news of the Soviet invasion of Czechoslovakia, the presidential election campaign, and Chicago Mayor Richard Daley's press conference about the violence at the recent Democratic National Convention in Chicago. Given this slate of inherently newsworthy events, the dust-up two days earlier at the Miss America Pageant, mounted by a group of women who lacked status as representatives of a recognized independent movement, simply did not qualify for airtime.

2. The term "second wave" was given its first highly visible public use by a journalist (Lear, 1968), but it was not a term widely used by the women involved in it, who generally used labels such as "women's movement," "women's liberation," or "the movement."

3. Importantly, the second wave's success at pursuing their issues in the courts, Congress, and state legislatures in the 1970s meant that feminist topics were covered by reporters who worked those venues as routine "beats" for newsgathering.

For a discussion of this factor and others in the shift to issue-centered coverage, see Barakso and Schaffner, 2006.

4. NOW was created in June 1966 during the third annual meeting of women who had been active in state commissions that were part of the Presidential Commission on the Status of Women. Betty Friedan, based on her *Feminine Mystique* fame, had been invited to the meeting and became part of a group of women at the meeting that grew disgusted by the recently established Equal Employment Opportunity Commission's refusal to enforce regulations against gender discrimination in employment included in Title VII of the 1964 Civil Rights Act. They left the meeting and drew up plans for what became NOW, and the organization's founding conference was held that October (Coontz, 2011; Davis, 1991).

5. Some scholars, such as Linda Nicholson (2008), argue against understanding the two broad factions as constituting a single movement, a position linked to the profound differences in feminist identity and ideology held by the women involved in liberal and radical groups. In this project, I treat them as parts of the same movement for reasons related to my focus on 1970. First, at that point, many women, particularly in New York, held membership in both NOW and radical groups, and events that I treat in subsequent chapters were planned and participated in by members of both types of groups. In short, coalitions between radical and liberal groups, while difficult, were still possible in 1970 in a way that they shortly would not be.

Second, news reports, although sometimes making distinctions between liberal and radical groups and ideas, consistently treated them as constituent parts of one movement, which was usually labeled "women's liberation," although it was sometimes also called the "new feminism." For example, in 1975, Jo Freeman argued that "women's liberation" had developed a "generic meaning," was used to apply to both NOW and the small radical groups, and the terms "feminism" and "women's liberation" were synonymous for most women in the movement (p. 109). Because of reporters' broad use of the term "women's liberation," I retain "liberal" and "radical" as clarifying terms for the two broad types of movement groups. However, this broad distinction does not capture the distinctive emphases of groups that identified as socialist feminists, who linked their analyses of women's oppression to the historical development of capitalism, and who saw themselves as separate from radical feminism (Echols, 1989). Mass media accounts of the movement did not recognize such distinctions and when they included socialist feminists—as a couple of reports from 1970 did—they were generally implicitly or explicitly grouped under the "radical" rubric.

6. I use the term "radical feminism" rather loosely here to denote the younger branch of the movement that operated through small groups, most of which practiced CR; moreover, at least in 1970, many members of radical feminist groups had ties to other countercultural movements. But groups such as The Feminists, New York Radical Feminists, and Redstockings (to name three New York–based radical groups that existed in some form in 1970 and that were featured in network coverage) had distinct ideological differences among them and political conflicts within them. For example,

within early radical groups, there was tension between those who saw themselves primarily as feminists and those who identified as "politicos," women with socialist leanings who were committed to working on feminist issues from within the larger left (Echols, 1989). Those distinctions were of little interest to television news workers and are thus not that pertinent to my arguments, except to note that mainstream media largely failed to recognize the ideological complexity of radical feminism in its representations.

7. Kathryn Thoms Flannery (2005) has noted that feminists "were engaged in literate production on a remarkable scale" by 1968 through printed material such as periodicals, books, broadsides, and newsletters (p. 2), and Karlyn Kohrs Campbell (1973) has argued that much of this discourse can be understood as the adaptation of the theory and practice of CR to written form, a point Hogeland (1998) also makes with regard to feminist novels of the 1970s. By 1970, anthologies of feminist writing had begun to appear, such as Robin Morgan's *Sisterhood is Powerful* (1970) and Toni Cade Bambara's (1970) *The Black Woman* (see also Tanner, 1970; Stambler, 1970), and 1970 also saw the publication of single-authored works of feminist theory and analysis that became best sellers, such as Kate Millett's *Sexual Politics* and Shulamith Firestone's *The Dialectic of Sex*. For a discussion of the conditions of production (and decline) of feminist print culture, see Rhodes, 2005.

8. Although the *Times*'s coverage of the early second wave was consistent and often sympathetic, it, like other national media, would eventually come under fire for both its employment practices (female employees filed a sex discrimination suit in 1974) and for editorial choices, such as the refusal to adopt Ms. as a generic title for women (see Robertson, 1992; Atkins-Sayre, 2005).

9. Sasha Torres (2003) argues that black women were similarly erased from television coverage of the civil rights movement, despite their centrality to movement politics. As she puts it, "if television is ambivalent about the politicized black male subjects it generates and cannibalizes, it generally exiles black women from its frame altogether" (p. 107).

10. Bradley (2003) argues that NOW's use of a civil rights model was problematic for several pragmatic reasons, including its implication of "white co-optation of black life" (pp. 43–46) that alienated many black Americans. She also implies that the model was a failure for NOW, a conclusion from which I differ. Although NOW failed to establish sexism as a moral issue in the same way that the civil rights movement had done for racism, the organization's success by the mid-1970s at gaining sustained and favorable coverage for its issues indicated that its emphasis on public, legal discrimination, modeled on the NAACP, produced results (see Barker-Plummer, 2002).

11. Another consistent limitation of national television news was its strong regional focus on East Coast, primarily New York City–based, activity. That focus indicated New York's centrality to national media culture as well as feminism's sizeable presence there, but women involved in the movement had different experiences and priorities in different parts of the country (in less urban locations, for example, the distinction

between radical and liberal ideology and practices was much less clear-cut). News reports rarely took note of this, although I discuss some sympathetic reporting that appeared purposely designed to intervene in a mediated narrative of what Judith Ezekiel (2002) terms "big-city feminism" (p. viii). For analyses of movement discourse and activism in specifically regional contexts, see Enke, 2003; Ezekiel, 2002; Pearson, 1999; Stokes, 2005; Valk, 2008; Whittier, 1995.

12. Video of the broadcast stories examined in later chapters was obtained from the Television News Archives at Vanderbilt University, with two exceptions. I obtained the video of the ABC "Women's Liberation" documentary broadcast in May 1970 from the Peabody Awards Archives at the University of Georgia, and the *Gloria: In Her Own Words* documentary was obtained from HBO. All quotations from these programs that appear in this book are from my own transcription.

Chapter 1. The Movement Meets the Press

1. Bradley (2005) discusses zap actions in terms of their participation in the Marxist tradition of "agitprop" (agitation propaganda) that members of NYRW learned from their participation in and exposure to other movements: "the civil rights movement had seemed to gather its sympathy from its public action—marches, sit-ins, the 'freedom rides' through the South and the violence they provoked—that dramatically illustrated the barriers to integration," and "as the anti–Vietnam War movement took hold, its young male leadership adopted the strategies, they believed, that had worked so well for civil rights" (p. 228). By 1968, feminists, in turn, were adapting such publicity-driven tactics to their own purposes.

2. The consensus about the importance of the protest, in memoirs of second wavers as well as in chronicles of the period, is striking. In her 1999 memoir of the movement, Susan Brownmiller (1999) wrote, "the boardwalk hijinks and civil disobedience of the Miss America protest had global ripples as both national and foreign journalists seized on the story" (p. 41). Flora Davis (1991) called the protest the moment that "feminism suddenly burst into the headlines" (p. 107), and, in *The Sisterhood*, Marcia Cohen (1988) described it as "a moment that changed the world's view of this rebellion—and therefore perhaps the rebellion itself—forever" (p. 149).

3. For discussions of the bra-burning myth, see Dicker, 2008; Martin, 1971; Morgan, 1992; Rosen, 2000; Van Gelder, 1992; Zeisler, 2008.

4. All subsequent quotations from the press release are taken from "No More Miss America" (1970). Widely distributed prior to the protest, its opening paragraph was directed at potential protestors: "Women's Liberation Groups, black women, high-school and college women, women's peace groups, women's welfare and social-work groups, women's job-equality groups, pro-birth control and pro-abortion groups— women of every political persuasion—all are invited to join us in a day-long boardwalk-theater event, starting at 1:00 P.M. on the Boardwalk in front of Atlantic City's Convention Hall. We will protest the image of Miss America, an image that oppresses women in every area in which it purports to represent us."

5. Todd Gitlin (1980) has discussed the powerful role of the *New York Times* as an agenda-setter during the 1960s, when it developed frames that guided subsequent reporting in print media and also served as a central channel "through which network news workers form[ed] pictures of the world, what [was] happening there, and what, within that world, deserve[d] investigating" (p. 299).

6. All subsequent quotations from the *New York Times*'s September 8 story on the Miss America Pageant protest are from Curtis, 1968a, p. 81.

7. Kathy Amatniek would later change her name to Kathie Sarachild, the name used for her publications that I cite at various points.

8. In fact, by 1968, the pageant had *never* had a black contestant. Pageant Rule 7, added in the 1930s, specified that contestants had to be members of the white race. The Miss America Pageant would include a black judge for the first time in 1969, and its first black contestant, representing Iowa, in 1970. Black women first entered the list of top ten finalists in 1980, and the first black Miss America, Vanessa Williams, was crowned in 1983 (Kinloch, 2004).

9. Although 1968 saw the first Miss Black America Pageant, all-black beauty pageants had a long history before 1968. Similarly, a number of civil rights groups, including the NAACP, had already engaged in various efforts to draw attention to the racism of all-white pageants, including the Miss America Pageant, before 1968 (Craig, 2002).

10. Generally traced to an origin in the Combahee River Collective Statement of 1977, a central document in the development of black feminist thought, intersectionality is the term used to describe the perspective that "the major systems of oppression are interlocking" and "the synthesis of these oppressions creates the conditions of our lives" (Combahee River Collective, 2000, p. 264). Important scholarly treatments of intersectionality include Collins (1990) and Crenshaw (1991).

11. Subsequent quotations from these two stories are taken from Curtis (1968b) and Klemesrud (1968).

12. Although Women's International Terrorist Conspiracy from Hell is the most often cited meaning behind W.I.T.C.H., the referent for the acronym for the short-lived group was somewhat elastic and could also refer to "Women Inspired to Tell their Collective History, Women Interested in Toppling Consumer Holidays and a host of other imaginative variations" (Brownmiller, 1999, p. 49).

Chapter 2. The Movement Makes the News

1. NYRF was founded in 1969 by Shulamith Firestone (who left Redstockings) and Anne Koedt (who left The Feminists). NYRF held that men obtained ego satisfaction from the oppression of women, and that women internalized their subordination, a position distinct from that of Redstockings or The Feminists. Multiple CR groups operated under the umbrella of NYRF, which, as a whole, was the largest radical group in New York City (Echols, 1989).

2. D.C. Women's Liberation formed in the winter of 1968 and disintegrated around 1971, partially because the gay-straight split arose later in Washington than it did in

New York. Some members of D.C. Women's Liberation would go on to form a lesbian collective called The Furies (Echols, 1989).

3. In addition to their outrage at the fact that no women were invited to testify at the hearings, the feminists also charged the Food and Drug Administration with failing to disseminate the results of studies that showed side effects from the pill, with using women as guinea pigs by selling the drug before sufficient testing was completed, and with failing to urge doctors to discuss the costs and benefits of the pill (Wolfson, 1998).

4. I use the term "social problem" here to denote a negative condition with collective implications; that is, a condition that conflicts with a society's ideal understanding of itself and that is recognized as affecting a large number of people. However, I understand social problems as rhetorical constructions and as the product of claims-making, not as objective entities (Best, 1993).

5. This footage likely had been filmed at a March 1969 production of a "satirical cabaret of feminist material," performed by the New Feminist Repertory Theater to benefit New York NOW (Hole and Levine, 1971, p. 369; see also dell'Olio, 1998).

6. The Berghoff protest in February 1969 was part of NOW's Public Accommodations Week, during which they mounted demonstrations at men-only restaurants, bars, and public transportation (Hickey, 2008). The incident is recounted in *The Berghoff Family Cookbook* (Berghoff and Ryan, 2007) in which the protestors are correctly identified as members of NOW. The cookbook goes on to note that the "men only" bar was discontinued after the protest, at which point "feminist Gloria Steinem came in for a much-publicized drink" (Berghoff and Ryan, 2007, p. 28).

7. Culhane probably took his reference to slavery from the "No More Miss America" (1970) press release, which included the charge that the pageant "exercises thought control . . . to enslave us all the more in high-heeled, low-status roles" (p. 588). Another clue indicating Culhane's familiarity with the "No More Miss America" document was his pairing of Miss America and Playboy Bunnies as targets of the radical movement in his second report in the series. The press release also contained a line claiming, "Miss America and *Playboy*'s centerfold are sisters over the skin" ("No More Miss America," 1970, p. 587).

8. The Feminists described themselves as "a group of radical feminists committed to intense study of the persecution of women and direct action to eliminate this persecution" (1969/1973, p. 370). Their most well-known action was a protest at the New York City Marriage License Bureau in September 1969. The event generated a few inches in the *New York Times,* which was dismissive even in the headline ("Five women protest the 'slavery' of marriage") and ran the story on page 93 of a ninety-six–page edition (Clark, 1969, p. 93).

9. Pierce was African American, and she was hired by CBS as a special correspondent in 1968 after a stint as an editor at *Ebony*. Her primary duty was contributing soft news reports and interviews to the *CBS Morning News,* although she also contributed occasionally to the *CBS Evening News* (Garrett, 1992).

10. dell'Olio was an experienced activist, although she was interviewed here through her status as founder of the New Feminist Repertory Theater, which was featured several times in the CBS series. In her memoir, dell'Olio (1998) claims membership in NOW, in New York Radical Women, and in New York Radical Feminists, but not The Feminists. She was, however, a longtime friend of Ti-Grace Atkinson's, which may have had some influence on her discourse here.

11. For examples of *New York Times* stories that included mentions of Atkinson, and sometimes quoted her extensively, see Bender, 1968, 1970a; Brownmiller, 1970b; Lear, 1968. Atkinson's oft-repeated comment that "marriage is slavery" was featured in *Life*'s first article on the movement (Davidson, 1969), and Bradley (2003) describes Atkinson's appearance on a 1969 radio show during which she made the same marriage-cancer comparison that she made in the March 1970 CBS story. For a collection of Atkinson's speeches, see her book, *Amazon Odyssey* (1974).

12. Although television reports on women's liberation failed to emphasize CR's importance to the movement, this was not true for all mass media. For example, women's magazines' attentiveness to the practice and its possibilities for women's self-awareness was no doubt a factor in the rapid growth of CR groups (see Dow, 1996).

13. "Mr. President, how long must women wait for liberty?" was a query that National Woman's Party members had prominently featured on signs they carried while picketing the White House in 1917 and 1918 as part of their strategy to pressure President Woodrow Wilson to publicly support the Nineteenth Amendment (Southard, 2007).

14. The feminist critique of the Playboy Club was well developed by 1970, and it went beyond sexual objectification to include analysis of the poor pay and working conditions Bunnies endured. In 1963, Gloria Steinem published an exposé of the Playboy Club that detailed the exploitative nature of work as a Bunny, although she did not identify as a feminist when she wrote it. For a discussion of *Playboy*'s sometimes surprising relationship to feminism in the 1970s, see Pitzulo, 2011.

15. In *The Way We Never Were* (1992), Coontz argues that nostalgia for the stable (white and middle-class) patriarchal nuclear family of the 1950s relies on a mythical vision of the past that only a small segment of Americans experienced; for example, the poverty rate in the 1950s was approximately the same for two-parent and one-parent black families. Although an increase in (white) women working outside the home often has been attributed to feminism, the rise in women's employment was steady throughout the second half of the twentieth century and was due to women's desire for the rewards of work as well as economic need. In general, "married women's work entry was well underway before there was a significant rise in feminist values and consciousness" (Coontz, 1992, p. 166).

16. Conceived as a five-member, bipartisan commission charged with eliminating illegal employment discrimination, the EEOC's initial authority was enacted primarily through rulings on the intent and implications of Title VII, through attempted conciliation of disputes between employees and employers, through amicus (friend of

the court) briefs filed in lawsuits, and through its relationship with the Department of Labor, the official enforcer of presidential executive orders regarding employment practices. In 1972, pressured by feminists, Congress passed the Equal Opportunity Act, which expanded the EEOC's powers considerably by ending the exemption of state and local governments from the provisions of Title VII, by making educational institutions and federal agencies subject to Title VII, and by giving the agency litigation authority to sue employers, unions, and employment agencies on behalf of the government (Blumrosen, 1993).

17. The issue in Phillips's case was her status as the mother of young children, not simply her gender. The assembly line job for which she applied was overwhelmingly held by women, a point that the lower courts had used in their ruling that sex discrimination had not taken place (Mayeri, 2011).

18. A central claim in Rosenfeld's case was that she had long performed the duties of station agent (while being classified as a clerk and telegraph operator) at various rural railway stations since her 1953 divorce. Yet she had never been allowed to have the title or to receive the higher salary that came with the job classification, and her union largely ignored her complaints. The EEOC advised her to sue, and she filed a lawsuit in 1968 against the state of California, the Southern Pacific Railroad, and the Transportation Communications International Union (Burman, 2009).

19. Phillips's case would be the first sex discrimination case under Title VII to be ruled on by the Supreme Court, with mixed results. The court's brief 1971 opinion agreed with the EEOC's position that Martin Marietta's refusal to consider Philips's application, while the company accepted those of men with young children, constituted sex discrimination under the terms of Title VII. However, the court also remanded the case back to the lower court to more fully consider whether or not family responsibilities were more relevant for women's job performance than for men's and, if so, "whether that difference would constitute a BFOQ for the employer's policy" (Rhode, 1989, p. 93). In the next several years, additional cases in which BFOQs were central issues would reach the Supreme Court and would result in more definitive rulings on the limits of such exceptions.

20. Quarles was born to Trinidadian parents and has noted that she was generally categorized as black, although she was, in fact, multiracial, and also had Portuguese, Chinese, English, and Scottish ancestors (Vallens, 1986). In her career at NBC, Quarles worked at the network's owned and operated stations in Chicago, New York, and Cleveland and also contributed stories to the network's nightly newscast. In the early 1970s, she would become the first woman to coanchor a nightly news program in New York at WNBC (Ziegler, 1992).

21. Although AT&T as a whole generally resisted the EEOC's conciliation efforts, some subsidiaries were more attentive to sex discrimination than others were. In 1966, Ohio Bell became one of only three Bell subsidiaries (of twenty-plus total) that employed women in "craft" positions (nonmanagement operations jobs in the plant department, such as the one Genevieve Glass held) that paid far better than the

traditionally female jobs. Ohio Bell also began one of the Bell systems' earliest management training programs for women in 1967, several years before AT&T responded to pressure from the EEOC (Herr, 2003).

22. Myrna Lamb's short play, "What Have You Done for Me Lately," about a man who discovers he is pregnant, was included in the first production of the New Feminist Repertory Theater in 1969. The feminist theater group attracted a good amount of attention in New York and was positively reviewed in the *New York Times* (See Bender, 1970b; Regelson, 1969). An early performance of Lamb's play was staged as a benefit for Redstockings, a radical group with a strong focus on abortion rights (Case, 1988).

23. Anne Snitow (1992) has persuasively argued that the so-called demon texts of the second wave, such as Firestone's *Dialectic of Sex,* do not bear out their labeling as antimotherhood tracts, although she also suggests that the radicals were less attentive to motherhood issues because of their general youth and childlessness relative to the older, liberal branch of the movement, in which many leaders and members were mothers who worked for wages (p. 35). Two additional useful treatments of the second wave's complex relationship with motherhood are Hallstein, 2010, and Umansky, 1996.

24. The Clergy Consultation Service, composed of Protestant ministers and Jewish rabbis, began in 1967. By 1969, it was counseling about ten thousand women per year, the overwhelming majority of whom chose abortion (Davis, 2005).

25. Austin, Minnesota, was an interesting choice for a town that was clearly meant to represent "Anytown, USA." About a hundred miles south of Minneapolis, Austin was a somewhat isolated place. Dominated by the Hormel meatpacking plant that was the largest employer of Austin's predominantly white citizens, the town would be the site of a famous yearlong strike in 1985–86. The often brutal work at the plant paid excellent middle-class union wages to men, but meatpacking industry jobs were highly gender-segregated and women's jobs paid less than men's. This situation eventually became a focus of activism (resisted by male meatpackers), providing some context for the young man's comment that more opportunity for women would entail a negative impact for men (Hage and Klauda, 1989; Horowitz, 1997).

Chapter 3. Magazines and the Marketing of the Movement

1. In 1970, the Seven Sisters of women's magazines included *Ladies' Home Journal, Good Housekeeping, McCall's, Redbook, Family Circle, Woman's Day,* and *Better Homes and Gardens.* Founded in 1883, *Ladies' Home Journal* was the oldest of this group to maintain its original name. James McCall founded *The Queen: Illustrating McCall's Bazaar Glove-Fitting Patterns* as a catalog to sell fashion patterns in 1873, but it did not become *McCall's Magazine—The Queen of Fashion* until 1887. *Good Housekeeping* was founded in 1885. The other members of the Seven Sisters were not founded until well into the twentieth century (Zuckerman, 1998).

2. The list of participants in the sit-in reads like a Who's Who of the second wave: Ti-Grace Atkinson, Shulamith Firestone, Anne Koedt, Kathie Sarachild (formerly

Amatniek), Susan Brownmiller, Lucy Komisar, Karla Jay, Rosalyn Baxandall, Letty Cottin Pogrebin, Alix Kates Shulman, Minda Bikman, Sally Kempton, Alice Denham, and Jacqui Ceballos were all there. Several of them, including Sarachild, Koedt, Shulman, Baxandall, and Ceballos, had participated in the 1968 Miss America Pageant protest.

3. One protest participant, Vivian Leone (1993), heard a rumor that the magazine's management summoned a black female staffer (whom Leone described as "faintly beige" with green eyes) to the protest scene because they "got wind of our concern over lack of representation for its 1.2 million black readers" (p. 213). Although none of the accounts I have read discuss whether or not the protest participants included any women of color (and I have spotted none in the many images of the protest that I have seen), the attention given in the list of grievances to the problematic whiteness of the *LHJ* (in both content and magazine personnel)—and the absence of that issue in any of the media coverage—are additional indications that mass media, rather than movement members, consistently overlooked the topic of race.

4. Feminist scholars have challenged generalizations about the content and ideological bias of *LHJ* and other women's magazines in the postwar era. Joanne Meyerowitz (1993) has argued that women's magazines included a substantial number of stories praising women for public achievements, revealing "a tension between individual achievement and domestic ideals" (p. 1465). Similarly, Eva Moskowitz (1996) argues that women's magazines did not ignore the discontent of housewives, but instead "devoted considerable attention to the subject by focusing on the psychological tensions experienced by the housewife and her difficulties conforming to the domestic ideal" (p. 77). In fact, as Jean Hunter (1990) has observed, *LHJ* paid a sizable amount of attention to Friedan's *Feminine Mystique,* and Friedan herself would edit a special issue of the magazine in 1964 devoted to exploring the "daring new concept" that "there was more to life for women than housework and childcare" (p. 586).

5. Carter's composure, noted in most accounts, may have been due to his foreknowledge of the protest and his desire to look reasonable in media stories. *Time*'s story about the protest claimed that Carter had been tipped off the day before, and had worn a "TV-blue shirt for the occasion" ("Woman-Power," 1970, p. 59).

6. The March 17 *New York Times* story (Raymont, 1970) on the *Newsweek* complaint did not refer to the involvement of women's liberation, except for a mention that the *Newsweek* women timed their press conference to coincide with the release of the magazine's cover story on the feminist movement. However, Brownmiller (1999) recounted that, at the Media Women meetings, "a delegation of women from *Newsweek* usually sat by themselves in a little huddle, immersed in a secret plot that would soon become public" (p. 83). For an extensive insider's account of the *Newsweek* sex discrimination suit, see Povich, 2012.

7. This reference to trousers indicates how easily mass media conflated feminism and female masculinity, as well as how consistently feminism was explicitly and implicitly framed as an attack on and/or an appropriation of masculinity. Feminists in trousers were hard to spot in the television coverage, which was dominated by women

in conservative dresses. Indeed, several accounts of the protest discuss the participants' plans to dress as conservatively as possible in order not to attract attention on
the way into *LHJ*'s offices (Bradley, 2003). Both Brownmiller (1999) and Jay (1999),
for instance, specifically described what they wore, and both wore skirts. Perhaps
there were a few women in trousers who caught the eye of the *Time* reporter. Equally
as likely, however, is that, writing the story later, the reporter assumed that they must
have been wearing trousers simply because they were feminists.

8. Sanders's sympathies for the movement were no doubt at least somewhat derived from her own struggles in a male-dominated field. When she was hired as a
correspondent by ABC news in 1964, she was one of two women in such a position.
In December 1964, she became the first woman to anchor an evening network newscast, when she stepped in for ailing ABC anchor Ron Cochran for one broadcast. In
1976, she was the first woman to reach the rank of vice president at a network when
she was appointed vice president and director of television documentaries (Sanders
and Rock, 1988).

9. The literal translation of Kinder, Küche, & Kirche is "children, home, and church,"
but its colloquial meaning, as feminists used it, is best expressed as "home and family."
One reason the phrase had resonance for second wavers is that it was used in the title of
a widely disseminated feminist analysis of psychological research on women, "Kinder,
Küche, Kirche as Scientific Law: Psychology Constructs the Female," originally written
in 1968 by psychologist Naomi Weisstein (a member of Chicago's Westside group that
formed in 1967) and widely reprinted; it appeared, for instance, in *Sisterhood Is Powerful*
(Morgan, 1970). Weisstein (1970) concluded that psychology characterizes women
as "inconsistent, emotionally unstable, lacking in a strong conscience or superego,
weaker, 'nurturant' rather than productive, 'intuitive' rather than intelligent, and, if
they are at all 'normal,' suited to the home and the family. . . . If they know their place,
which is in the home, they are really quite lovable, happy, childlike, loving creatures"
(p. 244). Presumably, the *LHJ* protesters found this an apt description of the ways that
women's magazines characterized their readers.

10. In *Freedom Is an Endless Meeting* (2002), sociologist Francesca Polletta makes a
persuasive case that radical feminist groups often had friendship networks at their
core, and that the norms of friendship—informality, exclusivity, and emotional investment—tended to coincide with a homogeneity that made diversifying membership and ensuring equality of participation difficult. Jane Gerhard (2001) makes a
similar point in *Desiring Revolution* and also argues that CR had inherent limitations
as a methodology for radicalizing women: "Not all women felt comfortable openly
discussing sexual topics, nor did all women feel as articulate as the university-trained
white women who, for the most part, made up the groups" (p. 103).

11. In Susan Brownmiller's March 15 *NYT Magazine* essay, she mentioned Betty
Friedan's reference to lesbians in the movement as a "lavender menace," the infamous
appellation indicating Friedan's fear that the association of lesbianism with feminism
would harm the movement's image. Brownmiller (1970b) dismissed Friedan's paranoia, commenting that lesbians were more of a "lavender herring" that presented "no

clear and present danger," but lesbians would perceive the comment as dismissive of their relevance to the movement (p. 134). Jay (1999) claims that several members of the GLF withdrew from participation in the *LHJ* protest as a result of Brownmiller's article, although she herself still attended because "I had spent too much time and energy on this action to walk away from it now" (p. 116).

12. Louisa Knapp Curtis, who edited the magazine in its first six years of publication, 1883–1889, was the wife of its founder and publisher, Cyrus Curtis (Scanlon, 1995). Between 1935 and 1962, *LHJ* had a husband-and-wife team of editors, Bruce and Beatrice Blackmar Gould. Thus, Hershey was the second woman to helm the magazine as its sole editor-in-chief and the first to edit it without the help of her husband (Zuckerman, 1998).

13. Social movement scholars continue to debate what is termed the "radical flank effect," which refers to the helpful or harmful consequences for moderates of radicals' actions (Haines, 1988; Gupta, 2002). In the positive version of the effect, distaste for and/or fear of extremist elements aid in the acceptance of moderate ideas. On the other hand, the moderate goals of a movement may be tainted by their association with more radical ideas, thus leading to a decline in acceptance for the movement as a whole, a negative radical flank effect. In the case of the *LHJ* action, the evidence for a positive radical flank effect is considerable, but the effect did not operate consistently in reactions to the early second wave. In chapter 5, for instance, I argue that although the goals of the NOW-planned Women's Strike for Equality were moderate and had already received positive news coverage, mass media cast the event as radical in its intent and potential effects. I attribute this reaction, in part, to the fact that the action employed tactics associated with the radical arm of the movement, such as street protest and guerilla theater, leading to coverage that, in a mediated version of a negative radical flank effect, depicted an essentially liberal action as militant and threatening.

Chapter 4. Fixing the Meaning of the Movement

Epigraph: Sanders was interviewed by a student reporter while on the UNC campus to film portions of the "Women's Liberation" documentary. The full article is available in the Marlene Sanders papers at the Wisconsin Center for Film and Theater Research at the University of Wisconsin, Madison.

1. Hefner was perhaps reacting to an April 1970 demonstration of two hundred feminists, led by the Chicago Women's Liberation Union, outside his Playboy Mansion (and corporate headquarters) in Chicago, at which the women protested the corporation's objectification and exploitation of women (Bronstein, 2011).

2. The *NOW* series was a revival of a previous ABC documentary series, *ABC Scope,* that debuted in prime time in 1964. By 1966, *ABC Scope* was focusing exclusively on the war in Vietnam, but without much ratings success, and the series ended in 1968. *NOW* began in March of 1970, and by the end of May, the program had focused half-hour episodes on the Black Panthers, on Vietnam, and on women's liberation (Hammond, 1981).

3. Although Presidents Kennedy and Johnson are easily recalled for their support of civil rights measures (e.g., JFK's introduction of a civil rights bill after the violence in Birmingham in 1963 and LBJ's advocacy of the Civil Rights Act of 1964 and the Voting Rights Act of 1965), Richard Nixon's civil rights legacy is also noteworthy, particularly his support for affirmative action policies that took shape during his presidency, beginning in 1969. See Kotlowski, 2002.

4. In 1970, feminists were still hopeful about federal attention to child care. In 1971, the Comprehensive Child Development Act, which was supported by a coalition of feminists and would have provided for a national child care system, passed both houses of Congress. However, President Nixon vetoed the act, and its allies could not muster the votes to override (Rosen, 2000).

5. A couple of exceptions to mainstream media's general neglect of addressing the movement's potential benefits for men appeared in the summer of 1970. Both were written by Gloria Steinem, whose national media profile in relation to the movement was on the rise as a result of a number of speeches she had begun to give about feminism on college campuses and in other venues. Part of Steinem's appeal was her inclusive vision, which was on display in both of the essays she published that summer. The first, adapted from a commencement address at Vassar and published in the June 7 *Washington Post,* was titled "Women's Liberation Aims to Free Men, Too," and contained lines such as "We want to liberate men from those inhuman roles as well. We want to share the work and responsibility, and to have men share equal responsibility for the children" (Steinem, 1970a, p. 192). *Time*'s August 31 issue that focused on the movement included an essay by Steinem (1970c) titled "What It Would Be Like If Women Win" in which she wrote at length about the ways that men's lives would improve if feminism succeeded. Her claim that "men will have to give up ruling-class privileges, but in return they will no longer be the only ones to support the family, get drafted, bear the strain of power and responsibility" (1970c, p. 22) was an echo of the kind of statements that Sanders's interviewees made about the movement's benefits for men.

6. For example, an essay advocating the learning of karate, titled "Self Defense for Women," was originally published in 1969 in *Women: A Journal of Liberation* and then reprinted the following year in *Sisterhood Is Powerful* (Morgan, 1970) as well as in *Voices from Women's Liberation* (Tanner, 1970). It began as follows: "Women are attacked, beaten and raped every day. By men. . . . It's about time that we as women got strong in order to defend ourselves!" (Pascalé, Moon, and Tanner, 1970, p. 527; see also Pearson, 1999).

Chapter 5. Making a Spectacle of the Movement

1. When the ERA reached the Senate in the fall of 1971, various attempts were made to add provisions that would exempt women from the draft. Because these provisions did not receive the support of ERA proponents (partially because any changes would have sent the amendment back to committee, where its future was uncertain), none

passed. The ERA, with its original wording, passed the Senate in March 1972 by a vote of 84 to 8 (Mansbridge, 1986).

2. This is my verbatim transcript of what Cronkite said. My suspicion is that he misread his news script, which probably said: "child care centers for mothers and abortions for anyone who wants them."

3. Some feminist film critics have questioned Mulvey's (1975/1999) somewhat totalizing theory of the male gaze by, for instance, arguing for a feminine spectatorship (see the essays in Thornham, 1999). However, as Barbara Green (1997) argues, although such revision has modified Mulvey's original claims, "what has remained persuasive is the notion that feminine spectatorship is a problem in popular culture and that femininity is aligned with a certain kind of visual pleasure" (p. 189). Green (1997) herself uses Mulvey to analyze the function of spectacle in relation to British feminists in the early twentieth century, arguing that "the political power of the iconography and discourse of activism has relied on the close association of women with the realm of the visual" (p. 147).

Chapter 6. After 1970

Epigraph: In fact, Sally Ride had appeared on the January 1983 issue of *Ms.* magazine with a coverline that read: "Sally Ride, Astronaut: The World Is Watching." Ride took a copy of the issue with her on the shuttle (Bradley, 2003).

1. The elite press, particularly the *New York Times,* did a better job of recognizing the rise of a specific black feminism and ran several articles in the early 1970s about it. See, for example, B. Campbell, 1973; Hunter, 1970; Morrison, 1971; Neby, 1973.

2. The *Times* did a better job with lesbians as well. See, for example, Klemesrud, 1970, 1973, 1977.

3. Members of Redstockings picketed, passed out leaflets, and ultimately interrupted a meeting of the New York Assembly's Joint Legislative Committee on the Problems of Public Health that had convened to consider abortion law reform (Redstockings's position favored complete repeal of laws regulating abortion). All of the witnesses scheduled to testify were men, with the exception of a nun, and the lack of testimony from women with abortion experiences was the central grievance the group articulated to the chair of the hearings. Although the hearings were then closed and reconvened in executive session, three women were eventually allowed to testify about their experiences after waiting for several hours. On March 21, 1969, the Redstockings's abortion speakout, designed to dramatize and remediate the silencing of women at the hearings, showcased the testimony of women who had been denied abortion or who had experienced illegal abortion. See Dubriwny, 2005; Nelson, 2003; Willis, 1969.

4. Steinem (1983) recounts that audiences often directed questions about feminism to her, while directing questions about civil rights to her partner, reflecting a dynamic that I have discussed in earlier chapters in which intersectionality goes unrecognized and thus women of color tend to be seen as qualified to speak on issues of race but not gender.

References

Abbott, S., and Love, B. (1972). *Sappho was a right on woman: A liberated view of lesbianism*. New York: Stein and Day.

Alexander, S. (1970a, June). The feminine eye. *McCall's*, 12.

Alexander, S. (1970b, July). The feminine eye. *McCall's*, 8.

Andelin, H. (1963). *Fascinating womanhood*. Santa Barbara, CA: Pacific Press.

Anderson-Bricker, K. (1999). "Triple-jeopardy": Black women and the growth of feminist consciousness in SNCC, 1964–1975. In K. Springer (Ed.), *Still lifting, still climbing: African-American women's contemporary activism* (pp. 49–69). New York: New York University Press.

Ashley, L. and Olson, B. (1998). Constructing reality: Print media's framing of the women's movement, 1966–1986. *Journalism and Mass Communication Quarterly, 75*, 263–77.

Atkinson, T. (1974). *Amazon Odyssey*. New York: Links Press.

Atkins-Sayre, W. (2005). Naming women: The emergence of "Ms." as a liberatory title. *Women and Language, 28,* 8–16.

Babcox, P. (1969, February 9). Meet the women of the revolution, 1969. *New York Times Magazine*, 34–35, 85–88, 90–92.

Bambara, T. C. (Ed.). (1970). *The black woman: An anthology*. New York: Signet.

Banet-Weiser, S., and Portwood-Stacer, L. (2006). "I just want to be me again!": Beauty pageants, reality television and post-feminism. *Feminist Theory, 7,* 255–272.

Barakso, M., and Schaffner, B. (2006). Winning coverage: News media portrayals of the women's movement, 1969–2004. *The Harvard International Journal of Press/Politics, 11,* 22–44.

Barker-Plummer, B. (1995). News as a political resource: Media strategies and political identity in the U.S. women's movement. *Critical Studies in Mass Communication, 12,* 306–324.

Barker-Plummer, B. (2002). Producing public voice: Resource mobilization and media access in the National Organization for Women. *Journalism and Mass Communication Quarterly, 79,* 188–205.

Barker-Plummer, B. (2010). News and feminism: A historic dialog. *Journalism and Mass Communication Monographs, 12,* 145–203.

Barthes, R. (1972). *Mythologies.* New York: Hill and Wang.

Baxandall, R. F. (1998). Catching the fire. In R. B. DuPlessis and A. Snitow (Eds.), *The feminist memoir project: Voices from women's liberation* (pp. 208–224). New York: Three Rivers Press.

Beasley, M. H., and Gibbons, S. J. (Eds.). (1993). *Taking their place: A documentary history of women in journalism.* Washington, D.C.: The American University Press.

Bem, S. L. (1993). *The lenses of gender: Transforming the debate on sexual inequality.* New Haven, CT: Yale University Press.

Bender, M. (1968, June 14). Valeria Solanas a hero to feminists. *New York Times,* 52.

Bender, M. (1970a, February 4). The women who'd trade in the pedestal for total equality. *New York Times,* 30.

Bender, M. (1970b, March 26). Women's liberation taking to the stage. *New York Times,* 60.

Bennett, L. (1988). *News: The politics of illusion,* 2nd ed. White Plains, NY: Longman.

Berger, J. (1972). *Ways of seeing.* London: Penguin.

Berghoff, C. and Ryan, N. R. (2007). *The Berghoff family cookbook: From our table to yours, celebrating a century of entertaining.* Kansas City, MO: Andrews McMeel Publishing.

Best, J. (1993). *Threatened children: Rhetoric and concern about child-victims.* Chicago: University of Chicago Press.

Betterton, R. (1987). Introduction: Feminism, femininity, and representation. In Betterton, R. (Ed.), *Looking on: Images of femininity in the visual arts and media* (pp. 1–17). London: Pandora.

Bluem, W. (1965). *Documentary in American television.* New York: Hastings House.

Blumrosen, A. W. (1993). *Modern law: The law transmission system and equal employment opportunity.* Madison: University of Wisconsin Press.

Bodroghkozy, A. (2012). *Equal time: Television and the civil rights movement.* Urbana: University of Illinois Press.

Boeth, R. (1971, August 16). A liberated woman despite beauty, chic, and success. *Newsweek,* 51–55.

Bolotin, S. (1982, October 17). Voices from the postfeminist generation. *New York Times Magazine,* 29–31+.

Borda, J. L. (2002). The woman suffrage parades of 1910–1913: Possibilities and limitations of an early feminist rhetorical strategy. *Western Journal of Communication, 66,* 25–52.

Bradley, P. (1998). Mass communication and the shaping of U.S. feminism. In C. Carter, G. Branston, and S. Allen (Eds.), *News, gender and power* (pp. 160–173). New York: Routledge.

Bradley, P. (2003). *Mass media and the shaping of American feminism, 1963–1975*. Jackson: University of Mississippi Press.

Bradley, P. (2005). *Women and the press: The struggle for equality*. Evanston, IL: Northwestern University Press.

Breines, W. (2007). *The trouble between us: An uneasy history of white and black women in the feminist movement*. New York: Oxford.

Bronstein, C. (2011). *Battling pornography: The American feminist anti-pornography movement, 1976–1986*. New York: Cambridge.

Brooks, T. and Marsh, E. (1999). *The complete directory to prime-time network and cable TV shows, 1946–present*. New York: Ballantine Books.

Brown, R. M. (1997). *Rita will: Memoir of a literary rabble-rouser*. New York: Bantam.

Brownmiller, S. (1970a, February). "Woman is often her own worst enemy—the enemy within." *Mademoiselle*, 184, 267, 268.

Brownmiller, S. (1970b, March 15). Sisterhood is powerful: A member of the women's liberation movement explains what it's all about. *New York Times Magazine,* 26+.

Brownmiller, S. (1999). *In our time: Memoir of a revolution*. New York: The Dial Press.

Burman, S. (2009, November 16). Women and railroading. *Trains: The Magazine of Railroading*. Retrieved from: http://trn.trains.com/Railroad%20Reference/Railroad%20History/2009/11/Women%20and%20Railroading.aspx. Accessed December 10, 2013.

Butler, J. (1990). *Gender trouble: Feminism and the subversion of identity*. New York: Routledge.

Cameron, D. (1985). *Feminism and linguistic theory*. London: Macmillan.

Campbell, B. (1973). Black feminists form group here. *New York Times,* 36.

Campbell, K. K. (1973). The rhetoric of women's liberation: An oxymoron. *Quarterly Journal of Speech, 59,* 74–86.

Carabillo, T, Meuli, M., and Csida, J. B. (Eds.). (1993). *Feminist chronicles, 1953–1993*. Los Angeles: Women's Graphics.

Carden, M. L. (1974). *The new feminism*. New York: Russell Sage Foundation.

Carroll, M. (1981, January 16). Emmanuel Celler, former Brooklyn congressman, dies at 92. *New York Times,* D16.

Carter, J. M. (1970a, May). Editor's Diary. *Ladies' Home Journal*, 10.

Carter, J. M. (1970b, August). Why you find the next eight pages in the Ladies' Home Journal. *Ladies' Home Journal,* 63.

Case, S. E. (1988). *Feminism and theatre*. New York: Methuen.

Charlton, L. (1970, August 27). Women march down Fifth in equality drive. *New York Times,* 1, 30.

Chisholm, S. (1970). *Unbought and unbossed*. New York: Avon.

Chisholm, S. (1973). *The good fight*. New York: Harper and Row.

Clark, A. E. (1969, September 24). Five women protest the "slavery" of marriage. *New York Times*, 93.

Cohen, M. (1988). *The sisterhood: The true story of the women who changed the world*. New York: Simon and Schuster.

Collins, G. (2009). *When everything changed: The amazing journal of American women from 1960 to the present*. New York: Little, Brown.

Collins, P. H. (1990). *Black feminist thought: Knowledge, consciousness, and the politics of empowerment*. Boston: Unwin Hyman.

Combahee River Collective. (2000). Combahee River Collective Statement. In B. Smith (Ed.), *Home girls: A black feminist anthology* (pp. 264–274). New Brunswick, NJ: Rutgers University Press.

Condit, C. M. (1990). *Decoding abortion rhetoric: Communicating social change*. Urbana: University of Illinois Press.

Connell, N. and Wilson, C. (Eds.) (1974). *Rape: The first sourcebook for women*. New York: New American Library.

Coontz, S. (1992). *The way we never were: American families and the nostalgia trap*. New York: Basic Books.

Coontz, S. (2011). *A strange stirring: The feminine mystique and American women at the dawn of the 1960s*. New York: Basic.

Craig, M. L. (2002). *Aint' I a beauty queen?: Black women, beauty, and the politics of race*. New York: Oxford University Press.

Craig, S. (2003). Madison Avenue versus *The Feminine Mystique*: The advertising industry's response to the women's movement. In S. A. Inness (Ed.), *Disco divas: Women and popular culture in the 1970s* (pp. 13–23). Philadelphia: University of Pennsylvania Press.

Crenshaw, K. (1991). Mapping the margins: Intersectionality, identity politics, and violence against women of color. *Stanford Law Review*, *43*, 1241–1299.

Cuklanz, L. (1995). *Rape on trial: How the mass media construct legal reform and social change*. Philadelphia: University of Pennsylvania Press.

Curtin, M. (1993). Packaging reality: The influence of fictional forms on the early development of television documentary. *Journalism Monographs*, *137*, 1–37.

Curtis, C. (1968a, Sept. 8). Miss America is picketed by 100 women. *New York Times*, 81.

Curtis. C. (1968b, Sept. 9). Along with Miss America. *New York Times*, 54.

D'Acci, J. (1999). Leading up to *Roe v. Wade*: Television documentaries in the abortion debate. In M.B. Haralovich and L. Rabinovitz (Eds.), *Television, history and American culture: Feminist critical essays* (pp. 120–143). Durham: Duke University Press.

Davidson, S. (1969, Dec. 12). An "oppressed majority" demands its rights. *Life*, 66–78.

Davis, A. (2000, Sept. 18). A surprise hitch. *Newsweek*, 92.

Davis, B. (1988). To seize the moment: A retrospective on the National Black Feminist Organization. *Sage*, *5*, 43–47.

Davis, F. (1991). *Moving the mountain: The women's movement in America since 1960*. New York: Touchstone.

Davis, T. (2005). *Sacred work: Planned Parenthood and its clergy alliances*. New Brunswick, NJ: Rutgers University Press.

Davison, J. (1972). *I am a housewife: A housewife is the most important person in the world*. New York: Guild Books.

Dell'Olio. A, (1998). Home before sundown. In R. B. DuPlessis and A. Snitow (Eds.), *The feminist memoir project: Voices from women's liberation* (pp. 149–170). New York: Three Rivers Press.

Denham, A. (2006). *Sleeping with bad boys: A juicy tell-all of literary New York in the 1950s and 1960s*. New York: Cardoza.

Dever, C. (2004). *Skeptical feminism: Feminist theory, feminist practice*. Minneapolis: University of Minnesota.

Dicker, R. (2008). *A history of U.S. feminisms*. Berkeley, CA: Seal Press.

Douglas, S. (1994). *Where the girls are: Growing up female with the mass media*. New York: Random House.

Douglas, S. and Michaels, M. (2005). *The mommy myth: The idealization of motherhood and how it has undermined all women*. New York: Simon and Schuster.

Dow, B. J. (1996). *Prime-time feminism: Television, media culture, and the women's movement since 1970*. Philadelphia: University of Pennsylvania Press.

Dow, B. J. (1999). Spectacle, spectatorship, and gender anxiety in the television coverage of the 1970 Women's Strike for Equality. *Communication Studies, 50,* 143–157.

Dow, B. J. (2001). Criticism and authority in the artistic mode. *Western Journal of Communication, 65,* 336–348.

Dow, B. J. (2003). Feminism, Miss America, and media mythology. *Rhetoric and Public Affairs, 6,* 127–160.

Dow, B. J. (2004). "Fixing' feminism: Women's liberation and the rhetoric of television documentary. *Quarterly Journal of Speech, 90,* 55–80.

Dubriwny, T. N. (2005). Consciousness-raising as collective rhetoric: The articulation of experience in Redstockings' abortion speak-out of 1969. *Quarterly Journal of Speech, 95,* 395–422.

Dudar, H. (1970, March 23). Women's lib: The war on "sexism." *Newsweek,* 71–74, 78.

Duffett, J. (1968, October) WLM vs. Miss America. *Voice of the Women's Liberation Movement,* 1–7.

DuPlessis, R. B. and Snitow, A. (Eds.). (1998). The feminist memoir project: Voices from women's liberation. New York: Three Rivers Press.

Echols, A. (1989). *Daring to be bad: Radical feminism in America, 1969–1975*. Minneapolis: University of Minnesota Press.

Echols, A. (2002). *Shaky ground: The sixties and its aftershocks*. New York: Columbia University Press.

Ehrenreich, B. (1987). *The hearts of men: American dreams and the flight from commitment*. New York: Anchor.

Eisenmann, L. (2010). Thinking feminist in 1963: Challenges from Betty Friedan and the President's Commission on the Status of Women," in J. Spence, S. J. Aiston, and M. M. Meikle (Eds.), *Women, education, and agency, 1600–2000* (pp. 224–240). New York: Routledge.

Enke, A. (2003). Smuggling sex through the gates: Race, sexuality, and the politics of space in second wave feminism. *American Quarterly, 55,* 635–667.

Ephron, N. (1972, November). Women. *Esquire,* 10.

Evans, S. (1979). *Personal politics: The roots of women's liberation in the civil rights movement and the new left.* New York: Knopf.

Evans, S. (2003). *Tidal wave: How women changed America at century's end.* New York: Free Press.

Ezekiel, J. (2002). *Feminism in the heartland.* Columbus: Ohio State University Press.

Faderman, L. (1991). *Odd girls and twilight lovers: A history of lesbian life in twentieth-century America.* New York: Penguin.

Faludi, S. (1991). *Backlash: The undeclared war against American women.* New York: Crown.

Farrell, A. E. (1998). *Yours in sisterhood: Ms. magazine and the promise of popular feminism.* Chapel Hill: University of North Carolina Press.

Feminists, The. (1969/1973). The Feminists: A political organization to annihilate sex roles. In Koedt, E. Levine, and A. Rapone (Eds.), *Radical feminism* (pp. 368–378). New York: Quadrangle.

Firestone, S. (1968). Abortion rally speech. In *Notes from the First Year* (n.p.). New York: New York Radical Women.

Firestone, S. (1970). *The dialectic of sex: The case for feminist revolution.* New York: Bantam.

Fishman, M. (1980). *Manufacturing the news.* Austin: University of Texas Press.

Fiske, J. (1987). *Television culture.* London: Routledge.

Five passionate feminists. (1970, July). *McCall's,* 53–55, 115.

Flannery, K. T. (2005). *Feminist literacies, 1968–1975.* Urbana: University of Illinois Press.

Fosburgh, L. (1970, August 26). Traditional groups prefer to ignore women's lib. *New York Times,* 44.

Freeman, J. (1975). *The politics of women's liberation.* New York: Longman.

Friedan, B. (1981). *The second stage.* New York: Summit Books.

Friedan, B. (1985). *It changed my life: Writings on the women's movement.* New York: W. W. Norton.

Friedan, B. (2000). *Life so far: A memoir.* New York: Touchstone.

Gamson, W. A. and Wolfsfeld, G. (1993, July). Movements and media as interacting systems. *Annals, AAPSS, 528,* 114–125.

Gans, H. J. (1979). *Deciding what's news: A study of* CBS Evening News, NBC Nightly News, Newsweek *and* Time. New York: Random House.

Garrett, M. (1992). Ponchitta Pierce. In J. Carney (Ed.), *Notable black American women,* vol. 2 (pp. 526–528). Detroit: Gale Research.

Gelfman, J. S. (1976). *Women in television news.* New York: Columbia University Press.

Gerhard, J. (2001). *Desiring revolution: Second wave feminism and the rewriting of American sexual thought, 1920–1982.* New York: Columbia.

Gerrity, D. (1970, March). Miss superfist. *Atlantic Monthly*, 91–93.

Giardina, C. (2010). *Freedom for women: Forging the women's liberation movement, 1953–1970*. Gainesville: University Press of Florida.

Gilmore, S., and Kaminski, E. (2007). A part and apart: Lesbian and straight feminist activists negotiate identity in a second-wave organization. *Journal of the History of Sexuality, 16*, 95–113.

Gitlin, T. (1980). *The whole world is watching: Mass media in the making and unmaking of the new left*. Berkeley: University of California.

Gloria Steinem tries to lower her famed profile. (1974, September 23). *People Magazine*, 8–9.

Graham, B. (1970, December). Jesus and the liberated woman. *Ladies' Home Journal*, 40–44, 114.

Gray, H. (1997). Remembering civil rights: Television, memory, and the 1960s. In L. Spigel and M. Curtin (Eds.), *The revolution wasn't televised: Sixties television and social conflict* (pp. 349–358). New York: Routledge.

Green, B. (1997). *Spectacular confessions: Autobiography, performative activism, and the sites of suffrage, 1905–1938*. New York: St. Martin's.

Griffin, S. (1971, September). Rape: The all-American crime. *Ramparts, 10*, 26–35.

Gupta, D. (2002, March 14–16). *Radical flank effects: The effect of radical-moderate splits in regional nationalist movements.* Paper presented at the Conference of Europeanists, Chicago, IL. Retrieved from: http://www.yumpu.com/en/document/view/6310445/radical-flank-effects-the-effect-of-radical-cornell-university. Accessed December 13, 2013.

Hage, D., and Klauda, P. (1989). *No retreat, no surrender: Labor's war at Hormel*. New York: William Morrow and Co.

Haines, H. (1988). *Black radicals and the civil rights mainstream, 1954–1970*. Knoxville: University of Tennessee Press.

Hallin, D. C. (1986). *"The uncensored war": The media and Vietnam*. New York: Oxford University Press.

Hallstein, D. L. O. (2010). *White feminists and contemporary maternity: Purging matrophobia*. New York: Palgrave Macmillan.

Hammond, C. M. (1981). *The image decade: Television documentary, 1965–1975*. New York: Hastings House.

Hanisch, C. (1970). What can be learned: A critique of the Miss America protest. In L. Tanner (Ed.), *Voices from women's liberation* (pp. 131–134). New York: Signet.

Hanisch, C. (1978a). The liberal takeover of women's liberation. In Redstockings (Eds.), *Feminist revolution: An abridged edition with additional writings* (pp. 163–167). New York: Random House.

Hanisch, C. (1978b). The personal is political. In Redstockings (Eds.), *Feminist revolution: An abridged edition with additional writings* (pp. 204–205). New York: Random House.

Hanisch, C. (1998). Two letters from the women's liberation movement. In R. B. DuPlessis and A. Snitow (Eds.), *The feminist memoir project: Voices from women's liberation* (pp. 197–207). New York: Three Rivers Press.

Hartmann, S. M. (1998). *The other feminists: Activists in the liberal establishment.* New Haven, CT: Yale University Press.

Hayden, C., and King, M. (1965/1979). Sex and caste: A kind of memo to a number of other women in the peace and freedom movements. In S. Evans (Ed.), *Personal politics: The roots of women's liberation in the civil rights movement and the new left* (pp. 235–238). New York: Knopf.

Heilbrun, C. (1996). *Gloria Steinem: The education of a woman.* New York: Ballantine.

Hepola, S. (2012, March 8). A woman like no other. *New York Times,* ST2, ST10.

Herr, L. K. (2003). *Women, power, and AT&T: Winning rights in the workplace.* Boston: Northeastern University Press.

Hershey, L. (1983). *Between the covers: The lady's own journal.* New York: Coward-Mc-Cann.

Hickey, G. (2008). Barred from the barroom: Second wave feminists and public accommodations in U.S. cities. *Feminist Studies, 34,* 382–408.

Hinds, H., and Stacey, J. (2001). Imaging feminism, imaging femininity: The bra-burner, Diana, and the woman who kills. *Feminist Media Studies, 1,* 153–177.

Hogeland, L. M. (1998). *Feminism and its fictions: The consciousness-raising novel and the women's liberation movement.* Philadelphia: University of Pennsylvania Press.

Hole, J., and Levine, E. (1971). *Rebirth of feminism.* New York: Quadrangle.

hooks, b. (1984). *Feminist theory: From margin to center.* Boston: South End Press.

Horowitz, R. (1997). *"Negro and white, unite and fight": A social history of industrial unionism in meatpacking, 1930–1990.* Urbana: University of Illinois Press.

Huddy, L. (1997). Feminists and feminism in the news. In P. Norris (Ed.), *Women, media, and politics* (pp. 183–204). New York: Oxford University Press.

Hull, G. T., Scott, P.B., and Smith, B. (Eds.). (1982). *All the women are white, all the blacks are men, but some of us are brave: Black women's studies.* New York: The Feminist Press.

Hunter, C. (1970, November 18). Many blacks wary of "women's liberation" movement in U.S. *New York Times,* 47.

Hunter, J. E. (1990). "A daring new concept": The *Ladies Home Journal* and modern feminism. *NWSA Journal, 2,* 583–602.

Illinois girl named Miss America. (1968, September 8). *New York Times,* 81.

Jamieson, K. H., and Campbell, K. K. (2006). *The interplay of influence: News, advertising, politics, and the internet,* 6th ed. Belmont, CA: Thomson Wadsworth.

Janeway, E. (1970, March 3). Happiness and the right to choose. *Atlantic Monthly,* 118–126.

Jay, K. (1970, April 4–18). *Ladies' Home Journal,* 1. *RAT,* 4, 22.

Jay, K. (1999). *Tales of the lavender menace: A memoir of revolution.* New York: Basic Books.

Jensen, E. (2011, August 14). Steinem's story, for a new generation. *New York Times,* AR16.

Jesus & Women: Readers answer Dr. Billy Graham. (1971, March). *Ladies' Home Journal*, 80–81.

Kaplan, L. (1995). *The story of Jane, the legendary underground feminist abortion service*. New York: Pantheon.

Kappeler, S. (1986). *The pornography of representation*. Minneapolis: University of Minnesota Press.

Kearon, P. (1973). Man-hating. In A. Koedt, E. Levine, and A. Rapone (Eds.), *Radical feminism* (pp. 78–80). New York: Quadrangle.

Kearon, P., and Mehrhof, B. (1973). Rape: An act of terror. In A. Koedt, E. Levine, and A. Rapone (Eds.), *Radical feminism* (pp. 228–233). New York: Quadrangle.

Kelly, C. A. (2000). Whatever happened to women's liberation? Feminist legacies of '68. *New Political Science, 22*, 161–175.

King, C. S. (2007). Acting up and sounding off: Sacrifice and performativity in *Alice, Sweet Alice. Text and Performance Quarterly, 27*, 127–142.

Kinloch, V. F. (2004). The rhetoric of black bodies: Race, beauty, and representation. In E. Watson and D. Martin (Eds.), *"There she is, Miss America": The politics of sex, beauty, and race in America's most famous pageant* (pp. 93–109). New York: Palgrave Macmillan.

Klemesrud, J. (1968, September 9). There's now Miss Black America. *New York Times*, 54.

Klemesrud, J. (1969, February 17). It was a special show—and the audience was special, too. *New York Times, 39*.

Klemesrud, J. (1970, December 18). The lesbian issue and women's lib. *New York Times, 47*.

Klemesrud, J. (1973, January 31). Lesbians who try to be good mothers. *New York Times, 46*.

Klemesrud, J. (1977, September 26). Underground book brings fame to a lesbian author. *New York Times, 42*.

Kline, W. (2010). *Bodies of knowledge: Sexuality, reproduction, and women's health in the second wave*. Chicago: University of Chicago Press.

Komisar, L. (1970, February 21). The new feminism. *Saturday Review, 27–30*.

Kotlowski, D. J. (2002). *Nixon's civil rights: Politics, principle, and policy*. Cambridge, MA: Harvard University Press.

Ladies' journal has "lib" section. (1970, July 28). *New York Times*, L13.

Ladner, L. (1970, July). A national guide to legal abortion. *Ladies' Home Journal, 73*.

Lardner, Jr. G. (1970, May 7). Women press rights on hill. *Washington Post*, B12.

Leading feminist puts hairdo before strike. (1970, August 27). *New York Times*, 30.

Lear, M. W. (1968, March 10). What do these women want? The second feminist wave. *New York Times Magazine*, 24–25, 50–62.

Leone, V. (1993). Occupying the Ladies' Home Journal: My first hurrah. In M. H. Beasley and S. J. Gibbons (Eds.), *Taking their place: A documentary history of women in journalism* (pp. 212–217). Washington, D.C.: The American University Press.

Lehman, K. (2011). *Those girls: Single women in sixties and seventies popular culture*. Lawrence: University Press of Kansas.

Levitt, L. (1971, October). She: The awesome power of Gloria Steinem. *Esquire*, 88–90+.

Liberating the journal. (1970, August 3). *Newsweek,* 44.

Liberating the magazines. (1971, February 8). *Newsweek,* 101.

Lib rip-off? (1972, February 9). *Washington Post,* D2.

Lichtenstein, G. (1970a, March 19). Feminists demand "liberation" in *Ladies' Home Journal* sit-in. *New York Times,* 51.

Lichtenstein, G. (1970b, August 27). For most women, "strike day" was just a topic of conversation. *New York Times,* 30.

Luker, K. (1985). *Abortion and the politics of motherhood.* Berkeley: University of California Press.

Lumsden, L. (2009). "Women's lib has no soul"? Analysis of women's movement coverage in black periodicals, 1968–73. *Journalism History, 35,* 118–130.

MacDougall, A. K. (1970, August 3). Keepers of the faith: *Ladies' Home Journal, McCall's* fight it out with sugar and spice. *Wall Street Journal,* 1, 11.

Male and Female (1970, May 18). *Newsweek,* 74, 76.

Mansbridge, J. J. (1986). *Why we lost the ERA.* Chicago: University of Chicago Press.

Martin, J. F. (1971, July). Confessions of a non-bra-burner. *Chicago Journalism Review, 4,* 11, 15.

Martindale, C. (1989). Selected newspaper coverage of causes of black protest. *Journalism Quarterly, 66* (4), 920–923, 964.

Matthews, N. A. (1994). *Confronting rape: The feminist anti-rape movement and the state.* New York: Routledge.

May, E. T. (2010). *America and the pill: A history of promise, peril, and liberation.* New York: Basic Books.

Mayeri, S. (2011). *Reasoning from race: Feminism, law, and the civil rights revolution.* Cambridge, MA: Harvard University Press.

McCall, M. (1970, April 8). ABC newswoman pictures WLM. *Daily Tarheel,* n.p.

Mendes, K. (2011). *Feminism in the news: Representations of the women's movement since the 1960s.* New York: Palgrave Macmillan.

Mercer, M. (1972, January). Gloria: The unhidden persuader. *McCall's,* 68–69+.

Messer-Davidow, E. (2002). *Disciplining feminism: From social activism to academic discourse.* Durham, NC: Duke University Press.

Meyer, K. E. (1970, March 19). Women invade *Ladies' Home Journal,* demand end to demeaning articles. *Washington Post,* A3.

Meyerowitz, J. (1993). Beyond the feminine mystique: A reassessment of postwar mass culture, 1946–1958. *Journal of American History, 79,* 1455–1482.

Millet, K. (1970). *Sexual politics.* New York: Avon.

Mills, K. (1990). *A place in the news: From the women's pages to the front page.* New York: Columbia University Press.

Mills, K. (1997). What difference do women journalists make? In In P. Norris (Ed.), *Women, media, and politics* (pp. 41–55). New York: Oxford University Press.

Molotoch, H. L. (1978). The news of women and the work of men. In G. Tuchman, A. K. Daniels, and J. Benet (Eds.), *Hearth and home: Images of women in the mass media* (pp. 176–185). New York: Oxford.

Moore, S. J. (1997). Making a spectacle of suffrage: The National Woman Suffrage Pageant, 1913. *Journal of American Culture, 20,* 89–103.

Moraga, C., and Anzaldúa, G. (Eds.). (1981). *This bridge called my back: Writings by radical women of color.* Watertown, MA: Persephone Press.

Morgan, R. (Ed.). (1970). *Sisterhood is powerful: An anthology of writings from the women's liberation movement.* New York: Vintage.

Morgan, R. (1978). *Going too far: Personal chronicle of a feminist.* New York: Vintage.

Morgan, R. (1992). *The word of a woman: Feminist dispatches, 1968–1992.* New York: W. W. Norton.

Morgan, R. (1999, September 26). A lady and a feminist. *New York Times,* 399.

Morgan, R. (2001). *Saturday's child: A memoir.* New York: W. W. Norton.

Morrison, T. (1971, August 22). What the black woman thinks about women's liberation. *New York Times Magazine,* 14–15, 63–66.

Moskowitz, E. (1996). "It's good to blow your top": Women's magazines and a discourse of discontent, 1945–1965. *Journal of Women's History, 8,* 66–98.

Mulvey, L. (1975/1999). Visual pleasure and narrative cinema. In S. Thornham (Ed.), *Feminist film theory: A reader* (pp. 58–69). New York: New York University Press.

Neby, E. (1973, November 7). They're black, so feminism has even more obstacles than usual. *New York Times,* 42.

Nelson, J. (2003). *Women of color and the reproductive rights movement.* New York: New York University Press.

Nichols, B. (1991). *Representing reality: Issues and concepts in documentary.* Bloomington: Indiana University Press.

Nicholson, L. (2008). *Identity before identity politics.* New York: Cambridge.

No more Miss America. (1970). In R. Morgan (Ed.), *Sisterhood is powerful: An anthology of writings from the women's liberation movement* (pp. 584–588). New York: Vintage.

North, S. (1970, March 3). Reporting the movement. *Atlantic Monthly,* 105–106.

NOW Bill of Rights. (1970). In R. Morgan (Ed.), *Sisterhood is powerful: An anthology of writings from the women's liberation movement* (pp. 575–577). New York: Vintage.

On the march for what they still haven't got, women arise. (1970, September 4). *Life,* 16–23.

Pascalé, S, Moon, R., and Tanner, L. (1970). Self-defense for women. In R. Morgan (Ed.), *Sisterhood is powerful: An anthology of writings from the women's liberation movement* (pp. 527–536). New York: Vintage.

Pearson, K. (1999). Mapping rhetorical interventions in "national" feminist histories: Second-wave feminism and *Ain't I A Woman. Communication Studies, 50,* 158–173.

Perlman, A. (2007). Feminists in the wasteland: The National Organization for Women and television reform. *Feminist Media Studies, 7,* 413–441.

Pitzulo, C. (2011). *Bachelors and bunnies: The sexual politics of Playboy.* Chicago: University of Chicago Press.

Plantinga, C. (1997). *Rhetoric and representation in nonfiction film.* Cambridge, UK: Cambridge University Press.

Poirot, K. (2004). Mediating a movement, authorizing discourse: Kate Millett, *Sexual Politics,* and feminism's second wave. *Women's Studies in Communication, 27,* 205–235.

Poirot, K. (2009). Domesticating the liberated woman: Containment rhetorics of second wave radical/lesbian feminism. *Women's Studies in Communication, 32,* 263–292.

Polatnick, M. R. (1996). Diversity in women's liberation ideology: How a black and a white group of the 1960s viewed motherhood. *Signs: Journal of Women in Culture and Society, 21,* 679–706.

Polletta, F. (2002). *Freedom is an endless meeting: Democracy in American social movements.* Chicago: University of Chicago Press.

Povich, L. (2012). *The good girls revolt: How the women of* Newsweek *sued their bosses and changed the workplace.* New York: PublicAffairs.

Prial, F. (1970, August 27). Feminist philosopher Katherine Murray Millett. *New York Times,* 30.

Rakow L., and Kranich, K. (1991). Woman as sign in television news. *Journal of Communication, 41,* 8–23

Raymont, H. (1970, March 17). As *Newsweek* says, women are in revolt, even on *Newsweek. New York Times,* 30.

Regelson, R. (1969, May 18). Is motherhood holy? Not anymore. *New York Times,* D1.

Rhode, D. L. (1989). *Justice and gender: Sex discrimination and the law.* Cambridge, MA: Harvard University Press.

Rhode, D. L. (1995). Media images, feminist issues. *Signs: Journal of Women in Culture and Society, 20,* 685–710.

Rhodes, J. (2005). *Radical feminism, writing, and critical agency: From manifesto to modem.* Albany: State University of New York Press.

Rhodes, J. (2007). *Framing the Black Panthers: The spectacular rise of a black power icon.* New York: The Free Press.

Roberts, D. (1997). *Killing the black body: race, reproduction, and the meaning of liberty.* New York: Vintage.

Roberts, G., and Klibanoff, H. (2007). *The race beat: The press, the civil rights struggle, and the awakening of a nation.* New York: Vintage.

Robertson, N. (1992). *The girls in the balcony: Women, men, and the* New York Times. New York: Random House.

Rosen, R. (2000). *The world split open: How the modern women's movement changed America.* New York: Viking.

Rosteck, T. (1994). See It Now *Confronts McCarthyism: Television documentary and the politics of representation.* Tuscaloosa: University of Alabama Press.

Roth, B. (2003). *Separate roads to feminism: Black, Chicana, and white feminist movements in America's second wave.* New York: Cambridge University Press.

Sanders, M., and Rock, M. (1988). *Waiting for prime-time: The women of television news.* New York: Harper and Row.

Sarachild, K. (1978). A program for feminist consciousness-raising. In Redstockings (Eds.), *Feminist revolution: An abridged edition with additional writings* (pp. 202–203). New York: Random House.

Scanlon, J. (1995). Inarticulate longings: *The* Ladies' Home Journal, *gender, and the promises of consumer culture*. New York: Routledge.

Schudson, M. (1995). *The power of news*. Cambridge, MA: Harvard University Press.

Seaman, B. (1995, rpt. 1969). *The doctor's case against the pill*. Alameda, CA: Hunter House.

Shreve, A. (1989). *Women together, women alone: The legacy of the consciousness raising movement*. New York: Viking.

Shuit, D. (1970, August 22). Mother of 7 fights women's lib movement. *Los Angeles Times*, A1.

Smith, L. (1972, January). Gloria Steinem, writer and social critic, talks about sex, politics and marriage. *Redbook*, 69–76.

SNCC position paper (Women in the movement). (1964/1979). In S. Evans, *Personal politics: The roots of women's liberation in the civil rights movement and the new left* (pp. 233–235). New York: Knopf.

Snitow, A. (1992). Feminism and motherhood: An American reading. *Feminist Studies, 40*, 32–51.

Solomon, M. (1979). The "positive woman's" journey: A mythic analysis of the rhetoric of STOP ERA, *Quarterly Journal of Speech, 65*, 262–274.

Southard, B. S. (2007). Miltancy, power, and identity: The Silent Sentinels as women fighting for political voice. *Rhetoric and Public Affairs, 10*, 399–418.

Springer, K. (2005). *Living for the revolution: Black feminist organizations, 1968–1980*. Durham, NC: Duke University Press.

Stambler, S. (Ed.), (1970). *Women's liberation: Blueprint for the future*. New York: Ace Books.

Steinem, G. (1963, May 1). A bunny's tale. *Show Magazine*, 90, 92, 94, 118.

Steinem, G. (1969, April 4). After black power, women's liberation. *New York*, 8–10.

Steinem, G. (1970a, June 7). Women's liberation aims to free men, too. *Washington Post*, 192.

Steinem, G. (1970b, July). After too much moving . . . cheerful rooms to live in, a private place to work. *House and Garden*, 52–55.

Steinem, G. (1970c, August 31). What it would be like if women win. *Time*, 22–23.

Steinem, G. (1970d, October). What "Playboy" doesn't know about women could fill a book. *McCall's*, 76–77, 139.

Steinem, G. (1971, August 26). A new egalitarian lifestyle. *New York Times*, 37.

Steinem, G. (1983). *Outrageous acts and everyday rebellions*. New York: Holt, Rinehart, and Winston.

Steinem, G. (1990, July/August). Sex, lies, and advertising. *Ms.*, 18–28.

Stephens, M. (1998). *The rise of the image, the fall of the word*. New York: Oxford University Press.

Stern, S. L. (1997). *Gloria Steinem: Her passions, politics, and mystique*. Secaucus, NJ: Birch Lane Press.

Stimpson, C. (1988). *Where the meanings are: Feminism and cultural spaces*. New York: Routledge.

Stokes, A. Q. (2005). Constituting southern feminists: Women's liberation newsletters in the South. *Southern Communication Journal, 70,* 91–108.

Tanner, L. (Ed.), (1970). *Voices from women's liberation.* New York: Signet.

Tate, H. (2005). The ideological effects of a failed constitutive rhetoric: The co-option of the rhetoric of white lesbian feminism. *Women's Studies in Communication, 28,* 1–31.

The new feminism: A special section prepared for the *Ladies' Home Journal* by the women's liberation movement. (1970, August). *Ladies' Home Journal,* 63–71.

The new feminists: Revolt against "sexism." (1969, November 21). *Time,* pp. 53–56.

The power of a woman: The journal's newsletter of involvement. (1970, August). *The Ladies' Home Journal,* 50.

The price of protest. (1968, September 27). *New York Times,* 25.

Thornham, S. (Ed.) (1999). *Feminist film theory: A reader.* New York: New York University.

Thornham, S. (2007). *Women, feminism and media.* Edinburgh: Edinburgh University Press.

Tobias, S. (1997). *Faces of feminism: An activist's reflections on the women's movement.* Boulder, Co: Westview.

Tomasson, V. (1970, April 4–18). *Ladies' Home Journal,* 2. *RAT,* 5, 22.

Torres, S. (2003). *Black, white, and in color: Television and black civil rights.* Princeton, NJ: Princeton University Press.

Trotta, L. (1991). *Fighting for air: In the trenches with television news.* New York: Simon and Schuster.

Tuchman, G. (1978a). The newspaper as a social movement's resource. In G. Tuchman, A. K. Daniels, and J. Benet (Eds.), *Hearth and home: Images of women in the mass media* (pp. 186–215). New York: Oxford.

Tuchman, G. (1978b). *Making news: A study in the construction of reality.* New York: The Free Press.

Tucker, L. R. (1988). The framing of Calvin Klein: A framing analysis of media discourse about the August 1995 Calvin Klein Jeans advertising campaign. *Critical Studies in Mass Communication, 15,* 141–157.

Umansky, L. (1996). *Motherhood reconceived: Feminism and the legacy of the sixties.* New York: New York University Press.

Valk, A. M. (2008). *Radical sisters: Second-wave feminism and black liberation in Washington, D.C.* Urbana: University of Illinois Press.

Vallens, A. (1986, October). The world of the multi-racial woman. *Cosmopolitan,* 260–263, 271.

Van Gelder, L. (1992, September/October). The truth about bra-burners. *Ms.,* 80–81.

Van Horne, H. (1968, September 9). Female firebrands. *New York Post,* 38.

van Zoonen, L. (1992). The women's movement and the media: Constructing a public identity. *European Journal of Communication, 7,* 453–476.

Vavrus, M. D. (2002). *Postfeminist news: Political women in media culture.* Albany: State University of New York Press.

Walters, S. D. (1995). *Material girls: Making sense of feminist cultural theory.* Berkeley: University of California.

Ward, A. (1970, March 8). Women hold own hearing on pill. *Washington Post,* 121.

Ware, C. (1970). *Woman power: The movement for women's liberation.* New York: Tower Books.

Watson, E., and Martin, D. (2004). Introduction. In E. Watson and D. Martin (Eds.), *"There she is, Miss America": The politics of sex, beauty, and race in America's most famous pageant* (pp. 1–23). New York: Palgrave Macmillan.

Weaver, D. (1997). Women as journalists. In P. Norris (Ed.), *Women, media, and politics* (pp. 21–40). New York: Oxford University Press.

Weber, M. (1970). Masters & Johnson: Their new cures for sex problems. *Ladies' Home Journal,* 51, 107.

Weisstein, N. (1970). "Kinde, küche, kirche" as scientific law: Psychology constructs the female. In R. Morgan (Ed.), *Sisterhood is powerful: An anthology of writings from the women's liberation movement* (pp. 228–245). New York: Vintage.

Whittier, N. (1995). *Feminist generations: The persistence of the radical women's movement.* Philadelphia, PA: Temple University Press.

Wilkes, P. (1970, November 29). Mother superior to women's lib. *New York Times Magazine,* 27–29, 149–150, 157.

Williams, B. (2008). AT&T and the private-sector origins of private-sector affirmative action. *Journal of Policy History, 20,* 542–568.

Willis, E. (1969, February 22). Hearing. *The New Yorker,* 28–29.

Willis, E. (1978). The conservatism of *Ms.* In Redstockings (Eds.), *Feminist revolution: An abridged edition with additional writings* (pp. 170–173). New York: Random House.

Willis, E. (1992). *No more nice girls: Countercultural essays.* Hanover, NH: Wesleyan University Press.

Wolfson, A. J. (1998). Clenched fist, open heart. In R. B. DuPlessis and A. Snitow (Eds.), *The Feminist Memoir Project* (pp. 268–283). New York: Three Rivers Press.

Woman of the year: Gloria Steinem. (1972, January). *McCall's,* 67.

Woman-Power. (1970, March 30). *Time,* 59.

Woman Power. (1970, March 30). *Newsweek,* 61.

Women's lib and me! (1970, November). *Ladies' Home Journal,* 69, 74.

Women's lib: A second look. (1970, December 4). *Time,* p. 50.

Wood, J. T. (2010). *Gendered lives: Communication, gender, and culture,* 9th ed. Belmont, CA: Wadsworth.

Zeisler, A. (2008). *Feminism and pop culture.* Berkeley, CA: Seal Press.

Ziegler D. (1992). Norma Quarles. In J. Carney (Ed.), *Notable black American women,* vol. 1 (pp. 909–910). Detroit: Gale Research.

Zuckerman, M.E. (1998). *A history of popular women's magazines in the United States, 1792–1995.* Westport, CT: Greenwood Press.

Index

ABC: coverage of birth control hearings, 55; coverage of House passage of ERA, 144, 145–46; coverage of *LHJ* sit-in, 26, 118; coverage of Liberty Island protest, 145; coverage of Strike, 151, 153, 155, 156, 160, 167; ERA documentary, 189; *NOW* series, 212n2; "Women's Liberation" (*see* "Women's Liberation"). *See also* Sanders, Marlene

abortion: article in *LHJ*, 112; clergy counseling service, 85, 87, 209n24; hearings on, 214n3; in news series, 57, 82–88; opposition to, 174, 177; as public policy concern, 84; Redstockings' focus on, 209n22; speakout, 192, 214n3; in Strike, 149–50, 154; in "Women's Liberation," 128

Abzug, Bella, 148, 151, 195

activism, 16–17, 43–46, 156–58, 164, 172

activism, civil rights, 42

activism, media, 146–47, 173

African Americans. *See* women of color

agitprop, 204n1

Alexander, Shana, 99, 113

Allen, Bonnie, 38, 39

Amatniek, Kathy, 34, 205n7. *See also* Sarachild, Kathie

Andelin, Helen, 157

Anthony, Susan B., 70, 191

antifeminism, 156–57, 158–59, 176–77, 178–79, 189

antifeminists, 156–58, 162, 163, 191. *See also* Schlafly, Phyllis

appearance, 60, 62, 73, 76, 160, 182, 194. *See also* beauty images; politics, beauty; visuals

Atkinson, Ti-Grace, 62, 63–64, 83, 103–4, 116, 117, 207n11

AT&T, 80, 208n21

audience: assumed for news, 12, 16; of CBS series, 57, 72, 93; of NBC series, 57, 85, 93; of print media, 16; of radicals, 65; and rhetorical choices, 170; in Strike coverage, 151, 155–56, 163; and visual representation of women, 13–14; of "Women's Liberation," 123, 133, 141–42; of women's magazines, 117

Austin, Minnesota, 209n25

Bambara, Toni Cade, 19

Barker-Plummer, Bernadette, 9, 50

Barthes, Roland, 56

Baxandall, Rosalyn, 46, 116

Bayh, Birch, 129–30, 133, 183
beauty images, in Strike coverage, 155–58
behavior, 60–61, 104, 164, 172, 195–96
Berger, John, 14, 156, 162–63
Berghoff restaurant, 60, 193, 206n6
binaries, gender, 49, 50
birth control hearings, 54–55, 60, 84–85, 206n3
birth control pill, 85, 206n3
Black Panthers, 131, 212n2
Bluem, William, 123
Bodroghkozy, A., 18
bona fide occupational qualification (BFOQ), 79, 208n19
Borda, Jennifer, 159
bra burning, 2, 17, 30–32, 45, 49, 159–60
Bradley, Patricia, 15, 47, 150, 203n10, 204n1, 207n11
Breines, Wini, 19
Brown, Rita Mae, 122
Brownmiller, Susan: accused of using movement for gain, 114, 115; *Against Our Will,* 175; article in *NYT Magazine,* 53, 99; on complaint against *Newsweek,* 210n6; on Friedan, 211n11; on importance of Miss America Pageant protest, 204n2; as leader of *LHJ* sit-in, 102; on lesbians, 211n11; on *LHJ* sit-in, 97, 101, 104, 116, 211n7; on Sanders, 121, 122

camera work. *See* visuals
Campbell, Karlyn Kohrs, 203n7
Carbine, Pat, 113
Carter, John Mack. See *Ladies' Home Journal (LHJ)* sit-in
CBS: audience of series of, 170; characterizations of movement, 58–65, 70–71; comparison-contrast strategy used by, 71; construction of antifeminism, 158–59; coverage of birth control hearings, 54, 55; coverage of House passage of ERA, 144, 145–46; issues in series of, 58–59, 71–76, 81, 82–84, 88, 137; lack of male opposition in series of, 73; marginalization of radicals, 92, 94; narrative of movement, 56; nature of coverage by, 169; representation of radicals' ideology, 88–89; rhetorical strategies of, 25–26,
71, 88; Strike coverage, 153, 158, 160–61, 166; use of visuals, 71–76
Ceballos, Jacqui, 148
Celler, Emanuel ("Manny"), 144, 145
Chancellor, John, 152
Chicago Women's Liberation Union (CWLU), 86–87, 92
child care, 74, 135, 136, 213n4
Chisholm, Shirley, 68, 75–76, 84, 148, 173
Civil Rights Act of 1964, 77, 79, 129, 144–45, 207n16
civil rights movement: feminism analogized with, 26–27 (*see also* sex-race analogy); feminism's links with, 37, 39; March on Washington, 153; *New York Times*'s coverage of, 42; oversimplification of, 132; presidents' support of, 213n3
class, 84, 86, 92, 110, 141
Cohen, Marcia, 204n2
Collins, Gail, 173
Combahee River Collective Statement, 205n10
combat, women serving in, 146, 213n1
Comprehensive Child Development Act, 213n4
consciousness-raising (CR): in CBS series, 62; difficulty in representing in news stories, 15, 65, 172; drawbacks of, 109–10, 211n10; functions of, 15; about Miss America Pageant, 32; in NBC series, 67; radicals' use of, 8; and transition of theorizing to academy, 186–87; in women's magazines, 109–10, 207n12
Coontz, Stephanie, 75, 207n15
coverage, news: after 1970, 175; decline in, 178; levels of analysis of, 12; regional focus of, 203n11; types of, 11
CR. *See* consciousness-raising
Craig, Maxine Leeds, 38
Cronkite, Walter, 61, 71, 153, 193, 214n2
Culhane, David, 57, 93, 137, 138, 170. *See also* CBS
Curtis, Charlotte, 34–35, 36, 38–39, 40–41, 42, 48

Davis, Flora, 204n2
Davison, Jaquie, 156–58, 160

D.C. Women's Liberation, 54, 205n2
dell'Olio, Anselma, 63, 207n10
Denham, Alice, 73–74
deviance, 153, 158, 168–69, 172
The Dialectic of Sex (Firestone), 83, 88
discrimination, economic, 65. *See also* employment
divorce, and feminism, 74–75
The Doctor's Case against the Pill (Seaman), 55
documentary, 123, 169, 189. See also *Gloria: In Her Own Words;* "Women's Liberation"
Dornan, Robert, 176
Douglas, Susan, 63, 153
draft, military, 213n1
Duffett, Judith, 32, 44

Ehrenreich, Barbara, 75
employment: and abortion law repeal, 88; in *LHJ* sit-in, 100, 101, 118–19; male evaluation of women's capabilities, 81; motivations for, 75; opportunity, 75, 79, 82 (*see also* sex discrimination); pay inequality, 59, 66, 79, 82, 101, 129; of women of color, 66, 81–82, 92; in "Women's Liberation," 129. *See also* child care; Equal Employment Opportunity Commission; sex discrimination; women, working
enemy, 134–36, 142
Equal Employment Opportunity Commission (EEOC), 76, 77, 81, 202n4, 207n16, 208n21
equality, 140, 145, 146, 174, 178, 213n1. *See also* Equal Rights Amendment
Equal Opportunity Act, 208n16
Equal Pay Act of 1963, 129
Equal Rights Amendment (ERA): coverage of, 69–70; documentary on, 189; failure of, 179, 180; goals of, 130; House's passage of, 27, 144, 145–46, 164; as key feminist goal, 3; in *LHJ* column, 107–8; opposition to, 144–45, 157, 174, 177; as policy solution, 128, 129; representation of, 179–80; in Strike coverage, 167; support for, 70, 144; symbolic power of, 178; in "Women's Liberation," 122, 128–30

ERA. *See* Equal Rights Amendment
Esquire, 194, 195
Evans, Sara, 51
event-centered reporting, 33, 36, 166
Evers, Myrlie, 173
Ezekiel, Judith, 204n11

family, different attitudes of black and white women toward, 84, 110
Fascinating Womanhood, 157
Feigen, Brenda, 183
The Feminine Mystique (Friedan), 7, 134, 210n4
femininity, 16–17, 43–46, 94, 151, 155–58, 160
feminism: in 1980s, 180; backlash against, 167, 174, 176–77; contradictions in, 200; image problems, 46, 137; negative frames for representing, 94; opposition to, 36–37 (*see also* antifeminism; antifeminists); pathologizing of, 17, 46; problematic media strategies attached to, 178; representing through individuals, 199; Steinem's definition of, 191
feminism, big-city, 204n11
feminism, first wave, 69–70, 159, 166, 170
feminism, liberal: and abortion rights, 82, 88; ascendancy of, 28, 142, 173–74; in CBS series, 56, 59; coherent rationale for, 59; Culhane on, 83; development of, 7; goals of, 81, 82, 88; images of, 14; in mass media representation, 88; media strategies, 8, 9; movement into mainstream, 187; in NBC series, 56, 67–68; practices of, 7; relation with radicals, 26, 92, 171; in Strike, 148; use of term, 202n5; in "Women's Liberation," 122. *See also* National Organization for Women
feminism, lifestyle, 189
feminism, radical: audience of, 65; in CBS series, 56, 60–65, 93; characterizations of, 9–10; composition of, 7; Culhane on, 83; demonization of, 92; development of, 7; difficulty in representing ideology of, 14, 65; disappointment in outcomes of *LHJ* sit-in, 114–17; ERA represented as symbol of, 179–80; factions in, 3;

feminism, radical (*continued*): goals of, 82, 114, 166, 171; images of, 14–15; legacy of, 174; in liberal vision of women's liberation, 92; mainstreaming of issues raised by, 82; marginalization of, 94, 171–72; and media, 8–9, 61, 64, 83; in NBC series, 56, 65–70, 92, 93; practices of, 7–8 (*see also* consciousness-raising); publications by, 9; in Strike, 149–50; struggle for legitimacy, 51; threatening aspects of, 142–43; used to make liberals seems reasonable, 116–17; use of term, 202n5, 202n6; view of ERA, 70; view of Steinem, 185–86, 187; view of using movement for personal gain, 114–15; in "Women's Liberation," 119, 132, 135, 140. *See also* consciousness-raising

feminism, second wave: connections to first wave, 70; context of interaction with mass media, 4; factions in, 3, 7, 67, 116, 202n5 (*see also* feminism, liberal; feminism, radical); linked to first wave, 126; misconceptions about, 18, 30–32; as movement, 3; struggle for legitimacy, 49–51; use of term, 201n2. *See also* women's liberation movement

feminism/civil rights analogies. *See* sex-race analogy

Feminist Repertory Theater, 206n5, 207n10, 209n22

The Feminists, 62–64, 70, 99, 135, 136, 205n1, 206n8

feminists, socialist, 202n5. *See also* Chicago Women's Liberation Union; socialist-feminist analysis

Firestone, Shulamith, 83, 88, 102, 116, 117, 172, 205n1

Fisher, Linda, 133, 134

Fiske, John, 154

Flannery, Kathryn Thomas, 203n7

Food and Drug Administration, 54, 55, 206n3

Ford, Judith Anne, 34, 40, 41

Fourteenth Amendment, 178

Freedom Trash Can, 30, 34

Freeman, Jo, 147, 162, 202n5

Friedan, Betty: on absence of women from leadership positions, 58–59; Brown-

miller on, 211n11; editing of special *LHJ* issue, 210n4; on ERA, 107–8; *The Feminine Mystique,* 7, 134, 210n4; and founding of NOW, 202n4; founding of NWPC, 173; as leader, 165; in *McCall's,* 113; motivations for Strike, 147; in *New York Times,* 181; personality, 188; *The Second Stage,* 187; on sexual politics, 68, 147; and Steinem, 187, 191, 192, 199; in Strike coverage, 151, 166; in "Women's Liberation," 135, 136

Gay Liberation Front (GLF), 99, 212n11. *See also* Jay, Karla

gaze, male, 72, 155, 162, 214n3

gender, 16–18, 61

gender anxiety: and abortion, 57; provoked by radicals, 64; and rebirth of political conservatism, 167; in reporting, 17–18, 27; in Strike coverage, 17, 148–49, 151–52, 157, 160–61, 166

gender expectations, 36–37, 61

gender identity, as performative, 163

gender roles, 83, 84, 89–91, 100–101, 126–27, 169

Gerhard, Jane, 211n10

Gitlin, Todd, 205n5

Glass, Genevieve, 80, 208n21

GLF (Gay Liberation Front), 99, 212n11. *See also* Jay, Karla

Gloria: In Her Own Words, 28, 189, 190–99. *See also* Steinem, Gloria

GOP, 178

Graham, Billy, 112

Green, Barbara, 214n3

Grierson, John, 123

Griffin, Susan, 175

Griffiths, Martha, 144

Grimm, Edith, 80

Grove Press, 97–98

guerilla theater, 127, 155

Hamer, Fannie Lou, 173

Hammer, Signe, 99, 102

Hanisch, Carol, 29, 30, 35, 37, 186

Happiness of Womanhood, 157, 158, 160

HBO. *See Gloria: In Her Own Words*

health, women's, 55. *See also* abortion; birth control hearings

Hefner, Hugh, 120, 212n1
Height, Dorothy, 165
Hernández, Aileen, 19, 147
Hershey, Lenore, 102, 113–14, 212n12
Hinds, Hilary, 30
Hogeland, Lisa Maria, 142, 203n7
housewives, 158, 166
Hunter, Jean, 210n4

identity, feminist, 167
intersectionality: Chisholm's, 68; defined, 205n10; elision of, 43, 76; lack of recognition of, 214n4; in Mackin's report, 87; news workers' difficulty with, 39, 50
issued-centered coverage, 202n3

"Jane," 85
Jay, Karla, 23–24, 102, 110, 115, 116, 117, 211n7
journalists, 47–48. *See also* individual journalists
journalists, female: in CBS series, 62; complaints against media organizations by, 103; in *LHJ* sit-in, 116; at NWC, 175; presentation of issues, 93; social trend stories by, 53; in Strike coverage, 155, 159, 165–66, 167. *See also* individual journalists

Kappeler, Suzanne, 154
Kearon, Pam, 175
Kennedy, Flo, 19, 39, 148, 195
Klemesrud, Judy, 39, 40–42, 47, 48
Koedt, Anne, 113, 205n1
Komisar, Lucy, 20, 53, 98, 114
Kunhardt, Peter, 190

Ladies' Home Journal (LHJ) sit-in: clothing of protesters, 210n7; coverage of, 97, 102–7, 110–11; description of, 96; effects of, 26, 112–18; goals of, 115–16; interpretation of, 97; issues in, 100, 105–6, 118–19; leadership of, 102, 103–4; participants in, 209n2, 210n3; planning of, 99; publicity value of, 108; radical flank effect, 212n13; responses to, 107–14; timing of, 97
Ladner, Lawrence, 112

Lamb, Myrna, 209n22
lavender menace. *See* lesbianism; lesbians
leaders/leadership, 10, 18, 35, 102, 103–4, 186. *See also* Atkinson, Ti-Grace; Friedan, Betty; Millett, Kate; Steinem, Gloria
lesbianism: absence of from coverage, 24; as accusation, 44–45; conflicts over, 22–24; in coverage, 171; in *Gloria: In Her Own Words*, 196, 198–99; in *LHJ* sit-in, 109–10, 212n11; in *New York Times*, 214n2; radicals' position on, 63; and Second Congress to Unite Women, 23–24; in splintering of groups, 205n2
lesbianism, political, 63
lesbians: Brownmiller on, 211n11; in coverage, 179; feminists labeled as, 68; at NWC, 176; purged from NOW, 23; rights of, opposition to, 177; in "Women's Liberation," 122, 132
liberalism, 92, 141
Lichtenstein, Grace, 103
Life, 48, 164
Lumsden, Linda, 41

Mackin, Catherine, 57, 76, 81–88, 98, 170
magazines, women's: characteristics of, 100; content of, 108–9, 113, 117–18, 210n4; CR in, 109–10, 207n12; founding of, 209n1; staffs of, 99, 212n12. See also *Ladies' Home Journal (LHJ)* sit-in; *McCall's*
man-hating, 142. *See also* politics, sexual
Mansbridge, Jane, 129, 178
March for Equality, 178
marriage: Atkinson on, 63–64, 83, 207n11; breakdown of, 74–75; "Can This Marriage Be Saved?" column, 109; in CBS series, 137; Friedan on, 187; in "Women's Liberation," 135, 136
martial arts, 61, 138–39, 213n6
Martin Marietta, 78, 208n19
McCall's, 99, 111, 113, 117–18, 183, 187. *See also* magazines, women's
McGee, Frank, 161
McLaughlin, Marya, 159, 165–66
media, 5–7. *See also* journalists; news
Media Women, 99, 110, 114, 116, 210n6
Mehrhof, Barbara, 63, 175

men: attitudes toward feminism, 121; evaluation of women's capabilities, 81; making feminism palatable to, 133–38; movement's benefits for, 134, 137, 213n5; in news series, 57; in NYRF ideology, 205n1; perceived as enemy, 134–36, 142; relationship to sexism, 91; and "Women's Liberation," 127–28, 133, 141–42

Meyerowitz, Joanne, 210n4

militancy, 61, 105, 153, 165

Millett, Kate, 22, 148, 150, 151, 181, 183, 198

Miss America Pageant, 29, 32–33, 40–42, 48–49, 200

Miss America Pageant protest: absence of leader, 35; in CBS series, 71–72; coverage of, 1–2, 201n1; and depoliticization of feminism, 46; as deviant, 172; effects of, 46–47, 48; and femininity, 43–46; Freedom Trash Can, 30–31, 34; and gender expectations, 43–46; goals of, 29, 36; Hanisch's critique of, 45–46; hecklers, 44–45; lack of message coherence, 35–36; misconceptions about, 30–31, 34, 46 (*see also* bra burning); motivations for, 45; as origin story, 29–30; press release, 37, 41–42, 43–44, 204n4, 206n7; print media coverage of, 16, 17, 31–32, 33, 34–35, 36, 38; purposes of, 35; reaction to, 36, 52; role of in movement, 72; sex-race analogy in, 90; strategy of, 9; Williams on, 41

Miss Black America Pageant, 25, 37–43

Morgan, Robin: in Babcox's article, 52; at Bridal Fair, 47; in coverage of Miss America protest, 35; on Curtis, 48; on Miss America protest, 30, 32, 44–45; on Miss Black America, 38; on *RAT Subterranean News,* 95–96; sit-in at Grove Press, 97–98

Moskowitz, Eva, 210n4

motherhood, 209n23

movements, 5–7

Ms., 118, 175, 183, 186, 214

Mulvey, Laura, 13, 72, 155, 214n3

Murray, Pauli, 19

National Black Feminist Organization, 171, 179

National Council of Negro Women, 165

National Organization for Women (NOW): African Americans in, 19; Berghoff protest, 60, 193, 206n6; boycott against sexist advertisers, 98; in CBS series, 75; classified as militants, 61; description of, 67–68; founding of, 77, 202n4; involvement in sex-discrimination lawsuits, 79; lesbian purge, 23; in *LHJ* sit-in, 99; media strategies, 8, 9, 125, 131, 149, 166; membership, 7, 133, 166, 173; pressuring of EEOC, 77; use of civil rights model, 203n10; use of sex-race analogy, 21, 60. *See also* Atkinson, Ti-Grace; Equal Rights Amendment; Friedan, Betty; Women's Strike for Equality

National Press Club, 98

National Women's Conference (NWC), 175–78

National Women's Political Caucus (NWPC), 173, 175, 183

NBC: audience of, 170; characterizations of movement, 65–70; coverage of birth control hearings, 54–55; coverage of House passage of ERA, 144, 145–46; coverage of Strike, 152–54, 155, 158, 161; credence given to feminists' complaints by, 70, 94; decision to prepare series on movement, 66; issues in series of, 56, 66, 82–83, 84–87, 88; lack of feminists in series of, 170; rhetorical purpose of series of, 93; rhetorical strategies of, 25–26, 88; sex discrimination complaint against, 98; underplaying of differences between feminist groups, 70; use of sex/race analogy in series of, 131; use of visuals, 71; women of color in series of, 169

Nelson, Gaylord, 54–55, 60

Nessen, Ron, 55

Nevins, Sheila, 190

"The New Feminism" section in *LHJ* column, 108–9

New Feminist Repertory Theater, 62, 206n5, 207n10, 209n22

news: audience of, 4, 12, 16; selection of stories, 6, 36. *See also* media

news, print. *See* individual publications

news, television: audience of, 16; early coverage of movement, 54; legitimacy of, 53–54; regional focus of, 203n11; as rhetoric, 12; visuality of, 11, 13, 14–15. *See also* ABC; CBS; NBC

news values, 6, 16, 50

Newsweek: on bra burning, 49; coverage of *LHJ* sit-in, 103, 104, 110, 117; sex discrimination complaint against, 97, 103, 210n6

New York Bridal Fair, 47

New York Radical Feminists (NYRF), 83, 99, 175, 205n1

New York Radical Women (NYRW), 1, 3, 30, 46–47, 204n1. *See also* feminism, radical

New York Times: as agenda-setter, 205n5; black feminism in, 214n1; bra burning in, 49; coverage of Bridal Fair, 47; coverage of civil rights movement, 42; coverage of *LHJ* sit-in, 102, 103, 104, 110; coverage of Miss America Pageant protest, 33, 34–35, 36, 38–39; coverage of Miss Black America Pageant, 39, 40–42; coverage of Strike, 150; early coverage of movement, 16, 47, 203n8; lesbianism in, 214n2; Steinem in, 181

New York Times Magazine, 48, 52, 180

Nichols, Bill, 123, 125

Nicholson, Linda, 202n5

North, Sandie, 99

Norton, Eleanor Holmes, 19, 148, 151, 165

NOW. *See* National Organization for Women

objectivity, 90, 121–22, 123–24, 128, 142

Ohio Bell, 80, 208n21

Older Women's Liberation, 100

Paul, Alice, 69–70, 159, 166, 170

performance, feminist, 83. *See also* theater, feminist

personal is political, 8, 193, 196

Phillips, Ida, 77, 78–79, 80, 108, 208n17, 208n19

Pierce, Ponchitta, 62–63, 206n9

Plantinga, Carl, 123

Playboy, 75, 120

Playboy Club, 72, 182, 192, 207n14

Pogrebin, Letty Cottin, 112

politics, beauty, 49, 73

politics, reproductive, 86. *See also* abortion; birth control hearings

politics, sexual, 8, 68, 147, 151–52

Polletta, Francesca, 211n10

postfeminism, 180, 197

pregnancy, 83, 85. *See also* abortion; birth control hearings; birth control pill

press, feminist: *Ms.,* 118, 175, 183, 186; need for, 95

print culture, feminist, 9, 203n7

Professional Women's Caucus, 129

Quarles, Norma, 79–82, 92, 193, 208n20

race: and attraction to liberal groups, 110; in CBS series, 75; in consciousness-raising articles, 110; in coverage of Miss America Pageant protest, 39; in coverage of Miss Black America Pageant, 37–43; in dominant narrative of movement, 92; and feminism, 37–43; in *Gloria,* 198–99; in *LHJ* sit-in, 100, 101, 210n3; in media coverage, 171; in NBC series, 66, 92; in reproductive politics, 86; in second wave feminism, 18–22; in sex-discrimination lawsuits, 79; in Strike, 165; in "Women's Liberation," 141. *See also* intersectionality; sex-race analogy; women of color

race-sex analogy. *See* sex-race analogy

racism: in CBS series, 83–84; cultural authority attached to claims of, 33; legitimation of claims, 131; in Miss America Pageant, 32, 41, 205n8, 205n9; power in, 137–38; understanding of in framework of liberalism, 50

radical flank effect, 212n13

Rankin, Jeanette, 148

rape, 175

RAT Subterranean News, 95–96, 115

Reagan, Ronald, 176, 178

Reasoner, Harry, 194

Redstockings, 3, 99, 186, 192, 205n1, 209n22, 214n3

reporters. *See* journalists

respectability, 166–67

Reynolds, Frank, 105, 145

Ride, Sally, 214

Ridge, Mary Thad, 139

Rosen, Ruth, 140

Rosenfeld, Leah, 77–79, 80, 108, 208n18

Saarinen, Aline, 65–70, 91, 170
Sanders, Marlene: career, 211n8; commitment to equality narrative, 119; coverage
of *LHJ* sit-in, 26, 96, 104–7, 118; coverage
of Liberty Island protest, 145; intentions
of, 139; interview with, 212; and legitimacy of feminism, 169; on *LHJ* coverage, 121; media pragmatism of, 131, 132;
at Second Congress to Unite Women,
23–24; sympathy for protesters, 107;
tipped off to *LHJ* sit-in, 97; on "Women's
Liberation," 27, 91, 121. *See also* "Wom-
en's Liberation"
Sarachild, Kathie, 205n7. *See also* Amatniek, Kathy
Schlafly, Phyllis, 174, 176, 177, 189, 191
Schudson, Michael, 168
Sculley, Pat, 135
Seaman, Barbara, 55
Second Congress to Unite Women, 23–24,
114
The Second Stage (Friedan), 187
second wave feminism. *See* feminism, second wave; women's liberation movement
Sevareid, Eric, 161, 163
sex discrimination: Berghoff protest, 60,
193, 206n6; complaints against media
organizations, 97–99, 103, 203n8; and
founding of NOW, 202n4; lawsuits, 77–
79, 108, 208n17, 208n18, 208n19; legislation on, 129; in *LHJ* sit-in demands, 100,
101; in meatpacking plant, 209n25; in
radicals' ideology, 88; as social problem,
76–81. *See also* Equal Employment Opportunity Commission; sexism
sexism: in CBS series, 56; in civil rights
movement, 21; cultural authority attached to claims of, 33; in Left, 95–96,
99; in NBC series, 56, 57, 89–91, 92–93;
power in, 137–39; refusal to recognize as
political issue, 17; as social problem, 89,
92–93, 169; Steinem's experiences with,
192. *See also* sex discrimination
sex-race analogy: in coverage of Liberty
Island protest, 145; as legitimation strategy, 130–31; in Miss America Pageant
protest, 33, 90; problems of, 137; reliance
on, 26–27; in sex-discrimination law-

suits, 79; use of, 21–22, 60; in "Women's
Liberation," 26–27, 122, 125–33
sex roles, 83, 84, 89–91, 100–101, 126–27,
169
sexuality, 22–24, 141, 205n2. *See also* lesbianism; lesbians
sexual objectification, 71–75
Sexual Politics (Millett), 22, 150
Sherwood, Virginia, 155, 165–66, 167
sit-ins, 60, 105, 115, 193, 206n6. See also
Ladies' Home Journal (LHJ) sit-in
Smith, Howard K., 17, 151, 160, 163
Snitow, Anne, 209n23
socialist-feminist analysis, 136
socialist feminists, 202n5
social problem, 206n4
social problem stories, 169
social trend stories, 53
spectacle, 154–55, 163, 214n3
spectator, male, 155–56, 162–64. *See also*
audience
Stacey, Jackie, 30
status quo, 94, 104
Steinem, Gloria: appeal of, 10, 18, 213n5; "A
Bunny's Tale," 182, 192, 207n14; emergence of, 28, 167, 180–89; founding of
NWPC, 173; *Gloria: In Her Own Words*, 28,
190–99; in *McCall's*, 113; on questions,
214n4; in Strike, 148; wedding of, 49
stereotypes, of women, 66
sterilization, forced, 84, 86
stridency, 165, 166
Strike Day. *See* Women's Strike for Equality
Strike for Equality. *See* Women's Strike for
Equality
subjects: credible/worthy, 71, 74, 75, 76,
78; preferred, in lifestyle feminism, 189;
preferred by media, 56; women as, 162,
163; women of color as, 92
suffrage, 58, 69
suffragists, 159. *See also* Paul, Alice
surveillance, women as objects of, 156

Temple, Jean, 74, 81
theater, feminist, 62, 206n5, 207n10,
209n22
theater, guerrilla, 127, 155
Third World Women's Alliance, 19, 165

Time, 22, 49, 102, 103, 183
Tobias, Sheila, 30
Tomasson, Verna, 115
Torres, Sasha, 18, 73, 137, 203n8
Trotta, Liz, 89–91, 93, 169
Tuchman, Gaye, 15

Van Gelder, Lindsy, 31–32, 50
Van Zoonen, Liesbet, 161
visuality, 11, 13–15
visuals: in CBS series, 56, 59–60, 71–76,
    94; in coverage of birth control hearings,
    55; in *Gloria: In Her Own Words,* 191; in *LHJ*
    coverage, 105, 106; in NBC series, 56–57,
    66, 67, 71, 76–80, 81, 89; in Strike cover-
    age, 152, 154, 155–56, 157, 162; in "Wom-
    en's Liberation," 124, 129, 134, 138–39

Walters, Barbara, 191
Ware, Cellestine, 19
Waters, Mary Alice, 135, 136
Weisstein, Naomi, 211n9
Why We Lost the ERA (Mansbridge), 178
Williams, Saundra, 40, 41, 42, 43
Willis, Ellen, 9, 113, 186
W.I.T.CH. (Women's International Terror-
    ist Conspiracy from Hell), 47, 67, 205n12
Wolf, Tom, 121
women: in CBS series, 57; characterized by
    psychology, 211n9; crowds of, 159, 164;
    as entertainment, 163; in NBC series,
    57; as objects of visual pleasure, 151; as
    spectacle, 155, 163
women, working, 71, 76–79, 207n15. *See
    also* employment
women of color, 203n9; black feminism in
    New York Times, 214n1; as breadwinners,
    66; Combahee River Collective State-
    ment, 205n10; in coverage of movement,
    20, 179; and family, 84, 110; forced ster-
    ilization of, 86; in *Gloria,* 195; journalists
    (*see* Pierce, Ponchitta; Quarles, Norma);
    as legitimate feminist subjects, 92; Miss
    Black America Pageant, 25, 37–43; in
    NBC series, 79–80, 169; at NWC, 176;
    organizations, 19, 165, 171, 179; relation
    with second wave feminism, 18–22, 84,
    110; in sex discrimination stories, 81–82,

92; in Strike coverage, 152; in "Women's
    Liberation," 122, 132, 141. *See also* race;
    racism
"Women's Liberation" (documentary), 26–
    27; audience of, 133, 141–42; equality
    narrative in, 140; The Feminists in, 64;
    focus of, 122; form of, 123–25, 130, 133;
    goals of, 122–23, 125, 139–40, 141; inter-
    views in, 124, 134–35; issues in, 124, 127,
    128–29, 132, 136, 140; lack of feminists
    in, 170; liberal tone of, 134, 141; men in,
    127–28, 141–42; narration of, 124; ob-
    jectivity in, 121–22, 128, 142; radicals in,
    135, 140; Sanders' view of, 26–27; strate-
    gies, 122–23, 125–33, 136–38; structure
    of, 124; subtitle, 132; vision of movement
    in, 64
women's liberation movement: awareness
    of, 5; changes in, 187; in collective con-
    sciousness, 163–64; cooptation of, 117,
    118; diversity of, 126; elements of con-
    sonant with liberalism, 92; interest in, 5;
    as legitimate story, 125; momentum of,
    145, 146, 173; roots of in left, 52; sympa-
    thetic treatment of, 169–71; use of term,
    202n5; using for personal gain, 114–15.
    See also feminism, second wave
Women's Strike for Equality: actions of,
    146; as attack on femininity, 160; cover-
    age of, 27–28, 146–47, 150–51, 156–57,
    164; demands in, 153–54, 161–62; de-
    sign of, 149; diversity of, 165; as enter-
    tainment, 151, 152–53, 155, 156, 162, 163;
    framing, 149–63; and gender anxiety,
    17, 148–49, 151–52, 157, 160–61, 166;
    impact of, 149, 166, 167, 173; issues in,
    70, 88, 136, 147, 149–50, 153–54, 161–62;
    male spectator of, 162–64; motivation
    for, 147; opposition to, 150, 156–58, 164–
    65; purpose of, 2; reactions to, 164; turn-
    out, 148; women's groups in, 148, 165
"women *vs.* women" tactic, 164–65, 189
The World Split Open (Rosen), 140

Youth International Party (Yippies), 30,
    31, 50

zap actions, 29, 47, 204n1

BONNIE J. DOW is an associate professor and chair of communication studies and an associate professor of women's and gender studies at Vanderbilt University. She is the author of *Prime-Time Feminism: Television, Media Culture, and the Women's Movement Since 1970*.

The University of Illinois Press
is a founding member of the
Association of American University Presses.

Composed in 10.5/13 Marat Pro
by Lisa Connery
at the University of Illinois Press
Manufactured by Sheridan Books, Inc.

University of Illinois Press
1325 South Oak Street
Champaign, IL 61820-6903
www.press.uillinois.edu